THE WITHERING AWAY OF THE STATE?

SAGE *Modern Politics Series* **Volume 6**
sponsored by the European Consortium for Political Research/ECPR

THE WITHERING AWAY OF THE STATE?

Party and State under Communism

Edited by

Leslie Holmes

SAGE Publications ● London and Beverly Hills

Copyright © 1981 by
SAGE Publications Ltd.

For information address:
SAGE Publications Ltd, 28 Banner Street, London EC1Y 8QE
SAGE Publications Inc, 275 South Beverly Drive Beverly Hills
California 90212

British Library Cataloguing in Publication Data
The withering away of the state? — (Sage modern
politics series; vol. 6)
1. Communist state
2. Communism
I. Holmes, Leslie
321.92   JC474   80-41954

ISBN 0-8039-9796-5
ISBN 0-8039-9797-3 Pbk

For Nolly, my late father,
Kim, Christine & Paul

Contents

Preface

Changes in the role and relationship — both de jure and de facto — of the party and state in societies allegedly building communism have not received the attention they deserve. According to Marx and particularly Engels, the state would eventually 'wither away' (or, sometimes, 'be abolished') following a socialist revolution, whilst it is often argued that Lenin's conception of the strong, compact and elitist party in *What is to be Done?* related specifically to Russian conditions of the early twentieth century. Despite this, approximately one third of the world's population lives in political systems having a dominant ideology called Marxism-Leninism in which it often appears either that the state itself is becoming stronger or that it is yielding power to the party apparatus. In the latter case, ideologists can claim that 'the state' is withering away; but this is true only in a highly formalistic sense, in that the functions of the state are taken over by an equally small — or even smaller — group of party officials. Hence the distribution of power in society (in the sense of allocative decision-making and the ability to enforce decisions) is not significantly altered. Such phenomena lead many people to conceive of 'communism' as a highly centralized and bureaucratic type of political system, very different from the better world Marx and Lenin considered inevitable. It was with the intention of analyzing this phenomenon and possible discrepancy that, in April 1979, a workshop was held in Brussels under the auspices of the European Consortium for Political Research (ECPR); the theme of this workshop was 'Changes in the Party and State under Communism', and the present volume is largely the outcome of this meeting.

Atypically, the collection of writers here is largely self-chosen; the policy for accepting applicants to the workshop was to ensure that as many communist states as possible were covered by academics from as many Western countries as possible — beyond which it was largely a matter of 'first come, first served'. On balance, this was beneficial; the reader will discover, for instance, that there are some perceptible differences of political orientation amongst the writers jostling between these covers. Whilst I have attempted to standardize the format of the chapters — to the extent that academics will permit themselves to be standardized — no attempt has been made to incorporate any ideological framework as such.

Particular emphasis has been placed on developments occurring within the past decade, so that, in addition to its main raison d'être, the book should also serve as a useful guideline to the latest political, economic and social situation in communist states.

Ideally, each sub-section (see details on the format below) would have been treated cross-nationally by one author. However, the study was intended to include the latest original research findings rather than being a summary of secondary sources; consequently, contributions had to be from specialists rather than generalists. Clearly, given inter alia the many different languages used in the various communist states, such specialists almost exclusively concentrate on one country or area. This does not mean that the book represents merely a collection of country-studies, however. Rather, the 'chequer-board' format has been used, which represents the optimal blend of specialized and comparative studies. In other words, although each of the empirical chapters focuses on only one country or area, a common framework of sub-sections is used in all of them. Hence, if one is primarily interested in looking at the total package of changes in the USSR or Cuba, one merely reads the relevant chapter. Conversely, if the reader is primarily interested in changes in the structure of the state, he/she can look up this subsection in each of the individual country-studies, and hence use the book in a genuinely comparative, thematic way. Moreover, the final chapter attempts to draw together the main findings of the preceding chapters, as well as offering various explanations for the phenomena described.

Not all communist states are included here; to have covered Poland or North Korea or Benin, for example, would have been attractive but is not of fundamental necessity to one of the basic exercises, viz. to show that there are some significant differences between communist states and their approaches to Party and State. Although the 'self-appointing' exercise outlined above largely explains the present selection of countries, the participants in Brussels felt that two particularly important gaps would have to be filled if the papers were to appear as a book. Thus Yugoslavia is so clearly sui generis in the communist world that, although no paper on it was presented in Belgium, a chapter is included here; I am very grateful to Dr Ralph Pervan for having agreed at short notice to produce this. The other glaring omission was a paper giving details on what Marx, Engels and Lenin had actually said about the Party and the State under socialism and communism; I am indebted to my colleague, Professor David McLellan, for having produced such a chapter. The one other contributor I would like to single out for special thanks is Dr Lourdes Casal, who came from the USA just to attend the workshop (thanks to a generous grant from the German Marshall Fund) and who produced her chapter on Cuba in the face of considerable personal problems.*

More generally, I would like to thank all of the contributors for having kept (reasonably) close to the methodological guidelines, and for having taken heed of many of the comments made on their original papers in Brussels. Thanks, too, to the former Executive Director of ECPR, Professor Jean Blondel, and his personal assistant, Val Stewart, for their encouragement and help at all stages of this project. And finally, of course, thanks are due to the small army of secretaries and typists who made the participants' ideas at least legible to each other in Brussels, and who subsequently made the Sage typesetters' lives a little less difficult.

A few words on definitions are necessary. In this book, 'communist' states (or societies) are simply states (or societies) claiming to be building communism, unless specified otherwise; no existing state suggests that it has already achieved communism. By 'communist party' is meant that political organization calling itself a party (in the case of Yugoslavia a 'league'), which adheres to a version of Marxist-Leninist ideology, is organized on the principles of democratic centralism, claims to be the vanguard of society and leading that society towards communism; the word 'communist' need not be included in the party's title. The 'party apparatus' comprises full-time, professional functionaries of the party (party *apparatchiki*) and is to be distinguished from ordinary members who have non-party jobs. The concept of state is more problematic. In much of the discussion in these chapters, it is fused in a general sense to mean the set of institutions claiming the sole legitimate right to 'govern' society; this includes the rights to direct and coerce, plus the responsibility to defend that society. However, because of the particular nature of communist states, some functions normally associated primarily with 'the state' in liberal-democracies are technically the responsibility of the party in the communist world; this aspect of party-state relations forms a major component of this volume. In analyzing the detailed functions of 'the state', we have followed Marx's own preference for concentrating on the state administrative apparatus (or bureaucracy) — the government, the ministerial staffs, etc. However, in societies in which the means of production have been fully or largely taken into state ownership, it is often unclear where to draw the boundaries of this apparatus. It can be argued, for instance, that the director of a state-owned enterprise is part of the state apparatus in the same way as a minister is. It would be ingenuous to suppose that a watertight definition, acceptable to all, can be produced — but it was felt that for most purposes, and unless otherwise specified, the 'state administrative apparatus' should be understood as consisting of the full-time, professional functionaries of central and local state executive organs which are not directly part of the production process. Of course, the executive organs are not the only important institutions of the state, so that other important branches considered here include the coercive/defensive organs (the police, the military) and the representative organs (e.g. parliaments).

In order that the reader may understand the methodological framework used for the country-studies in this book, it will be useful to finish this preface by reproducing below the guidelines that were issued to all contributors. It must be emphasized, however, that contributors were urged to use their own discretion in deciding whether a particular point should be analyzed briefly or in depth — or indeed omitted altogether — and were also encouraged to include other factors they considered relevant to their particular object of study.

THE FORMAT

All of the country-studies are to use the following framework:

A General Introduction

This section should include a brief history and analysis of the political culture of the country/area being examined, before proceeding to the details of changes in the party and state.

The Party

Here, the primary concern is with the dominant party in each communist state, irrespective of whether the party includes the word 'communist' in its title. The main areas to be considered are:

(a) Changes in the theory of its role. Reference should be made both to formal documents (party statutes, party programmes, constitutions) and to debates at conferences, in journals, etc. Where possible, analysis of indigenous criticism of the party's role and radical proposals for change should be included.

(b) Changes in its structure and functions. Does the number and importance of functions performed by the party appear to be increasing or decreasing? Do structural changes reflect an attempt to shift the locus of decision-making and implementation, and, if so, on what sort of question? Do these changes represent decentralization or centralization — both within the party and in society?

(c) Changes in its composition, including its overall social structure. Has there been any attempt at 're-proletarianization' in the 1970s? If so, has this been only at the level of mass membership, or is it also reflected in senior bodies such as the Central Committee? How do such changes relate to the 'dictatorship of the proletariat'?

(d) Changes in the role of the non-hegemonic parties (in those communist states having multi-party systems). In particular any significant change in the balance of power between the dominant party and the lesser parties is to be noted.

The State

(a) Changes in the theory of its role. Basically the same approach as in (a) above is to be adopted.

(b) Changes in its structure and functions. Which functions has the state taken over from or transferred to the party? Again, have attempts to shift the focus of decision-making and/or implementation been reflected in structural changes (e.g. the abolition of some state bodies or the creation of others) or in changes in the roles of existing bodies? If the latter, have transfers of powers from one state organ to another been essentially horizontal (e.g. from the State Council to the Council of Ministers in the GDR) or vertical (e.g. from an all-union to a republican body in the USSR)?

(c) Changes in the methods and scale of mass political participation (e.g. electoral reform, the use of referenda, use of the media, involvement in decision-making, etc.). Both proposals for and implemented change are to be considered.

Changes in the Party-State Relationship/Conclusions

This section should consist mainly of a summary of, integration of and attempted explanation for the information contained in parts one and two. Moreover, it is most important that contributors reach a conclusion here — however brief — as to whether the party and/or the state is in fact withering away, remaining static, or expanding its role in the country or countries analyzed; obviously, your conclusion might be that a decision on this depends on one's conception of the term 'withering away' — but if so, state this explicitly.

This, then, has been the framework for analysis. Not all of the chapters can be expected to answer these questions in the same depth, of course — one major reason being that it is much easier to obtain information about Yugoslavia and the USSR, for example, than it is about Albania or Kampuchea/Cambodia. Nevertheless, we feel that at least a start has been made on tackling a singularly important and much neglected problem of political theory and practice.

Leslie Holmes
Canterbury, England
July 1980

*It is with deep sadness that I have to report that Lourdes Casal died shortly before the publication of this book; she will not be forgotten.

1 Marx, Engels and Lenin on Party and State

David McLellan
University of Kent at Canterbury, UK

This introductory chapter attempts — in a necessarily brief and sketchy manner — to outline the inheritance of classical Marxism as one element which may help to illuminate subsequent Marxist practice.[1] In dealing with Marx and Engels on the one hand and Lenin on the other, the large contextual differences between nineteenth century Western Europe and twentieth century Russia make comparison extremely difficult. The most evident divergence of view is on the party — whereas the post-revolutionary state, lying in the future, allowed a greater degree of harmony. As I hope the following exposition will show, the concepts of betrayal or contradiction are too sharp to fit the relationship of the three thinkers here under consideration; but, equally, the successors to 1917 were far from having an integrated body of doctrine on which to build.

THE PARTY

In contradistinction to Lenin, Marx has very little to say on the party. He offered no more systematic an account of the political party that he conceived to be necessary for working-class action than he did of his views on classes or on the state. Marx never founded a party and was only a member of any party organization for a few years. Although from very early on he saw the proletariat as the agent of social change, he always based his political activity on existing organizations, and particularly in his later years offered much advice to the growing workers' parties. Two difficulties inherent in giving an account of Marx's views are, firstly, that it was only during Marx's lifetime that the idea of the political party in the modern sense developed; secondly, that Marx himself used the term in widely differing senses. The two periods in which he was most active were those of the Communist League (1847-52) and the First International (1864-73).

The communist correspondence committees that Marx and Engels initiated in 1846 were not political parties, but only means of exchanging ideas among revolutionary groups in the European cities. Describing the organization in a letter to Proudhon, Marx said that the aim was 'to link German socialists with French and English socialists, to keep foreigners informed of the socialist movements that will develop in Germany, and Germans informed of the progress of socialism in France and England'.[2] In 1847, however, on the invitation of its leaders, Marx became a member of the League of the Just, though he insisted that it abandon its character as a small international conspiratorial organization. He wrote much later: 'When for the first time Engels and I joined the secret society of communists, we did so on the condition sine qua non that everything that could favour a cult of authority be banished from the statutes'.[3] In 1847, it was renamed the Communist League and given a new and thoroughly democratic constitution stipulating that all officers were elected by, and continually responsible to, the members, the sovereign body being the annual congress.

It was the League that commissioned *The Communist Manifesto* in which Marx and Engels outline their conception of the communist party. The communists' claim to be the vanguard of the working class was not based, according to Marx, on any interests separate from those of the proletariat as a whole or on any sectarian principles of their own.

> The communists are distinguished from other working-class parties by this only:
> 1. In the national struggles of the proletarians of the different countries they point out and bring to the front the common interests of the entire proletariat, independent of all nationality.
> 2. In the various stages of development which the struggle of the working class against the bourgeoisie has to pass through, they always and everywhere represent the interests of the movement as a whole.

Thus they were both 'the most advanced and resolute section' of the working class and also 'theoretically, they have over the great mass of the proletariat the advantage of clearly understanding the line of march, the conditions and the ultimate general results of the proletarian movement'.[4] With regard to other opposition parties, the communists, while instilling into their members the exclusiveness of their class interests, 'support every revolutionary movement against the existing social and political order of things'. In France they supported the social democrats, in Switzerland the radicals, in Germany the liberal bourgeoisie, etc. In spite of its programme being called the Manifesto of the Communist Party, the League in 1848-49 never functioned as a real political party, even in the sense in which Marx and Engels used the term in *The Communist Manifesto*, nor could it have done so in the circumstances: it had only 300 members at most, and was always forced to operate in a semi-clandestine manner. The League appears to have been dissolved by Marx in June 1848 since he preferred to work through the Press; and when, in April 1849, Marx for the first time saw the need and potential for a separate organized workers' party, it was already too late, for the defeat of the insurrection in south-east Germany meant the end of the revolution.

In 1850 the League was reorganized with London as its centre. During the two years of its existence, Marx was responsible for several directives from the Central Committee to the groups. The most important of these, the Address written in March 1850, called for the establishment of an 'independent, secret and public organization of the workers' party'. This party would be separate from other opposition parties and formed from the nucleus of already existing workers' associations which were normally of a social or educational nature. Marx did conclude an abortive alliance with Blanqui at about this time, but his conception of the communist party was very different from Blanqui's: in Marx's view the party should aim at being a party of the masses and should not try to gain power by a revolutionary putsch, nor be highly centralized; he also warned the workers of a lengthy revolutionary struggle to achieve class consciousness. 'They themselves', he wrote, 'must do the utmost for their final victory by clarifying their minds as to what their class interests are, by taking up their position as an independent party as soon as possible and by not allowing themselves to be seduced for a single moment by the hypocritical phrases of the democratic petty bourgeoisie . . .'[5] By the summer of 1850, Marx had become convinced that an immediate revolution was not possible. The League split into two factions on this issue: a minority of the Central Committee wished to continue activities aimed at promoting an immediate revolution, whereas Marx told the workers that they might have as much as fifty years of civil war to go through before they were ready for revolution. Marx subsequently referred to the League as only an 'episode in the history of the Party which grows naturally from the soil of modern society'.[6]

From the early 1850s until the mid-1860s, Marx was not a member of any party. He wrote to Engels in February 1851: 'I am very happy with the public and authentic isolation in which we two, you and I, now find ourselves. It entirely corresponds to our position and our principles. The system of mutual concessions, of inadequacies endured for the sake of appearances, and the obligation of appearing ridiculous before the public in the party with all these asses, has now ceased'.[7] Marx did, however, continue to refer to his 'party', and that in two senses. Firstly, when he talked about 'recruiting our party afresh' or 'insisting on party discipline', he was referring to his small group of intimate followers often called by their acquaintances the 'Marx party'. Secondly, Marx used the term in a wider sense, as when, in the letter to Freiligrath quoted above, he talks of 'the party in the great historical sense' or later talks of the Paris Commune as 'the most glorious deed of our Party since the June insurrection in Paris'.[8]

The second period of Marx's activity as a member of the political party was occasioned by the First International. Marx's policies here give a fair indication of his ideas on the organization of working-class parties. The International Association of Working Men was not founded by Marx; it sprang up spontaneously, and its chief purpose originally was to protect English trade unions against the importations of foreign labour. It was in no way a communist party, nor did Marx's followers form a separate group inside it. Marx opposed secret groupings inside the International even in countries where no right of association existed. 'This type of organization', he declared, 'is opposed to the proletarian movement because these associations, instead of educating the workers, subject them to authoritarian and mystical laws that impede their independence and misguide their minds.'[9] The rules of the Association were intended by Marx to have as wide a scope as possible, including, for example, the followers of Proudhon and Lassalle. Marx wished the International only to deal with those matters, as he wrote to Kugelmann, 'which allow of immediate agreement and concerted action by the workers and give direct nourishment and impetus to the requirements of the class struggle and the organization of the workers into a class'.[10] Even after the defeat of the Paris Commune in 1871 had convinced Marx of the need for more discipline and independence in proletarian parties, he still did not press for further centralization of the International: the demand of the London Conference of 1871 for the 'constitution of the working class into a political party' only referred to independent national parties. The quarrel with Bakunin and his followers which brought about the end of the International was a quarrel about organization, not about ideology: Marx was for a democratic, open organization guided by decisions taken by majority vote at annual congresses, whereas Bakunin was in favour of a secret society with a hierarchical organization. In its later years, owing to the growth of reaction outside the International and of disruptive elements inside it, Marx was forced to fight for a more effective central control.

Marx's comments on the German Social Democratic Party and its forerunners show the same concerns. He strongly criticized the followers of Lassalle for creating too disciplined and dogmatic a party. But for all his misgivings about the Gotha Programme of 1875 (which united the two hitherto opposed wings of the German workers), Marx recognized the German Social Democratic Party as a genuinely socialist party and even referred to it as 'our party'. In one of his last pronouncements on this theme, Marx sent a circular to the party leaders in 1879 urging them to preserve the party from all contamination with foreign values.[11]

Some interpretations of Marx[12] see his political attitudes as changing from Jacobin in the late 1840s to an emphasis on the possibilities of peaceful transition to socialism by means of radical democratic and even parliamentary strategies. The above account would obviously dispute this. The claim for Engels is, however, stronger. Circumstances prevented Engels from exercising his very considerable gifts as a practical politician, living as he did in enforced isolation from the leaders of the SPD. Towards the end of his life, the growing electoral success of the Social Democrats led Engels to stress the evolutionary rather than the revolutionary side of Marxism and declare the tactics of 1848 to be outmoded in every respect. In his Preface to a re-edition of Marx's *Class Struggles in France*, written in 1895 shortly before he died, Engels stated that the growth of Social Democracy 'proceeds as spontaneously, as steadily, as irresistibly, and at the same time as tranquilly as a natural process', and continued·

We can count even today on two and a quarter million voters. If it continues in this fashion, by the end of the century we shall conquer the greater part of the middle strata of society, petty bourgeois and small peasants, and grow into the decisive power in the land, before which all other powers will have to bow, whether they like it or not. To keep this growth going without interruption until it of itself gets beyond the control of the prevailing governmental system, not to fritter away this daily increasing shock force in vanguard skirmishes, but to keep it intact until the decisive day, that is out main task. And there is only one means by which the steady rise of the socialist fighting forces in Germany could be temporarily halted, and even thrown back some time: a clash on a big scale with the military, a blood-letting like that of 1871 in Paris. In the long run that would also be overcome. To shoot a party which numbers millions out of existence is too much even for all the magazine rifles of Europe and America. But the normal development would be impeded, the shock force would, perhaps, not be available at the critical moment, the decisive combat would be delayed, protracted and attended by heavier sacrifices.[13]

Such passages, regarded as Engels's political 'testament', certainly played a role in influencing the leaders of the SPD, though it should be noted that Engels agreed (very reluctantly) to excise certain more revolutionary passages under pressure from the Berlin leaders.[14] In any event, it can readily be appreciated that Engels' rather ambivalent position provided ammunition for both sides in the great debate on whether Marx's political doctrines needed to be revised in the light of changing circumstances.

Of the dispute over Engels' 'political testament' in the SPD, Lenin was only a distant observer. The Russian social formation consisted of economic backwardness, rapid incipient industrialization, lack of borgeois culture, political autocracy — in short all the factors contained in the notion of 'combined and overall development'. This necessitated a different approach to party organization. (It is, of course, no accident that the passages in Marx's writings which most closely parallel Lenin's approach are from the 1840s when German society had many similarities to early twentieth century Russia.)

In the context of Russian politics Lenin was far from being innovatory. In his fundamental work on the Party — *What is to be Done?* — Lenin was out to reassert the Plekhanov orthodoxy of the pre-1894 period against later developments; and so far from revealing a break of confidence in the masses, the book was designed to remedy 'the lag of the leaders behind the spontaneous upsurge of the masses'.[15] The first three chapters criticized the 'Economists' and terrorists, and described the disarray of the movement in the late 1890s, and so on. Lenin attacked the Credo of Kuskova and the two Russian workers' newspapers *Rabochaia Mysl* and *Rabochee Delo* as typical of 'Economism'.[16] His main point was that these groups showed inadequate leadership and inability to articulate the role of the proletariat as leader of all classes in the struggle against the autocracy. Basing himself on his conclusions in *The Development of Capitalism in Russia,* Lenin declared that they could not produce the initial organization of the Party necessary to parallel politically the transition from Kustar (handicraft) production to national capitalism. The Economists could only duplicate the proletariat's isolated and local efforts. In subsequent chapters and in line with Plekhanov and Axelrod, Lenin elaborated his ideas on Social Democratic consciousness. This involved an intensive knowledge of the socio-economic situation and prospects of every class. It was therefore impossible for the proletariat, whose 'economic' struggle was too narrow, to achieve this consciousness (Lenin never talked of 'class consciousness' with regard to the proletariat). Echoing Plekhanov and Axelrod, Lenin maintained that the proletariat, left to itself, would inevitably follow bourgeois ideology. In this connection, Lenin quoted Kautsky at length and then continued in the key passage:

> Since there can be no talk of an independent ideology formulated by the working masses themselves in the process of their movement the only choice is — either bourgeois or socialist ideology. There is no middle course (for mankind has not created a 'third' ideology, and, moreover, in a society torn by class antagonisms there can never be a non-class or an above-class ideology). Hence, to belittle the socialist ideology in any way, to turn aside from it in the slightest degree means to strengthen bourgeois ideology. There is much talk of spontaneity. But the spontaneous development of the working-class movement leads to its subordination to bourgeois ideology, to its development along the lines of the Credo programme; for the spontaneous working-class movement is trade-unionism, is Nur-Gewerkschaftlerei, and trade-unionism means the ideological enslavement of the workers by the bourgeoisie. Hence, our task, the task of Social-Democracy, is to combat spontaneity, to divert the working-class movement from this spontaneous, trade-unionist striving to come under the wing of the bourgeoisie, and to bring it under the wing of revolutionary Social-Democracy.[17]

In Chapter Four, Lenin moved to his positive proposals. Given the Party's task of assuming the role of leading all exploited classes in the democratic revolution (the 'hegemony of the proletariat in the democratic revolution' to use Plekhanov's phrase), it must have an all-Russian organization. This was best centered on an all-Russian newspaper such as *Iskra* aspired to be. Such an organization could maintain contacts and doctrinal cohesion on an all-Russian basis, ensure specialization and non-duplication, and maintain the hegemonic position of the proletariat. Such an organization would also have the attributes of secrecy, centralization, specialization, and exclusivity. But all these attributes would be dependent on Lenin's fundamental idea, which was the real point at issue in the Bolshevik-Menshevik split: that the organization should be composed of professional revolutionaries. They would be professional in two senses: they would devote themselves full-time to party work and they would be fully trained: 'the struggle against the political police requires special qualities; it requires professional revolutionaries'.[18]

Lenin was not against mass organizations — on the contrary — but he insisted that they must be quite separate from the party elite:

> We must have such circles, trade unions, and organizations everywhere in _as large a number as possible_ and with the widest variety of functions; but it would be absurd and harmful to _confound_ them with the organization of _revolutionaries_, to efface the border-line between them, to make still more hazy the all too faint recognition of the fact that in order to 'serve' the mass movement we must have people who will devote themselves exclusively to Social-Democratic activities, and that such people must _train_ themselves patiently and steadfastly to be professional revolutionaries.[19] (original emphasis)

Nor was Lenin against inner-party democracy, but this implied full publicity and election to all offices, and only an 'incorrigible utopian' could advocate this under present conditions in Russia. The leadership would therefore have to be chosen through the oligarchical principle of co-option.[20]

It should be stressed that Lenin's views represented the whole of the Emancipation of Labour Group, including Plekhanov and Axelrod; _What is to be Done?_ was therefore the last major publication carrying the assent of all the orthodox Marxists. After the split at the Second Congress, Plekhanov and Martov both accused Lenin of 'dictatorship'. Luxemburg published a biting critique of Lenin's ideas,[21] as did Trotsky. Yet, at least until 1905, there was not much difference between Bolsheviks and Mensheviks as regards internal party democracy.[22] The difference between Lenin and his critics was not one of principle but of approach, and certainly accusations of Blanquism were quite misplaced: influence over, and support of, the masses were absolutely essential to his theory.

It would, in any case, be wrong to overemphasize the importance of _What is to be Done?_ Lenin wrote later that his pamphlet 'should not be treated apart from its connection with the concrete historical situation of a definite, and now long past, period in the development of our Party'.[23] The Economists, he said at the 1903 congress, 'have gone to one extreme. To straighten matters out somebody had to pull in the other direction — and that is what I have done'.[24] He never republished the book after 1917 — though it was canonized, for obvious reasons, by Stalin.

The wave of strikes and unrest that swept Russia in 1905 rendered much of *What is to be Done?* completely out of date: Lenin's pessimism was refuted by the revolutionary spontaneity of the masses.[25] Whereas in *What is to be Done?* Lenin had been against a Party that was open to mass membership, the changed conditions of 1905 brought floods of new members. Party membership increased ten times and the distinction between an elitist party and mass organization became less rigid. Although Lenin did not abandon the idea of a clandestine party, he did concede that 'our party has stagnated while working underground'.[26] He urged his followers 'to extend your bases, rally all the worker social democrats round yourselves, incorporate them in the ranks of the party organization by hundreds and thousands',[27] and stated that 'the new form of the basic organization or nucleus of the workers' party must be definitely much broader than were the old circles. Apart from this, the new nucleus will most likely have to be a less rigid, more free, more loose organization'.[28] This entailed changes in a party structure: Lenin committed himself to the introduction of the elective principle and the curtailment of the powers of the Central Committee and even advocated the principle of referendum.[29]

The new party structure was summed up in the phrase 'democratic centralism'. The phrase was of Menshevik origin and, on Lenin's proposal, was incorporated into the statutes of the party at the Stockholm Congress of 1906 which temporarily reunited the two factions.[30] In his Report on the Congress, Lenin explained that the principle of democratic centralism consisted in 'working tirelessly to make the local organizations the principal organizational units of the party in fact, and not merely in name, and to see to it that all the highest standing bodies are elected, accountable, and subject to recall'.[31] The rights of a minority within the party were also guaranteed. Lenin stated his principle as 'freedom of discussion, unity of action'[32] — and the call to action could only be issued by the Congress, not the Central Committee.

It is, of course, true that the new democratic centralism of 1905-06 was not only due to the revolutionary fervour of the times:

Lenin cannot have been uninfluenced by the fact that the Bolsheviks were in a minority at the Stockholm Unity Congress of 1906 and that the Central Committee there elected was under Menshevik control. With the failure of the revolution, the renewed split between the Bolsheviks and the Mensheviks, and the period of reaction from 1908 to 1912, the sectarian spirit inside the Bolshevik party came back in force. Under Lenin's impulsion, the Party, persecuted inside Russia and internally divided abroad, became increasingly monolithic. Lenin came to insist on the 'party' line.[33]

Once again, however, just as 1905 had swept away the rigid organization of the Bolshevik Party, so 1917 inaugurated the most open and 'liberal' period in the Party's life. Once again, the party membership increased tenfold in a few months and the monolithic, highly centralized structure of the Party could not survive the heady atmosphere of new-found liberty. Different tendencies operated inside the Party, whose organization was 'necessarily somewhat loose and fluid',[34] and vigorous debates on policy options occurred at every level. Trotsky, previously vilified by Lenin, but now welcome as a comrade in arms, went as far as to declare the party to be de-Bolshevized'.[35]

But this state of affairs did not, and could not, last long. The civil war and severe dislocation that confronted the Bolsheviks from 1918 to 1921 necessitated a clamp-down on previous liberties. There had been a very open debate on the sort of peace to be concluded with the Germans, and until 1921 there was much discussion of economic policies and relationships to the Soviets and Trade Unions, with Bukharin and Lenin on opposite sides. But the end of the civil war found the country completely exhausted. The proletariat had been decimated and the majority of the population were hostile to the Communist Party — as it had been renamed. The Central Committee found itself contested by the Workers' Opposition, led by Shliapnikov and Kollontai, who demanded the uninhibited right for the workers to elect their own Trade Union leaders and an independence vis-à-vis the Party. Almost as much opposed to the current Party tendencies were the Democratic Centralists, who wished for more internal democracy in the party and real powers for local Soviets. Their opposition was based on all too real grievances,[36] and Lenin had, as late as the end of 1920, reiterated the right of all tendencies within the Party to free expression and their proportional representation in the Party Congress. But the Tenth Party Congress, meeting in March 1921 only weeks after the brutal repression of the Kronstadt rising,[37] marked the definite break with this tradition. On Lenin's proposal two resolutions were adopted; the first ordered 'the immediate dissolution of all groups without exception formed on the basis of one platform or another (such as the Workers' Opposition Group, the Democratic Centralists Group etc)',[38] with a two-thirds majority to expel members from the Party. The second resolution specifically condemned the Workers' Opposition and declared, in a spirit quite alien to the confidence in the masses expressed in 1917, that 'only the political party of the working class, i.e. the Communist Party, is capable of uniting, training and organizing a vanguard of the proletariat and of the whole mass of the working people that alone will be capable of withstanding the inevitable petty-bourgeois vacillations of this mass, and the inevitable traditions and relapses of narrow craft unionism or craft prejudices among the proletariat'.[39] Expulsions duly followed and shortly afterwards Stalin became the Party's General Secretary.

THE STATE

The very different context of the political thought of Marx, Engels and Lenin is again brought out in their respective views on the State. Lenin was interested in the capture of state power and his most significant contribution lies in his views on post-revolutionary society. Marx and Engels (apart from the brief period after the Paris Commune) were chiefly occupied in analyzing the bourgeois state. Marx was first led to formulate his views on the state, which was in many ways for him the most characteristic institution of man's alienated condition, by his early journalistic experiences. Marx experienced the impact of the state chiefly as censor of his articles for the *Rheinische Zeitung*. In opposition to the contemporary Prussian state, Marx conceived of the possibility of forming a truly free association of men in an idealized state conceived, on the Hegelian model, as the incarnation of reason.

By the summer of 1843, two factors led Marx to modify this view: one was his reading of Feuerbach's critique of Hegel's philosophy, the second his practical experience as editor of the *Rheinische Zeitung* which showed him the importance of socio-economic factors in the framing of legislation. With this in mind,

Marx elaborated his ideas on the state in a long manuscript which
was a critique of Hegel's political philosophy. According to Hegel,
the state was logically prior to, and ethically superior to its two constituent elements, the family and civil society. Marx set out to show
that it was an illusion to suppose that the state had a universal
character capable of harmonizing the discordant elements of civil
society and uniting them on a higher level. By describing the state
prior to any analysis of civil society, Hegel presupposed a gap
between them and so had to work out institutions to bridge the gap.
All these institutions, however — monarch, representative
assemblies, bureaucracy — were in fact cloaks for particular interests in civil society: the state was no more than an empty ideal
sphere which created the illusion of belonging to a community.
This opposition between civil society and the state was
characteristic of the bourgeois epoch but not of the Middle Ages.
The form of government that Marx recommended, in contrast to
Hegel, was one where there was no separation between civil society
and the state and which directly corresponded to 'the essence of
socialized man'. He called this 'true democracy' and characterized
it as follows:

> In all states that are not democracies, the state, the law, the constitution is the
> dominant factor without really dominating. i.e. materially penetrating all the
> other spheres that are not political. In a democracty the constitution, the law and
> the state itself are only a self-determination of the people and a particular con-
> tent of them in so far as it is a political constitution.[40]

With his conversion to communism in 1844, Marx came to the
conclusion that the state was essentially the negation of man. In the
Paris Manuscripts he declared the state to be an expression of
human alienation similar to religion, law and morality, and equally
based on a particular mode of production. But at the same time the
state did contain positive elements. Marx's analysis here is similar
to his analysis of religion which in many respects acted as a
paradigm for his political views. Marx considered America as 'the
most perfect example of a modern state' and went as far as to say:

> . . . as regards actual life, the political state, even where it is not yet consciously
> impregnated with socialist principles, contains in all its modern forms the
> demands of reason . . . Inside its republican form the political state expresses all
> social struggles needs and truths.[41]

Thus Marx viewed the state, like religion, as a statement of man's ideal aims and also a compensation for their lack of realisation. The state was limited just because its aims remained ideal. Marx found confirmation of his view in the documents of the French and American revolutions which claimed to emancipate man as a political citizen, but left him in bondage as a man, or member of civil society, i.e. economic society. It was this paradox that Marx analyzed in his 1843 essay 'On the Jewish Question' in which he gave his most accessible critique of liberalism. In his article against Ruge in 1844 Marx went as far as to say that the more political a state was, and the more it constituted a separate sphere, the more incapable it was of solving society's problems:

> The state cannot abolish the contradiction which exists between the role and good intentions of the administration on the one hand and the means at its disposal on the other, without abolishing itself, for it rests on this contradiction. It rests on the contrast between public and private life, on the contrast between general and particular interests. The administration must therefore limit itself to a formal and negative activity, for its power ceases just where civil life and work begin.

Thus:

> If the modern state wished to do away with the impotence of its administration, it would have to do away with the contemporary private sphere for it only exists in contrast to the private sphere.[42]

Marx actually signed a contract in 1844 for a book on politics which would have incorporated his *Critique of Hegel's Philosophy of the State* and readings on the French Revolution; but he seems to have got no further than the table of contents.

Although Marx in his later writings did not abandon the idea of the state as compensation, as alienated social power, he concentrated more and more on an analysis of the function of the state in society. Whereas in his earlier writings he had tended to emphasize the gap between the state and society, he later considered the state as part of society. His fullest formulation of this idea was in *The German Ideology*. Marx's programme of analysis, stated at the beginning of the work, was:

> definite individuals who are productively active in a specific way enter into these definite social and political relations. In each particular instance, empirical

observation must show empirically, without any mystification or speculation, the connection of the social and political structure with production. The social structure and the state continually evolve out of the life-process of definite individuals, individuals ... as they work, produce materially, and act under definite material limitations, presuppositions, and conditions independent of their work.[43]

In *The German Ideology* Marx traced the origin of the state, together with other social institutions, to the division of labour: the state was in contradiction to the real interests of all members of society, constituting as it did an illusory community serving as a screen for the real struggles waged by classes against each other. In the course of history each method of production gave rise to a typical political organization furthering the interests of the dominant class. The large-scale industry and universal competition of modern capitalism had created their own political organization — the modern state which was dependent on the bourgeoisie for taxes and public credit. The state in turn moulded other social institutions:

Since the state is the form in which the individuals of a ruling class assert their common interests and the entire civil society of an epoch is epitomized, the state acts as an intermediary in the formation of all communal institutions and gives them a political form. Hence, there is the illusion that law is based on will, that is, on will divorced from its real basis, on free will. In similar fashion, right in turn is reduced to statute law.[44]

This is the view that Marx summed up in *The Communist Manifesto:* 'The executive of the modern state is but a committee for managing the common affairs of the whole bourgeoisie.'[45] It should be noted, however, that Marx himself considered this correlation between economic substructure and political formations to be a very loose one: for example, though he thought England the most advanced country economically, France was for him politically more advanced in many respects.

Marx does admit exceptions to his general description of the state as an instrument of class domination, and especially in two of his most striking analyses of contemporary events — *The Class Struggles in France* and *The Eighteenth Brumaire of Louis Bonaparte.* Sometimes Marx says that the state need not be representative of the whole of a class but only of a section of that class (for example, the financiers under Louis-Philippe); or that one class can control the state for the benefit of another class (for example, the Whigs on behalf of the middle class in England). In relatively backward countries, where classes were not fully developed, Marx thought that the state could play a relatively independent role; also in the European absolute monarchies in the transition between feudal and bourgeois classes. He says of France under Louis Bonaparte, in contrast to his predecessors: 'only under the second Bonaparte does the state seem to have made itself completely independent'. He goes on: 'And yet the state power is not suspended in mid-air. Bonaparte represents a class, and the most numerous class of French society at that, the small-holding peasants'.[46]

Yet Bonaparte was not controlled by the peasants and governed by no means exclusively in their interests. Indeed, Marx said that the state simply as an instrument of class domination was to be found only in North America, 'where the state, unlike all other national structures, was from the start subordinated to bourgeois society and bourgeois production'.[47]

The second broad exception in Marx to the idea of the state as an instrument of class domination occurs in Asian societies — India, China, and to some extent Russia. Owing to the lack of private property in land, 'the despot here appears as the father of all the numerous lesser communities, thus revealing the common unity of all'.[48]

Marx considered bureaucracy to be the most essential part of this modern state apparatus. His views on bureaucracy are contained chiefly in his *Critique of Hegel's Philosophy of the State* written in 1843 and in *The Eighteenth Brumaire of Louis Bonaparte* written in 1851. In the latter Marx writes of bureaucracy as originating with the rise of absolute monarchy and thus originally as a progressive force which destroyed the corporations of medieval society and made for centralization and equality of treatment for all citizens. In the 1843 manuscript, with his eye principally on Prussia, Marx described how the bureaucracy had eventually become a caste which claimed to possess, through higher education, the monopoly of the interpretation of the state's interests. The bureaucracy, finding itself challenged by the very spirit of equality that originally it had fostered, had turned itself into a medieval corporation, taking refuge in the trinity of mystery, hierarchy and authority. In France, Marx considered that the bureaucracy, which had prepared the way for the rule of the bourgeoisie, had largely become an instrument in their hands, though they conserved a tendency to independence, unlike the bureaucracies of Britain and the United States where parliaments were stronger and bureaucracy had not played such an important role in the transition from feudalism. Under Louis Napoleon, owing to the weakness of the bourgeoisie, the bureaucracy was able to control the state, being more than a match for the isolated peasantry that formed the basis of Bonaparte's power. This point is expanded in Marx's draft versions of *The Civil War in France*.

Any successful revolution was bound to involve the breaking of the power of the state and its bureaucracy. In 1871 Marx reminded Kugelmann of the passage in *The Eighteenth Brumaire* where he talked of the destruction of the bureaucratic-military machinery and described it as 'the precondition of any real popular revolution on the continent'.[49] In 1872 he wrote:

> What all socialists understand by anarchism is this: as soon as the goal of the proletarian movement, the abolition of classes, shall have been reached, the power of the state, whose function it is to keep the great majority of producers beneath the yoke of a small minority of exploiters, will disappear and governmental functions will be transformed into simple administrative functions.[50]

The distinction made here between 'government' and 'administration' is never completely spelled out by Marx but he seems to have thought that the abolition of the state would at least involve the disappearance of its most typical manifestations — the bureaucracy, the army and the judicature. The phrase that most often comes to mind in this connection is that 'the state is not abolished, it withers away', although the words are not actually by Marx but by Engels. Nevertheless, the variety of terms that Marx uses to refer to the disappearance of the state is too great to yield any precise meaning and the term most often employed is, in fact, 'abolition'.[51]

Marx's conception of the future role of the state has to be pieced together from remarks made solely en passant. Some statements of Marx seem to reveal an 'authoritarian' attitude, but these are usually devoted to what aspects of the bourgeois revolution the proletariat should support. When, for example, in the address of March 1850 he says 'the workers . . . must not only strive for a single and indivisible German republic, but also within this republic for the most determined centralization of power in the hands of the state authority', [52] this is a recommendation of policy in a country on the eve of a bourgeois revolution.

For Marx's view of the state after a successful proletarian revolution, there are two main sources. The first is Marx's comments on the Paris Commune, contained in his *The Civil War in France.* This essay cannot be taken as entirely representative of Marx's thought as it was written immediately after the bloody failure of the Commune and could not but have been an attempt at justification. Moreover, the rising had taken place against Marx's advice, he knew that the majority of its leaders were not communist and he went so far later as to say that its policies 'were not socialist, nor in the circumstances could they have been'.[53] Nevertheless, some of the policies of the Commune seem to have met with Marx's approval and he also considered it to have important potentialities. Marx welcomed the Commune's proposals to have all officials, including judges, elected by universal suffrage and revocable at any time; to pay officials the same wages as workmen; to replace the standing army by the armed people; and to divest the police and the clergy of their political influence. Marx also considered that the initiative of the Commune could have yielded a decentralized, federal political structure and an economy based on co-operatives united by a common plan.

Naturally during the arguments inside the International Marx rejected the anarchist views of Bakunin and his followers, but this does not support the view that he was an authoritarian.

The second main source for Marx's view of government after a proletarian revolution is in the *Critique of the Gotha Programme.* Here Marx asserts that 'freedom consists in converting the state from an organ superior to society into one completely subordinate to it.'[54] Commenting on the role of the state in communist society, Marx merely says that the question as to what social functions analogous to those of the contemporary state will still subsist in a communist society can only be answered scientifically. Marx's only further statement is that there will exist 'a period of revolutionary transformation' between capitalist and communist society and that in this period 'the state can be nothing but the revolutionary dictatorship of the proletariat'.[55] As has been previously pointed out, it is difficult to read any particular political implications into the term 'dictatorship'.

In the six-volume treatise he called his 'Economics', which Marx intended to write but never even half completed, the fourth volume was to have been devoted to the state; and it is the lack of this volume that constitutes the major gap in Marx's later writings. The general outline of its contents has to be reconstructed from the tangential remarks in writings devoted to other subjects.

The views of the later Engels on the state were directly informed by his attempt to produce an all-embracing materialist philosophy and by the political practice of the contemporary SPD. Both tended to issue in a technological approach illustrated at its most extreme in Engel's article 'On Authority', where he compares the discipline necessary in post-revolutionary society to that currently obtaining in factories. The emphasis on the non-subjective factors that had been present in his thought at least since the *Principles of Communism* of 1847 led him often to adopt a relatively mild attitude to the bourgeois state. Engels tended to avoid emphasizing the idea that the state needed to be smashed and considered the republic to be the 'ready-for-use political form for the future role of the proletariat'.[56] His view of the transition to communism is worth quoting at length:

> As soon as there is no longer any class of society to be held in subjection; as soon as, along with class domination and the struggle for individual existence based on the former anarchy of production, the collisions and excesses arising from these have also been abolished, there is nothing more to be repressed which would make a special repressive force, a state, necessary. The first act in which the state really comes forward as the representative of society as a whole — the taking possession of the means of production in the name of society — is at the same time its last independent act as a state. The interference of the state power in social relations becomes superfluous in one sphere after another, and then ceases of itself. The government of persons is replaced by the administration of things and the direction of the process of production. The state is not 'abolish-- ed', it withers away.[57]

This view of the state as 'withering away' is plainly a metaphor drawn from biology — with all that that implies.[58]

Lenin's ideas on the state are largely marked by the tension between pre-revolutionary theory and post-revolutionary practice. The theory goes back directly fifty years to the Marx of the Paris Commune. Lenin's most important work on the state was his *State and Revolution*; indeed, it has been called by Colletti far and away 'Lenin's greatest contribution to political theory'.[59] It is a sort of practical counterpart to his ideas on imperialism.

The book had its origin in Lenin's argument with Bukharin in the summer of 1916 over the existence of the state after a proletarian revolution. Bukharin had emphasized the 'withering' aspect, whereas Lenin insisted on the necessity of the state machinery to expropriate the expropriators. In fact, it was Lenin who changed his mind, and many of the ideas of *State and Revolution*, composed in the summer of 1917 — and particularly the anti-Statist theme — were those of Bukharin.[60]

Lenin's direct and simple definition of the state is that 'the State is a special organization of force: it is an organization of violence for the suppression of some class'.[61] Hence his denigration even of parliamentary democracy, which was influenced by what he saw as the recent increase of bureaucratic and military influences:

> To decide once every few years which member of the ruling class is to repress and crush the people through parliament — this is the real essence of bourgeois parliamentarism, not only in parliamentary-constitutional monarchies, but also in the most democratic republics.[62]

Thus, following Marx's conclusions on the Paris Commune, which Lenin took as his model,[63] Lenin declared that the task of the revolution was to smash the state. Although for a period under socialism 'there remains for a time not only bourgeois right but even the bourgeois state without the bourgeoisie',[64] Lenin believed that after a successful proletarian revolution the state had not only begun to wither,but was in an advanced condition of decomposition. But Lenin also called the state 'the armed and ruling proletariat'. Did this, too, wither? Yes, it did, in so far as it was in any way a power separate from, and opposed to, the masses (the influence on Lenin of his recent experience of the Soviets is clear here). He had little to say of the institutional form of this transition period. There was a strong emphasis on the dictatorship of the proletariat:

> A Marxist is solely someone who extends the recognition of the class struggle to the recognition of the dictatorship of the proletariat. This is what constitutes the most profound distinction between the Marxist and the ordinary petty (as well as big) bourgeois. This is the touchstone on which the real understanding and recognition of Marxism is to be tested.[65]

But there was little analysis of the shape this dictatorship might take, which is all the more tantalizing as Lenin's strong insistence on the withering of the state immediately after the revolution has libertarian or even anarchist overtones. His general view seemed to embody the classic socialist formula that the government of people could give way to the administration of things:

> We ourselves, the workers, will organize large-scale production on the basis of what capitalism has already created, relying on our own experience as workers, establishing strict, iron discipline backed up by the State power of the armed

workers; we will reduce the role of the state officials to that of simply carrying out our instructions as responsible, revocable, modestly paid 'foremen and accountants' (of course, with the aid of technicians of all sorts, types and degrees). This is our proletarian task, this is what we can and must start with in accomplishing the proletarian revolution. Such a beginning on the basis of large-scale production will of itself lead to the gradual 'withering away' of all bureaucracy, to the gradual creation of an order without quotation marks, an order bearing no similarity to wage slavery, an order in which the functions of control and accounting — becoming more and more simple — will be formed by each in turn, will then become a habit, and will finally die out as the special functions of a special section of the population.[66]

In the political sphere, what is most striking is the absence of reference to the agent of revolution — the Party itself. In his one serious reference to the Party Lenin said:

By educating the workers' Party, Marxism educates the vanguard of the proletariat which is capable of assuming power and of leading the whole people to Socialism, of directing and organizing the new order, of being the teacher, the guide, the leader of all the workers and exploited in the task of building up their social life without the bourgeoisie, and against the bourgeoisie.[67]

It is ambiguous here whether it is the vanguard or the proletariat which 'is capable of assuming power and of leading . . .'. Lenin's general cast of thought would tend to the former, but Lenin nowhere enlarged on the apparent clash which this entailed with his more liberal statements.

The optimism inherent in *State and Revolution* did not, however, long survive the success of the October revolution. The difficulties were enhanced by the isolation of the Soviet State among hostile powers, the failure of the revolutionary movement abroad and the consequent necessity for the Soviet government to sign a separate and humiliating peace with the Germans at Brest-Litovsk — a policy which Lenin had the greatest difficulty in getting adopted in the face of strong opposition from such Left Communists as Trotsky and Bukharin. Already a different emphasis was present in Lenin's reply to Bukharin at the Seventh Party Congress in March 1918. 'Just when will the State wither away?', he asked, and answered, 'We shall have managed to convene more than two Congresses before the time comes to say: see how our State is withering away. It is too early for that. To proclaim the withering away of the State prematurely would distort the historical perspective'.[68] The gradual shift from dictatorship of the proletariat to dictatorship of the Party and the equating of Party and state was aided and abetted by three main factors: the fact that the Party found power thrust into its hands; the growth of bureaucracy; and the lack of an effective workers' voice.

In late 1917 the Bolshevik Party was small and its organization ineffective. Some Bolsheviks, such as Preobrazhensky, even suggested that the Party be dissolved in the Soviets. But, as Liebman says,

> in proportion as the popular basis of the new regime got smaller and Soviet democracy became more formal, the Party, which offered a firmer resistance to social and political difficulties thanks to its greater cohesion, reinforced its authority and reestablished to its own advantage the previous disequilibrium.[69]

By 1919 the Party and the State were inextricably linked and the dictatorship of the proletariat became equated with the dictatorship of the Party — and Lenin was able to talk of class relationships being exercised 'under the leadership of the Party'.[70]

This Party domination was enhanced by the suppression of opposition, beginning with dissolution of the Constituent Assembly in January 1918. Before the revolution, Lenin had been in favour of the convocation of the Constituent Assembly, not apparently realising the inevitable clash with the slogan of 'all power to the Soviets'. The decision to dissolve the Constituent Assembly, for which the Bolsheviks had only obtained twenty-five percent of the votes, was unavoidable for a Party that claimed to be pursuing the proletarian socialist revolution. For the largest party in the Constituent Assembly represented peasant interests and the whole structure of the Assembly was much more appropriate to a bourgeois democracy.

But neither did the Soviets last long as an expression of popular will: the Civil War and the militarization of public life soon led to the *de facto* eclipse of Soviet power. The very existence of opposition parties was also gradually threatened. Before 1917, Lenin had never suggested a single-party state and the subsequent inability of the Bolsheviks to arrive at a coalition with their Socialist opponents was due just as much to their opponents' intransigence as to their own. But pressure of Civil War and the tendency to equate anti-Bolshevism with the counter-revolution led to the eventual suppression of all opposition parties. The Social Revolutionaries, representing as they did the better-off peasantry, were basically hostile to the Bolshevik programme; but this was not the case with the Mensheviks, whose popular support (despite the Bolshevik harrassment) tended to grow. In June 1918 they were excluded from the Pan-Russian Congress of Soviets and systematically suppressed at the end of 1920.

This tendency towards monolithism was increased by the growth of bureaucracy.[71] Bureaucracy was encouraged by the increased nationalization programme caused by confiscations and the war effort. There was also the influence of the traditional bureaucratic methods of Russian autocracy, and the desire to find work for the increasing number of unemployed by absorbing them into the state machine. By the end of 1920 this administrative machine had swollen to almost six million employees — a growth that was in inverse proportion to the productive capacity of the economy. Although Lenin was in favour of recruiting bourgeois technicians and specialists and indeed giving them special privileges, he was incessant in his conflict with bureaucracy. 'All of us', he wrote, 'are sunk in the rotten bureaucratic swamp of "department"'.[72] By early 1921 Lenin characterized the Soviet Union as 'a workers' state with bureaucratic distortion'.[73] And a year later, at the last Party Congress he attended, Lenin admitted:

> If we take that huge bureaucratic machine, that gigantic heap, we must ask: who is directing whom? I doubt very much whether it can truthfully be said that the Communists are directing that heap. To tell the truth, they are not directing, they are being directed.[74]

Even the famous Rabkrin (Workers' and Peasants' Inspectorate), designed to be a popular watchdog over the administration, became yet another body with all the deficiencies which it was supposed to combat. Lenin's remarks on the subject during the last months of his active life are akin to despair.

The growth in the power of the party and of the bureaucracy necessarily precluded the effective expression of grass-roots working-class opinion. Workers' control had been introduced in principle in November 1917, but was not an economic success and began to be abandoned after a few months. Under pressure of economic circumstances, Lenin called for piecework wages and even for Taylorism. The 'War Communism' in 1918-21 necessitated a highly centralized control and the subsequent NEP meant an (albeit necessary) step backwards. Strikes were seen as illogical in a state 'belonging' to the workers. On the crucial question of the status of Trade Unions there were two diametrically opposed views. Firstly, there were the views of the so-called Workers'

Opposition, represented by Kollontai and Shliapnikov, that the Trade Unions should have a decisive vote in the administration of economic matters. Secondly, there was the view of Trotsky that the Trade Unions should be simply an arm of political authority. Lenin accorded the Trade Unions a certain independence in the struggle against bureaucracy, but his view did not ultimately prevail.[75] The general inability of the Soviet government to put into practice the principles of *State and Revolution* filled Lenin's last years with gloom and pessimism. The conclusion from the above is inescapable: the fact that a proletarian revolution was successful in backward Russia and not supported by a similar revolution in the advanced West left the Bolsheviks in a political impasse for which their theory left them totally unprepared.

NOTES

1. The following draws substantially on my *Thought of Karl Marx* (2nd. edition London: Macmillan, 1980) and *Marxism after Marx* (London: Macmillan, 1979).

2. Marx to Proudhon, 5 May 1846, in K. Marx, F. Engels, *Werke* (Berlin: Dietz, 1957 ff) — hereafter *MEW* — Vol. XXVII, 442.

3. Marx to Blos, 10 November 1877, K. Marx, F. Engels, *Selected Correspondence* (Moscow: Foreign Languages Publishing House, 1961) — hereafter *MESC* — 310.

4. 'The Communist Manifesto', in K. Marx, F. Engels, *Selected Works,* (Moscow: Foreign Languages Publishing House, 1962) — hereafter *MESW* — Vol. I, 4-6.

5. K. Marx, 'Address of the Central Committee to the Communist League', *MESW*, Vol. I, 117.

6. Marx to Freiligrath, 29 February 1860, *MEW,* Vol. XXX, 490.

7. Marx to Engels, 11 February 1851, *MEW,* Vol. XXVII, 184 ff.

8. Marx to Kugelmann, 12 April 1871, *MEW,* Vol. XXXIII, 206.

9. Speech to the London Conference of 1871, *MEW,* Vol. XVII, 655.

10. Marx to Kugelmann, 9 October 1866, *MEW,* Vol. XXXI, 529.

11. Cf. *MESC,* 'Circular Letter of 1879', 375ff.

12. Of which the best is Lichtheim in his *Marxism* (London: Routledge, 1964).

13. F. Engels, in *MESW,* Vol. I, 135ff.

14. See further H. J. Steinberg, 'Revolution und Legalität. Ein unveröffentlichter Brief Engels an Richard Fischer', *International Review of Social History* (1967); and C. Elliott, *'Quis custodiet sacra?* Problems of Marxist Revisionism', *Journal of the History of Ideas,* Vol. 28 (1967), 73ff.

15. V. Lenin, 'What is to be Done?', in *Selected Works* (Moscow: Foreign Languages Publishing House, 1960), Vol. 1, 211.

16. On how Lenin in fact misrepresents the Economists, see A. Wildman, *The Making of a Workers' Revolution* (Chicago: Chicago University Press, 1967), 118ff.

17. V. Lenin, op. cit., 156ff.

18. Ibid., 215.

19. Ibid., 228ff.

20. See further, V. Lenin, *Collected Works*, Vol. 6, 229ff, spelling out the details of this centralization.

21. See R. Luxemburg, *Organizational Questions of Russian Social Democracy* (Berlin: Rote Verlag, 1904).

22. For the difficulties that, for example, Kautsky has in appreciating what points of principle could be involved in the split, see C. Weill, *Marxistes Russes et Social-democratie Allemande 1898-1904* (Paris: Maspero, 1977), 123ff.

23. V. Lenin, 'Preface to the Collection Twelve Years', *Collected Works*, Vol. 13, 101.

24. V. Lenin, 'Speech on the Party Programme', *Collected Works*, Vol. 6, 489.

25. See, in general, S. Schwarz, *The Russian Revolution of 1905* (Chicago: Chicago University Press, 1967), Ch. 4.

26. V. Lenin, 'The Reorganization of the Party', *Collected Works*, Vol. 10, 32.

27. Ibid.

28. Ibid., 34.

29. Cf. V. Lenin, 'The Social Democrats and the Duma Elections', *Collected Works*, Vol. 11, 434.

30. Cf. V. Lenin, 'A Tactical Platform for the Unity Congress', *Collected Works*, Vol. 10, 163.

31. V. Lenin, 'Report on the Unity Congress', *Collected Works*, Vol. 10, 376.

32. Ibid., 381.

33. See, for example, V. Lenin, 'Resolution Adopted by the Second Paris Group', *Collected Works*, Vol. 17, 221ff.

34. L. Schapiro, *The Communist Party of the Soviet Union*, 2nd edition (London: Eyre and Spottiswoode, 1970), 174.

35. Quoted in I. Deutscher, *The Prophet Armed: Trotsky, 1879-1921* (Oxford: Oxford University Press, 1954), 258. For a view stressing the radical alterations in the Bolshevik party in 1917, see R. Daniels, *The Conscience of the Revolution* (New York: Simon and Schuster, 1969), first two chapters.

36. R. Daniels, *The Conscience of the Revolution*, Chs. 5 and 6.

37. See P. Avrich, *Kronstadt 1921* (Princeton: Princeton University Press, 1970).

38. V. Lenin, 'Preliminary Draft Resolution of the Tenth Congress', *Collected Works*, Vol. 32, 244.

39. Ibid., 246.

40. D. McLellan (ed.), *K. Marx, The Early Texts* (Oxford: Blackwell, 1971) 66.

41. Ibid., 81.

42. Ibid., 213ff.

43. L. Easton and K. Guddat (eds.), *Writings of the Young Marx* (New York: Doubleday, 1967), 413ff.

44. Ibid., 470.

45. 'The Communist Manifesto', *MESW*, Vol. I, 36.

46. 'The Eighteenth Brumaire', *MESW*, Vol. I, 333.

47. D. McLellan (ed.), *Marx's Grundrisse* (London: Macmillan, 1971), 48.

48. K. Marx, *Pre-Capitalist Economic Formations* (London: Lawrence and Wishart, 1964), 69.

49. 'Marx to Kugelmann', 12 April 1871, *MEW*, Vol. XXXIII, 205.

50. K. Marx, 'The Alleged Splits in the International', in J. Freymond (ed.), *La*

Premiere Internationale (Geneva: Droz, 1926), Vol. II, 295.

51. Cf. M. Evans, 'Marx Studies', *Political Studies* (December 1970).

52. 'Address to the Communist League', *MESW*, Vol. I, 115.

53. Marx to Domela-Nieuwenhuis, 22 February 1881, *MESC*, 410.

54. K. Marx, 'Critique of the Gotha Programme', *MESW*, Vol II, 32.

55. Ibid., 33.

56. Engels to Lafargue, *MESC*, 472. See also Engels to von Patten, *MESC*, 363, where Engels specifically refers to the passage at the end of the second section of *The Communist Manifesto* which he and Marx had declared to be outmoded in their preface to the second German edition of 1872.

57. F. Engels, *Anti-Dühring* (Moscow: Foreign Language Publishing House, 1954), 315.

58. Marx never used this expression *(absterben)*, preferring the more direct 'abolish' *(abschaffen)*.

59. L. Colletti, *From Rousseau to Lenin* (London and New York: New Left Books, 1972), 224.

60. See S. Cohen, *Bukharin and the Bolshevik Revolution* (New York: Knopf, 1973), 39ff.

61. V. Lenin, *Selected Works* (Moscow, 1960), Vol. 2, 320.

62. Ibid., 338.

63. Cf. his very different view of the Commune as 'a government such as ours should not be' in 'Two Tactics', *Collected Works*, Vol. 9, 81.

64. V. Lenin, *Selected Works*, Vol. 2, 381.

65. Ibid., 328.

66. Ibid., 341.

67. Ibid., 322.

68. V. Lenin, 'Speech against Bukharin's Amendment', *Collected Works*, Vol. 27, 148.

69. M. Liebman, *Le Léninisme sous Lénine* (Paris: Seuil, 1973), Vol. 2, 109.

70. V. Lenin, 'Left-Wing Communism — An Infantile Disorder', *Collected Works*, Vol. 31, 48.

71. See Bukharin and Preobrazhensky's comments on this problem in *The ABC of Communism* (Harmondsworth: Penguin, 1969), 237ff.

72. V. Lenin, Letter to A. Tsyurupa, *Collected Works*, Vol. 36, 566. See also his letter to Bogdanov of December 1921, *Collected Works*, Vol. 38, 557.

73. V. Lenin, 'The Party Crisis', *Collected Works*, Vol. 32, 48.

74. V. Lenin, 'Report of the Central Committees to the Eleventh Congress', *Collected Works*, Vol. 33, 288.

75. See, for detail, R. Daniels, *The Conscience of the Revolution*.

2 Albania, Bulgaria, Romania: Political Innovations and the Party

Bogdan Szajkowski
University College, Cardiff, UK

Albania, Bulgaria and Romania constitute some of the most interesting examples of diversity in the development of communist political systems. In the three countries the theory and practice of the party, the state and party-state relations have undergone considerable changes since the early 1960s, resulting in the uniquely strengthened role of the party at the expense of the state, with the latter not withering away but becoming an indispensable appendage of the party.

The first part of this paper concentrates on the changes in the party role and functions and changes in party membership and social composition. The second part is devoted to changes in the structure and functions of the state, indicating which of its functions, de jure, de facto or both, have been taken over by the party. An attempt is also made to outline in broad terms (detailed analysis not being possible due to limited space) the reasons for these changes, which are further illustrated through the multiple holding of positions.

THE PARTY

In the 1960s the Party of Labour of Albania (PLA), the Bulgarian Communist Party (BCP) and the Romanian Communist (Workers') Party (RWP/RCP) all underwent processes of political innovation which, though differing in many respects, were similar in nature and served essentially as an instrument of continued party supremacy.

Albania, after her break with the Soviet Union in 1961 and the explicit rejection of the Soviet model of development, became increasingly ideologically, as well as politically and economically, dependent on China. In early 1966 Albania embarked on her own Cultural Revolution.[1] However, unlike its Chinese counterpart, the Albanian Ideological and Cultural Revolution (its official title) was not designed to mark an intra-party power struggle, but represented a unified effort by the Party leadership to reassert its authority over the regional and local party organizations, as well as to restore its influence in all sectors of Albanian life. During the first stage of the Revolution (February 1966-February 1967), following the Chinese example, military ranks were abolished and high-ranking party and state functionaries were assigned to work with local and regional party and state organs. Attempts were also made to reduce the bureaucracy by transferring administrative staff to work in factories and on farms.

The second period of the revolution was launched by Enver Hoxha on 6 February 1967 in his opening speech to the 5th Congress of the Party of Labour of Albania, and was designed to intensify the struggle against bureaucratism and to eliminate all remaining bourgeois traits from Albanian life. Again, as in China the Red Guards played a major part in it, but unlike the Chinese Red Guards they remained firmly under the control of the party. In March 1973, Hoxha concluded the third phase of the Revolution, designed to 'preserve Marxist-Leninist purity in all aspects of Albanian life'. This phase, according to Hoxha at its introduction, included elimination of all traces of religion, emancipation of women and eradication of undesirable foreign influences such as long hair, lack of respect for authority, modern styles in clothing, etc.[2]

The fourth period of the Revolution has been the anti-bureaucratism campaign, which began in 1975 and was aimed at reducing the staff of government agencies and the number of non-production employees in agriculture and industry. The main reason for this campaign is the fear on the part of the regime of the development of institutionalized opposition or competition to the Party in policy-making. In 1975 the Albanian leadership decided that the Revolution would become a permanent feature of Albanian life until the final victory of socialism had been achieved.

The Ideological and Cultural Revolution has formed a major

part in the uninterrupted development of the revolution conducted by the Party. This ongoing revolution has, since 1944, passed through three main stages: the anti-imperialist democratic stage of the victory of national independence and the establishment of the people's state power; the stage of the construction of the economic base of socialism; the stage of the complete construction of socialist society, which is still in progress. These three stages are a constituent part of a single revolution led by the PLA.[3]

The radical changes that took place in Albanian society during the Ideological and Cultural Revolution also gave the country an entry into the present stage of the complete construction of a socialist society. These developments are reflected in the latest Constitution of the People's Socialist Republic of Albania, which was approved by the People's Assembly on 28 December 1976. According to Hoxha, the document guarantees that Albania will follow the correct Marxist-Leninist path to the achievement of communism, and viewed through the prism of deep revolutionary changes, it is the most appropriate law in the present stage of the country's development.[4]

The Constitution[5] gives the Party of Labour of Albania, in comparison with other communist states, unprecedented control not only of the state apparatus but also of all its agencies as well as of mass organizations. Thus 'The People's Socialist Republic of Albania is a State of the dictatorship of the proletariat, which expresses and defends the interests of all the working people . . . ' (Article 2). Furthermore the document emphasizes that 'The Party of Labour of Albania, the vanguard of the working class, is the sole leading political force of the state and the society. In the People's Republic of Albania the dominant ideology is Marxism-Leninism. The entire socialist social order is developed on the basis of its principles.' (Article 3). The supervisory role of the Party is guaranteed by Article 10, which states: 'Under the leadership of the Party of Labour of Albania, the working class, as the leading class of the society, the cooperativist peasantry, as well as the other working people, exercise direct and organized control over the activity of state organs, economic and social organizations and their workers, for the purpose of defending the victories of the revolution and strengthening the socialist order.'

The Party also oversees the activities of the People's Assembly which, according to Article 66, is the 'supreme organ of state power, the bearer of the sovereignty of the people and the state and

TABLE 1
Membership of the Party of Labour of Albania;
Bulgarian Communist Party and Romanian Communist Party

Year	PLA	BCP	RCP
1943	700		
1944		25,000	less than 1,000
1945		254.000	over 200,000
1947			714,000
1948	45,382	495,658	
1952	44,418		
1954		455,251	
1955			593,398
1956	48,644	484,255	
1958			
1960			834,000
1961	53,659		
1962		528,674	1,100,000
1965			1,450,000
1966	66,327	611,179	
1969			1,924,500
1970			1,999,720
1971	86,985	699,476	
1972			2,230,000
1974			2,480,000 approx.
1976		788,211	
1977	101,500		
1978		817,000	2,747,110

Sources: All the tables in this chapter are based on tables contained in B. Szajkowski (ed.), *Marxist Governments: A World Survey*, 3 Vols. (London: Macmillan, 1981).

N.B.: The estimated population of Albania in 1976 was 2,458,600; the population of Bulgaria in 1976 was 8,761,000; the estimated population of Romania in 1978 was 21,855,000.

the sole law-making organ.' However, Article 67 of the Constitution states that the People's Assembly defines the main directions of the internal and external policies of the State 'in conformity with the general line and the orientation of the Party of Labour of Albania.'

The Party's grip on the state and society is further strengthened by Constitutional provisions that the 'Armed Forces are led by the Party of Labour of Albania' (Article 88) and Article 89 which specifies that the First Secretary of the Central Committee of the Party of Labour of Albania is the Commander-in-Chief of the Armed Forces and Chairman of the Defence Council.

In 1977 the membership of the PLA was just under three per cent of the population. Of the total number of party functionaries in all establishments, 40 per cent were under the age of 30; 31 per cent belonged to the 31-40 age group; 21 per cent were 41-50 and 8 per cent were over 51 years of age.[6] Although the membership of the Party has increased over the years (see Table 1) the PLA also underwent several small purges and at least one major purge during the various stages of the Ideological and Cultural Revolution. During the period between 1967-70, 1,323 members and 434 candidates were expelled from the Party, while 1,047 have been demoted to candidate status.

Only limited statistical data on the social composition of the Party of Labour of Albania are available. Table 2 shows that in accordance with the policy of 'revolutionization' the percentage of labourers in the Party has slightly increased over the years, although that of white-collar workers has only marginally declined. Also since 1967 there has been a deliberate drive to increase the representation of women, who in 1971 constituted 22.05 per cent, in 1972 24 per cent, in 1975 26 per cent and in 1976 27 per cent of the total membership.

TABLE 2
Social Composition of the Party of Labour
of Albania

	Labourers	Collective peasants	White collar workers
	%	%	%
1970	35.2	20.0	35.8
1971	36.4	29.7	33.9
1975	37.7	29.2	33.1
1976	37.5	29.0	33.5

The political innovation process in Bulgaria can be traced to the period of the Great Leap Forward that the country experienced at the end of the 1950s.[7] Although Chinese influence during this period of intensive activity has been subsequently denied, Maoist development policies clearly must have been an important factor. The main aim of the campaign was to fulfil the economic plan in advance. In the agricultural sector, for example, this was to be achieved through the merger of collectives into larger units thus improving territorial administration — in order both to decentralize industrial decision-making and to create jobs for the many unemployed. By December 1960 when the Great Leap Forward was terminated considerable improvements had been made in the economy. However, the policies of accelerated development invoked during the Great Leap Forward had also led to much hostility among sections of the general public, but particularly within the Party. In the purges that followed, the First Secretary of the Bulgarian Communist Party, Todor Zhivkov, secured his position by deposing two of his most serious rivals, Vulko Chervenkov in 1961 and Anton Yugov in 1962.

Since then, his position has been relatively secure, and it was further strengthened when he took over the presidency of the Council of State in 1971. When in 1965 a group of ten men, all with close Party and/or military connections, were found guilty on conspiracy charges against the regime another round of purges was carried out. Over the next three years there were various signs that the conspirators' aims of making Bulgaria more independent of the Soviet Union were shared by others. The Warsaw Pact invasion of Czechoslovakia in 1968 must have curtailed such aspirations. By 1971 when the Tenth Congress of the BCP met, the Party managed to secure its dominant position. This was further emphasized by the Second Bulgarian Constitution adopted in May 1971, which defined the party as 'the leading force in society and the state'.

In 1978 the membership of the Bulgarian Communist Party was just over 9 per cent of the total population (see Table 1) and has been steadily increasing over the years. As far as the social composition of the Party is concerned (see Table 3), it is worth noting that despite an official policy of increasing the proletarian element in the Party, in the 1970s the percentage of industrial workers rose at a lower rate than that of the white-collar workers.

Another policy pursued particularly in the 1970s has been that of increasing the number of young people in the Party; in January

1978 approximately 40 per cent of the Party members were less than forty years of age. Finally, although 50 per cent of the total population are female less than 30 per cent constitute the BCP membership.

TABLE 3
Social Composition of the BCP

	Industrial workers	Peasants	White-collar workers	Others
1948	26.5	44.7	16.3	12.5
1954	34.1	39.8	17.9	8.2
1958	36.1	34.2	21.7	8.0
1962	37.2	32.1	23.6	7.2
1966	38.4	29.2	?	?
1971	40.2	26.1	28.2	5.6
1976	41.1	23.1	35.6	—
1978	41.8	22.4	30.3	5.5

N.B.: The 1976 figure was not sub-divided into 'white-collar workers' and 'others'

In the case of Romania the political innovation process which led to the attainment of the RWP/RCP supremacy was much more radical in nature and ramifications than in Bulgaria, and in many respects — particularly in its appeal to nationalism — it has many features in common with Albania.

The first step in a search for a new political formula in Romania was the concerted campaign of 'de-Sovietization' and 're-Romanization' that began in the early 1960s.[8] Beginning with the restoration of original Romanian names to streets and places previously Russified, developing into the mass rehabilitation of historical and cultural figures associated with the struggle for political and economic independence and restoring 'Romanism' to the Romanians, the campaign culminated in the obvious endeavour to build a new image for the Party. The communists were now presented as direct descendants, followers and continuators of national ancestors, from Dacian Kings onwards. Particular emphasis was placed on the role of the communists in the events of August

1944 which led to the overthrow of the Antonescu regime. While formerly the Red Army had been credited with the liberation of Romania, from 1962 onwards the Romanian Communist Party was put forward as the main instigator of the anti-Antonescu putsch.[9] The publication in 1964 of Marx's hitherto unknown 'Notes on the Romanians'[10] was perhaps the most important step in the campaign for national legitimization of the Party. Communist ideology was proved perfectly compatible with anti-Russian nationalism, since the founder of scientific socialism had denounced in these 'Notes' Russia's encroachment on Romanian independence in general and the annexation of Bessarabia in particular.

In addition to its appeal to nationalism the Party increased its popularity as a result of an amnesty for former 'class enemies' and in 1962 by shortening, and in some cases totally abolishing, the candidacy or probation period. The new Party statutes adopted at the Ninth Congress in 1965 did away with the candidacy period altogether, resulting in a considerable number of intellectuals joining its ranks. The Romanian Party was changing from an essentially worker elite group into a nationally representative organization. The election of Nicolae Ceauşescu to the post of Secretary-General of the Party in March 1965 brought about new and radical dimensions to the political innovation process.

At the Fourth RWP Congress in July 1965, the first chaired by the new leader, it was decided to re-adopt the name Romanian Communist Party, thus emphasizing the Romanian roots of the Party and disassociating the Party from the Soviet-backed derivative image the RWP had been identified with. (The Fourth Congress of the RWP became the Ninth Congress of the RCP.) Perhaps even more important has been the change of name of the country from the People's Republic to Socialist Republic, putting Romania on an equal footing with the USSR.

The next (Tenth) Party Congress in 1969 instituted the 'rotation principle', according to which high Party officials are required periodically to exchange positions in the central Party apparatus for jobs at a lower level. The person who has so far remained unaffected by this principle is the Secretary-General of the Party, Nicolae Ceauşescu. Insofar as the application of the rotation principle has prevented the development of institutionalized opposition or competition to the top Party leadership, it has served in the same way as the first and fourth stages of the Albanian Ideological and Cultural Revolution.

Since Ceauşescu's advent to power there have been radical changes in the structure and role of the top Party body, the Political Bureau. In 1965 that body was replaced by the Standing Presidium, which headed the Central Committee's Executive Committee, a new intermediary body between the Central Committee and the top leadership of the RCP. The purpose of this innovation appears to have been the establishment of a mechanism for the smooth advance of Ceauseşcu's proteges. At the Eleventh Congress in 1974, under newly adopted statutes, the Standing Presidium — whose members were the most influential individuals in the Party — was replaced by a Permanent Bureau appointed by the Political Executive Committee (a new name for the former Executive Committee) from among its members. The Permanent Bureau has an ex-officio membership consisting of the Secretary-General of the Party (Ceauşescu), the President of the Republic (Ceauşescu), the Prime Minister and all the Secretaries of the Central Committee, five persons in all. In January 1977 the membership of the Bureau was increased to nine.

It appears that the evolution of the Permanent Bureau was a process aimed at the elimination of the former Standing Presidium, whose members might have become too influential and independent. Thus, firstly, most of the members of the former Presidium were removed from the new Bureau as a result of its new ex-officio membership and secondly Ceauşescu's closest collaborators were promoted to the Bureau, thereby ensuring his renewed domination of the decision-making process. Among the four promoted in January 1971, three were close relatives of the Secretary-General, including his wife Elena, his brother-in-law Ilie Verdet and his nephew Cornel Burtică. Another brother-in-law Manea Mănescu had been a member of the Bureau since its establishment. Mrs Ceauşescu nowadays appears to be the second highest-ranking Romanian official.[11]

In 1978 the membership of the RCP (see Table 1) was almost 13 per cent of the total population, one of the highest in any of the communist countries. The most dramatic expansion of Party membership in accordance with Party policies has occurred since the advent of Nicolae Ceauşescu to power. Between 1965 and 1978 the RCP membership has almost doubled.

The data on the Party's social composition (see Table 4) are sketchy. Three points, however, should be emphasized. Firstly, between 1965 and 1969 as the membership of intellectuals increased from 10 to 23 per cent, the percentage of workers decreased by only 1 per cent (from 44 to 43 per cent) and that of peasants by 6 per cent (from 34 to 28 per cent). This would suggest that the drive for new members has been successful in all three sections of the population, least among the peasantry. Secondly, since 1965 the percentage of peasant members of the Party has declined steadily over the years, from 34 to 20 per cent. This is more likely to reflect demographic and socio-occupational changes as a result of Romanian industrial growth rather than a lack of party appeal among the peasants. Thirdly, the RCP is one of the few communist parties that have attracted 50 per cent of its members from among industrial workers.

TABLE 4
Social Composition of the RWP/RCP, 1955-78

	Workers		Peasants		Intellectuals	
	No.	%	No.	%	No.	%
1955		42.6				
1960		51.0		34.0	70,000	
1965	630,000	44.0	500,000	34.0	145,000	10.0
1969		43.0		28.0		23.0
1972	1,060,000	46.5	526,589	23.1	430,000	18.8
1974		50.0		20.0		22.0
1975		approx. 50.0		approx. 20.0		approx. 22.0
1978	'over 73.26 per cent of members are engaged in material production'					

N.B.: The 'others' category can be approximately estimated in percentage terms by deducting the total of the above three categories for any given year from 100.

THE STATE

In Albania the vast expansion in the role of the Party during the past decade, through the application of the dictatorship of the proletariat, must have substantially limited the role of the executive. In the Albanian literature the state and its central and local agencies are discussed in conjunction with and in relation to the Party. The Party is always an undivided leader in the socialist state, according to Agim Popa, the editor of *Zeri i Populit*, who goes on to say:

In this connection our Party has expressed and rejected as the most flagrant departure from positions of Marxism-Leninism and as attempts at justifying the liquidation of the dictatorship of the proletariat, the revisionist theories and practices denying and eliminating the undivided role of the proletariat party in Socialism, beginning with the preaching on the 'independence' of the socialist state from the proletarian party and on the party being merely an ideological factor and ending with the opportunist justification of pluralism of political parties in the socialist system.[12]

Although the constitution determines the role of the Party of Labour of Albania within the political structure of the country, the percentage of population belonging to the PLA is very small indeed. The Party dominates and supervises the direction and activities of the central and local government, not only as of right but through a comprehensive system of multiple holding of positions, with considerable concentration of power among the members of the Political Bureau. Thus the most important governmental positions of Prime Minister, Deputy Prime Ministers and Ministers in charge of crucial ministries such as Defence, Interior and Finance are held by the top Party officials (see Table 5).

TABLE 5
Government Posts held by the Members of the PLA Political Bureau, July 1978

Enver Hoxha	(First Secretary of the Central Committee)
Ramiz Alia	(Secretary of the Central Committee)
Adil Carcani	First Deputy Prime Minister
Kadri Hazbiu	Minister for Internal Affairs
Hekuran Isai	(Secretary of the Central Committee)
Hysni Kapo	(Secretary of the Central Committee)
Spiro Koleka	Deputy Prime Minister, Deputy Chairman of the People's Assembly
Pali Miska	Deputy Prime Minister
Manush Myftiu	Deputy Prime Minister
Mehmet Shehu	Prime Minister, Minister for People's Defence
Haki Toska	Minister of Finance

N.B.: Posts in parentheses are purely Party positions.

The multiple holding of positions has been standard practice since the foundation of the new Albanian regime; for instance, in 1978 seven of the twenty-two members of the Council of Ministers were members or candidate members of the Central Committee. With every key position occupied by a Political Bureau member, the party elite maintained direct control over the entire governmental structure, applying the principle that 'the more the revolution advances and deepens, the more the leading role of the Party must be strengthened and perfected in every sphere of life and state and social activity'.[13]

Until 1971 the state structure of Bulgaria resembled closely that of the Soviet Union with a presidium of the National Assembly similar to the Presidium of the Supreme Soviet. In 1971, however, the Presidium was replaced by the more powerful State Council which is defined as a supreme permanent organ of state power. It includes representatives from the BCP and the other political party allowed to function, the Agrarian Union, and from the mass organizations. The Council fulfils executive and legislative functions when the National Assembly is not in session. It can initiate and pass decrees and resolutions entirely in its own right and without subsequent ratification by the National Assembly. One other example of the Council's considerable power, which is without parallel in the communist world, is that it supervises the work of the Council of Ministers. In other countries this function is performed de jure by the national parliament. The Bulgarian Council of State is presided over by the First Secretary of the BCP Central Committee, Todor Zhivkov, a fact that would suggest further strengthening of Party control over the state apparatus.

In addition, the BCP exercises direct control over some of the most important ministries in the Bulgarian government (see Table 6). In conformity with the pattern of multiple holdings of positions that exists in all the communist countries, the most important governmental positions are held by the members of the Political Bureau. Thus the posts of Prime Minister, Minister of Foreign Affairs, First Deputy Prime Minister, Minister of National Defence, Chairman of the Committee for State and People's Control and Minister of Public Education are held by top Party officials.

In Romania, like almost all the other European communist countries (with the exception of Albania and Czechoslovakia), constitutional provisions are made for a Council of State (Supreme Collegial State body). The Council's prerogatives, however, were substantially reduced with the creation in 1974 of the office of President of the Republic.

The President (who is elected, on the recommendation of the

TABLE 6
Posts held by the Members of the Political Bureau of the BCP July 1978

Full members

Ognyan Doinov	(Secretary of the Central Committee)
Tsola Drakoicheva	Member of the State Council
Dobri Dzhurov	Minister of National Defence
Grisha Filipov	Member of the State Council; (Secretary of the Central Committee)
Pencho Kubadinski	Member of the State Council; Chairman of the Fatherland Front
Aleksandr Lilov	Member of the State Council; (Secretary of the Central Committee)
Ivan Mihailov	Member of the State Council
Petar Mladenov	Minister of Foreign Affairs
Stanko Todorov	Chairman of the Council of Ministers
Tano Tsolov	First Deputy Chairman of the Council of Ministers
Todor Zhivkov	President of the State Council; (First Secretary of the Central Committee)

Candidate Members

Todor Stoichev	Member of the State Council
Peko Takov	Vice-President of the State Council
Krustyu Trichkov	Deputy Chairman of the Council of Ministers; Chairman of the Committee for State and People's Control
Drazha Vulcheva	Member of the State Council; Minister of Public Education

N.B.: Posts in parentheses are purely Party positions.

Central Committee of the RCP and the Socialist Unity Front, by two-thirds majority of the deputies to the Grand National Assembly) has prerogatives unmatched by any other communist head of state (with the possible exception of Yugoslavia and the Democratic People's Republic of Korea). The Constitution does not require him to submit his decisions for the approval of any organ of state authority. President Ceauşescu shares with President Kim Il Sung another characteristic, the ever growing cult of personality.[14]

Like the Party of Labour of Albania, the Romanian Communist Party has increased its dominant role, particularly during the past decade. According to its programme, adopted in 1974, the Party will continue to exist and lead society as long as the process of socialist edification and construction continues. It will only gradually wither away 'through its integration in the society's life; through an ever more organic participation of Party members in the entire social life.'[15] As pointed out earlier, there are signs that the take-over from within of societal structures has been the Party's main operational context. The control that is exercised from inside rather than outside is in marked contrast to most other ruling communist parties except possibly Albania and the Democratic People's Republic of Korea. In addition, since 1967 the tendency in Romania has been to merge Party and state (as in the two countries mentioned above) to avoid parallelism. This has given rise to several forms of Party domination over state activities, notably by the following means.

TABLE 7
State or Joint State-Party Positions held by
Members of the Romanian Permanent Bureau, 1978

Nicolae Ceauşescu	President of the Republic
	President, Council of State
	Chairman, National Defence Council
	Chairman, Supreme Council for Economic Development
	Chairman, Commission for Economic and Social Forecasting
Elena Ceauşescu	Chairman, Section for Chemical Industry, Supreme Council for Economic Development
Manea Mănescu	Prime Minister
Gheorghe Oprea	First Deputy Prime Minister
	Chairman, Section for Metallurgical Industry and Machine Building, Supreme Council for Economic Development
Ilie Verdet	First Deputy Prime Minister
	Chairman, State Planning Committee
Cornel Burtică	Deputy Prime Minister
	Minister of Foreign Trade and International Economic Co-operation
Paul Niculescu	Deputy Prime Minister
	Minister of Finance
	Chairman, Council for Co-ordination of Consumer Goods Production
Ion Pătan	Deputy Prime Minister
	Minister of Technical-Material Supply and Control of Fixed Assets
Gheorghe Rădulescu	Deputy Prime Minister
Stefan Andrei	Minister of Foreign Affairs
Iosif Banc	Chairman, Central Council of Workers' Control of Economic and Social Activities

Firstly through the process of multiple holding of positions, a practice standard to all communist countries (see Table 7). Of the forty members of the Romanian government in 1978 only three were not members of the Central Committee and of the remaining thirty-seven, all but one were full members of that body.

Secondly, through the 'rotation principle' the Party has been able to establish a mechanism of supervision at all levels.

In most recent years another institutional innovation has provided for the creation of joint Party-State organizations, such as the Supreme Council for Economic Development, the Central Council of Workers' Control of Economic and Social Activity, the Defence Council, the Council for Socialist Culture and Education and the Committee for Problems of People's Councils, among others. These organizations provide an infrastructure for blending Party and state activities.

CONCLUSIONS

The political innovation process initiated by the PLA, BCP and RCP in the later 1950s and early 1960s, which to a large extent was due to the political and social instabilities expressed to varying degrees in all the Eastern European countries, resulted in the Albanian, Bulgarian and Romanian cases in a marked strengthening of the dominant position of the respective parties.

Since in all three countries the Party occupies an even more dominant position than in other communist states, it was perhaps only too natural that political innovations involving the Party should occur in these countries first. However, analyzing the nature of these innovations, one is struck by their highly manipulative and personal nature.

While in Albania the PLA has remained an elitist group whose constitutional position is unique in the entire communist world, the BCP and RCP, by broadening their bases since the early 1960s, have lost their worker elite group content. Both the latter parties began a transformation process into nationally representative organizations, parties of the 'whole people'. By playing a leading role in the alliance between workers, peasants and intelligentsia, both have moved away from the traditional position of the vanguard of the proletariat. The RCP in particular has both in theory and in practice moved closer to Yugoslavia's League of Communists, thus perhaps beginning the process of withering away through its integration with society.

Albania and Romania present a unique and fascinating example of a political system where the Party and the state are de facto and de jure extremely closely interwoven. Albania is an even more clear cut example than Romania of the Party's complete monopoly of power. As Enver Hoxha explains, the Albanian State is the 'State of the dictatorship of the proletariat' where there is 'only one unified state power', that of the Party of Labour of Albania.[16]

Another interesting feature of two of the parties analyzed in this study are the family links among the top echelon of the RCP and PLA. Among the nine members of the RCP Permanent Bureau, four are close relatives, including the wife, of Nicolae Ceauşescu — who of course is also a member of that body. The Central Committee of the PLA, consisting of seventy-seven members, includes five married couples. In the Romanian and Albanian parties attempts have been made to prevent the development of institutionalized opposition by the introduction of the 'rotation principle', in the RCP in 1969 and in the PLA since 1966, and by assigning high-ranking functionaries to work with lower organs.

While the positions of the PLA, BCP and RCP have been strengthened at the expense of the state there is no sign that the latter has begun the withering away process. The state has become merely an appendage of the party.

Lastly, a word or two must be added about the leaders of the three parties.

In the case of Bulgaria and Romania the party leaders are also heads of state. But, irrespective of whether the party leadership is or is not combined with the top state positions, it is the party post that always remains the fountainhead of the regime leader's power. The relationship between the two jobs can also be gathered from the fact that it is the party leader who adds to his function that of head of state and never vice versa. This, in the cases of Ceauşescu and Zhivkov, was an extension not only of personal power but primarily of party control over the state.

In essence, the situation in Albania is similar: the centre of power is the party and the party leader is the effective leader of the country. Enver Hoxha is evidently not interested in accumulating more trappings of office.

NOTES

1. The following is based on B. Szajkowski, 'Socialist People's Republic of Albania', in B. Szajkowski (ed.), *Marxist Governments: A World Survey*, Vol. 1 (Albania-The Congo) (London: Macmillan, 1981), 34-61.

2. See *History of the Party of Labour of Albania* (Tirana: 'Naim Frashëri' Publishing House, 1971), 607-655.

3. Ibid., 656

4. Enver Hoxha, *Report to the 6th Congress of the Party of Labour of Albania* (Tirana: 'Naim Frashëri' Publishing House, 1971), 130.

5. *The Constitution of the People's Socialist Republic of Albania* (Tirana: The '8 Nëntori' Publishing House, 1977).

6. *History of the Party*, op. cit, 241.

7. The following is based on L. Holmes, 'People's Republic of Bulgaria' in *Marxist Governments*, Vol. 1, 116-144.

8. The following is based on M. Shafir 'Socialist Republic of Romania' in *Marxist Governments*, Vol. 3 (Mozambique-Yugoslavia), 589-639.

9. This new interpretation of historical events was first made public in a book review printed in the Party's historical periodical in 1962. See A. Niri's review of V.B. Ushakov, *The Foreign Policy of Nazi Germany* in *Analele Institutului de Studii Istorice al Partidului*, Vol. VIII, No. 5 (1962), 179-84. See also the series of articles entitled 'Pages of History' that appeared in *Lumea* in 1979 on the 35th anniversary of the August events — *Lumea* Nos. 27 (6 July, 24-26); 30 (27 July-2 August, 13-14, 31); 31 (3-9 August, 23-25); and 32 (10-16 August, 22-23). In addition see A. Simion, 'Romanian Communist Party's Decisive Role in the Historic Events of August 1944', *Lumea*, No. 34 (24-30 August 1979), 24-25.

10. K. Marx, *Insemnari despre Romani — Manuscrise inedite* (ed. A. Otetea and B. Schwann) (Bucharest: Editura Academeiei Republicii Populare Romine, 1964).

11. The list of family connections is long. Elena Ceauşescu is a member of the Party's Permanent Bureau, Political Executive Committee, Central Committee, member of the Grand National Assembly, member of the Technical Sciences section of the Romanian Academy, Director-General of the Central Institute of Chemical Research, chairman of the section for the Chemical Industry of the Supreme Council for Economic Development, member of the Executive Bureau of the National Council for Science and Technology.

Nicu Ceauşescu, one of the President's sons, is the Secretary of the Romanian Union of Communist Youth. Valentin Ceauşescu (son) is a leading member of the Institute of Inventions. Major-General Ilie Ceauşescu (brother) is a deputy secretary of the Higher Political Council of the Romanian Army and Professor of History at the Military Academy of Bucharest. Marin Ceauşescu (brother) is the head of the Romanian Economic Agency in Vienna. Florea Ceauşescu (brother) is editor-in-chief of an agricultural publication. Ion Ceauşescu (brother) is Secretary of State in the Ministry of Agriculture. Constantin Ceauşescu (brother) is head of the Directorate of Post, Radio and Television.

Cornel Burtică (nephew) is a member of the Party's Permanent Bureau, Political Executive Committee, Central Committee and also Deputy Prime Minister. Ion Ionita (nephew) is chief-of-staff of the Romanian Army and Minister of National Defence. Manea Mănescu (brother-in-law) until March 1979 was Prime Minister and was replaced by another brother-in-law Ilie Verdet, who is also a member of the Party's Permanent Bureau, Political Executive Committee and Central Committee. Gheorge Petrescu (brother-in-law) is a Minister of Metallurgical Industries and Janos Fazekas (father-in-law of Ceausescu's son, Valentin) is another Deputy Prime Minister and Minister of Internal Trade.

This list is far from complete. It does not include Mrs Ceauşescu's side of the family and other lesser officials.

12. Agim Popa, 'Comrade Enver Hoxha, On the Dictatorship of the Proletariat', *Albania Today*, Vol. 42 No. 5 (1978), 31.

13. Enver Hoxha, *Report to the 7th Congress of the Party of Labour of Albania* (Tirana: The '8 Nëntori' Publishing House, 1977), 23.

14. Over the years since 1965 Ceauşescu himself almost came to replace the party as the personification of the much-lauded 'Romanian national spirit' and 'Ceauşescu-Romania' — in precisely that order — became the slogan of mass rallies. A most recent example of this is the *Resolution of the Twelfth Congress of the Romanian Communist Party* from which the following passage is taken:

In full consensus with the ardent will of all the communists, unanimously expressed in the Party general meetings and conferences, voicing the loftiest feelings of everlasting love and esteem of our whole people, the Congress has re-elected — in an atmosphere of great enthusiasm — to the office of General Secretary of the Party, Comrade Nicolae Ceauşescu, the most beloved son of the people, who embodies the most distinguished virtues of our nation, a brilliant leader and remarkable revolutionary, an ardent patriot and consistent internationalist, an outstanding militant of the international working-class and communist movement, of the struggle for peace and collaboration among peoples, a highly prestigious and authoritative personality of the present-day political life. The Congress voices its conviction that this political act, of high communist responsibility, is the safest guarantee for the firm implementation of the Programme of Building the Multilaterally Developed Socialist Society and Romania's Advance to Communism, for the rise of our homeland to ever higher levels of progress and civilization, for the strengthening of the country's national independence and sovereignty and for the assertion of the Romanian people's lofty ideals of peace, freedom and international collaboration. (Bucharest: Agerpres, November 1979, 2.)

15. *Programul Partidului Comunist Roman de Faurire a Societatii Socialiste Multilateral Dezvoltate si Inaintare a Roman Spre Comunism*. (Bucharest: Editura Politica, 1975), 111.

16. Enver Hoxha, 'Proletarian Democracy is Genuine Democracy', *Albania Today*, Vol. 42 No. 5, (1978).

3 China — From Idealism To Pragmatism?

Barbara Krug
University of Saarland, Saarbrücken, FRG

INTRODUCTION

1. The Chinese Communist Party and the Struggle for Power[1]

The military weakness of the Chinese Empire, exposed in several wars with the Western powers and Japan[2] not only converted China into a semi-colony of those powers but also led Chinese youth to examine the reasons for their country's weakness.

The collapse of the Manchu dynasty in 1911-12, the destruction of the unity of the country and three great civil wars between 1850 and 1900,[3] in the eyes of those Chinese who had been educated abroad, rendered proof that the Confucian system as a whole had failed and that only the adaption to western thinking could save China. Hence, they realized that China had to find a new identity as a nation state to replace the old concept of China as a cultural entity.[4] Although the first president of the Chinese republic, Sun Yatsen, wanted to build a new China, modelled after western democracies, the first country which offered him and his party — the Guomindang — help and promised to revise the humiliating 'Unequal Treaties', was the newly established Soviet Union.[5] Lenin and the Comintern, who saw the implications of supporting national liberation movements for the expansion of communism,[6] provided help in two respects. On the one hand, they stimulated the establishment of a Communist Party in China (hereafter, CCP), which in 1921 was founded by different 'Marxist Study Groups'[7] of college students. On the other hand Russian advisors sent by the Comintern reorganized the Guomindang and helped Sun to build an efficient party-army. It was also due to the presence of the Russian advisors that both parties formed an 'United Front' in the form of the so-called 'Bloc from within',[8] which meant that members of the CCP joined the Guomindang as individuals. In the eyes of the Comintern, the United Front represented all the forces in the national revolution: workers, peasants, the petty bourgeoisie, and the national bourgeoisie.[9]

Both parties started together in the Northern Expedition of 1926 in which the country was to be united. The increasing influence, however, of the CCP members within the Guomindang,[10] as well as their success in building up communist mass organizations,[11] led Chiang Kaishek, the centrists and the right wing of the Guomindang to the coup d'état of 1927, in which the urban and industrial base of the CCP was completely smashed.[12] From now on, the Chinese Communists who retreated to the mountainous regions of Hunan and Jiangxi (Kiangsi) establishing 'Soviet Areas' there, became a movement recruited mainly from the peasantry.

Though in the 1930s Chiang Kaishek was able to unite the country he did not succeed in eliminating the Communist bases. After being forced to give up the Soviet Areas in the south, the CCP started the Long March to China's northern province of Shanxi (Shensi) where they established, in 1935, the new base at Yanan. After the outbreak of the war against Japan the CCP and the Guomindang formed a second United Front in order to fight the Japanese together.[13] After the end of World War II it became obvious that the Guomindang had lost popular support and the CCP had successfully mobilized the revolutionary potential of the Chinese peasantry.[14] After four years of civil war, the People's Republic of China (PRC) was established on 1 October 1949.

The experience of twenty-two years of armed struggle in a guerilla war, interrupted only by the war against Japan, influenced the perceptions of the Communists at least as much as Marxist-Leninist theory. Mao's vision of an identity between Party, army, and administration is obviously based on the experience of the Soviet Areas in Jiangxi, (1927-34)[15] and in Yanan (1935-45).[16] The need for military strength led to a highly motivated leadership by all-round cadres, who were able to accomplish military, administrative and political tasks at the same time, and who became afterwards the model for the whole country. These 'red' cadres were regarded by Mao as superior to the 'experts'. Such experts would be the type of leadership personnel required within a framework of a more institutionalized and diversified political system as was proposed by those members of the CCP who had worked in the trade unions and the urban underground and joined the CCP base after the Long March.[17] Hence, already in the 1940s the debate about the role of the Party had started. During the first Rectification (Zhengfeng) Movement, a compromise was found but, as the history of the PRC shows, both sides tried to put their respective concepts into practice whenever either dominated the political process.

2. The CCP in Power

In the history of the People's Republic of China (PRC) one can distinguish between periods of 'Transformation' and periods of 'Consolidation'. During the former, Mao Zedong attempted to implement his revolutionary aims through mass mobilization. The latter are characterized by Liu Shaoqi's approach of giving priority to more pragmatic administration and stability, in which economic factors and expertise as well as collective leadership within the Party and clearly institutionalized channels of conflict resolution would replace Mao's concept of the creativity of the masses and their ad hoc participation in the decision-making processes.[18] Although Liu Shaoqi personally played an active role in politics only until his purge in 1966 during the Great Proletarian Cultural Revolution (GPCR), his ideas continued to be upheld by a particular faction within the Party and state bureaucracy as well as in the military.

The history of the CCP since 1949 can be divided into the following periods:

1949-56 (First Period of Consolidation)

After the 'Period of Recovery' (1949-52), the CCP adopted a Soviet-type regime with collective leadership, centralized and specialized hierarchies in the State and Party organization as prescribed by the State Constitution of 1954 and the Party Constitution of 1956. The economy was to be planned and centrally directed.[19]

1957-60 (First Period of Transformation)

During the Great Leap Forward central planning was abolished, expertise of administrative cadres and intellectuals substituted by the so-called 'creativity of the masses', and collectivization in the agricultural sector completed. At the end of the 'Hundred Flowers' (1957) and 'Antirightist' movements most of the non-communist ministers and officials in state agencies were purged and many party-members, particularly intellectuals, were also dismissed.[20]

1961-65 (Second Period of Consolidation)

After the disaster of the Great Leap Forward a period of 'Readjustment' set in. Liu Shaoqi became Chairman (Head of State) of the People's Republic of China while Mao Zedong withdrew from all positions in state organizations; he remained Chairman of the Central Committee of the CCP, however. Many cadres were rehabilitated, Party as well as state organizations re-established, and the process of collectivization stopped.[21] But already by 1963 the attacks on party cadres who did not do physical labour had started again. At the same time the 'Learn from the People's Liberation Army' campaign began.[22]

1966-69 (Second Period of Transformation)

During this time the whole administration, including economic and party agencies as well as the central government, was rendered almost totally ineffective by the Red Guards and revolutionary rebels upon the exhortation of the Cultural Revolutionary leadership. At first sight, the GPCR thus turned out to be Mao Zedong's great success leading to the purge of Liu Shaoqi and many of his associates, and also to the destruction of the latter's conception of how the country should be ruled. But it soon became apparent that although it had been possible to destroy the bureaucratic apparatus, it was impossible to replace bureaucratic administration by the 'creativity of the masses'. In this situation of political chaos, Mao called out the army.[23] But only those sections of the army loyal to Lin Biao (Minister of Defence and newly-named successor) kept within the limits of Mao Zedong's wishes of subduing the Red Guards; while others, particularly in the provinces, used their newly-won political power to rebuild the administration and economic structures.[24]

1969-76

With the appearance of the army on the political scene, it becomes more and more difficult to distinguish only between 'transformation' and 'consolidation' periods. From now on the political struggle was no longer between the proponents of the 'two lines'. Now the army had become an important factor in its own right, without which neither of the traditional two groupings could hope to win an advantage over the other. As so often in Chinese history the conflicts that led to the GPCR were not resolved by the victory of one side but ended in a series of compromises. Reviewing the achievements of each faction in the post-GPCR era, one could argue that Mao and his associates had gained important advantages over their adversaries; but it would probably be more correct to say that in the long run the faction of Liu Shaoqi proved to be more successful. A catalogue of the more recent achievements of each faction would look as follows:

Mao Zedong and his followers had been successful in launching, in 1975, the 'Criticize Lin Biao, Criticize Confucius' campaign (which in fact had been an indirect attack on Zhou Enlai, who had become the major proponent of the Liu Shaoqi line); in placing a large number of their supporters in the newly constituted Politburo and Central Committee of the CCP (1973)[25] [this was the price Zhou Enlai had to pay for the rehabilitation of his close associate, Deng Xiaoping]; launching, in 1975, the campaign 'To exercise dictatorship over the bourgeoisie', which was another attempt to discredit party bureaucracy; and finally launching the campaign against 'the rightist storm of the reversal of verdicts' which attacked Deng Xiaoping and ended in 1976 with his dismissal from all positions inside and outside the party. But the spiritual heirs of Liu Shaoqi outperformed the former, as proven by the dismissal of Chen Boda, Mao Zedong's personal secretary, in 1970; the 'Lin Biao incident' ending with the death of Mao Zedong's successor and a large-scale reshuffle among Lin's followers in the Chinese officer corps, in 1971;[26] the first campaign of rehabilitation of party and bureaucratic cadres 1969-71; the 'new course' in economic policy 1971-73; the propagating of the 'Four Modernizations' in 1975, and the purge of the 'Gang of Four' on 6 October 1976.[27]

1976-80

The rehabilitation of Deng Xiaoping can be interpreted as a new phase of consolidation, if not the 'final' victory of Liu's and Deng's concept.[28] The period to the present can be described as the retreat of the Party from economic organizations; the re-installing of institutionalized leadership; the re-appearance of mass organizations, non-communist parties and religious organizations; limited chances to express personal opinions; the opening to the West, as far as technology is concerned; the re-installing of a wage and income system with payments according to individuals' work; and the re-introduction of university entrance examinations.[29]

THE PARTY

1. The Theoretical Debate

As mentioned above, even before the CCP's take-over in China there had been serious tensions among its leaders. However, most western observers regarded the CCP as monolithic. In fact, the disagreements between Liu Shaoqi and Mao Zedong came to the fore during the Yanan Period, between 1934 and 1945.[30] These differences were on the one hand based on the personal and career backgrounds of the two main proponents, but on the other, also on different conceptions regarding the possible contribution that not only the party but also the army could make to the construction of a socialist society.

As the leading figure of the communist underground in enemy-held areas during the war, Liu had to work with people of very different social backgrounds, attitudes and interests.[31] The only way he could weld together such a diverse group of supporters and enforce party discipline was to adopt a style of leadership that was conducive to a measure of debate without endangering the basically hierarchical order of his organization and its capacity to make swift decisions. Out of this historical necessity the communist underground movement around Liu Shaoqi came to be controlled by — and continued to uphold — the principles of 'democratic centralism'.[32]

On the other hand, Mao Zedong's approach to leadership reflected another historical experience: as one of the leading figures of the peasant movement and the Long March he believed in the unity of the armed, and the ideological struggle in which a strong and unified leadership was necessary and in which the partisan army was not necessarily subordinate to the party.

During the Long March, the CCP and the communist army, or class struggle and armed struggle, became identical. As Mao put it: 'We know that in China there would be no place for the proletariat . . . no place for the Communist Party and no victory for the revolution without armed struggle.'[33] Although in theory the guns should be commanded by the party, in reality there existed hardly anything worth the name of a party organization in the liberated areas which could command the army; all power rested effectively in the hands of Mao as the leader of both the party and the army.

The non-existence of a party organization in the liberated areas meant that, in the final analysis, the authority for interpreting policy and ideology also rested solely with the single leader, namely Mao Zedong. Mao's position of dominance since 1935 may not have been purposefully intended. But it was the reflection of Mao's sense of political practicability. For him it was not the theorist, not Marx or Lenin, who makes a real impact in furthering world revolution; rather it was an experienced leader of armed revolutionists who carried forward the revolution.[34] This strictly hierarchical concept of leadership clearly contradicted Liu Shaoqi's ideal of a Leninist-type of cadre party governed by collective leadership. Although in the Yanan period Liu supported Mao's concept of the unity of the armed and the ideological struggle,[35] with its inherent strong leadership position for Mao, he reluctantly pointed out somewhat lamely that 'Comrade Mao Tse-tung is the leader of the whole party, but he, too, obeys the party . . .'.[36]

To discuss the full range of the debate among 'Maoists' and 'Liuists' would be beyond the limits of this paper. Rather it will concentrate on what are considered to be the most important aspects of this debate, namely:

1. The issue of whom, and what, the Party represented within the Chinese revolution

2. The question of leadership within the Party
3. The problem of class struggle.

The Representation of the Party within the Chinese Revolution

One of the main problems facing communist parties in developing countries is the question of who they can claim rightfully to represent. If they claimed to represent primarily the industrial proletariat they would, in the virtual absence of industry and industrial labour in these countries, represent very little indeed. Their need to legitimize their claim to represent and fight for 'the people' or 'the masses' requires them to define their potential clientele differently from that of their comrades in industrial societies.

The Chinese translation for 'proletariat'[37] characterizes those who have no means of production or no control over the use of the products of their labour. There is no reference to any industrial production, or any industrial proletariat. Mao was very well aware that in the absence of a substantial industrial proletariat the Party would be the vanguard of only a very small fraction of the Chinese population.[38] Therefore the classical Marxian concept of the proletariat was intentionally rejected by Mao Zedong. Consequently, the Chinese definition of the proletariat showed already from its early beginnings a marked difference from Marx's definition: the Chinese understanding of the working class includes not only industrial workers but also the rural workers and small peasants.[39] Secondly the term 'proletariat' did not relate solely to class background but is, rather, a state of mind, or, to put it in Mao Zedong's words the 'right consciousness of the self-sacrificing "new" man'.[40] Therefore, the term 'proletariat' or the term 'revolutionary masses' stands for both, the working classes as well as the 'heroes' and other 'good people' (Yingxiong Haohan) who do not necessarily need to have the 'right' social origin.

The absence of an industrial proletariat led Mao Zedong to still another conclusion, namely the virtue of being 'poor and blank'.[41] Being 'blank' became the antithesis to the materialistic thinking of the west. 'Revolutionary zeal' was to be the main criterion by which cadres were to be recruited. In this sense the CCP came to claim to represent
— the relatively small industrial proletariat,
— the rural proletariat, small and lower middle peasants,
— the nationalist democratic forces,

— the people who have the 'right revolutionary spirit'.

'Relying on the poor and blank masses' became the slogan in the main thrusts against party bureaucracy and civilian or military experts. The Great Leap Forward as well as the GPCR had been expressions of the belief in the creativity and capability of correct judgement by the masses.[42] As the embourgeoisement of the party bureaucracy set in, Mao Zedong found himself confronted with what he called 'capitalist roaders' in the upper ranks of the party, while those he considered possessing the right revolutionary spirit were either outside or in the lower ranks of the party. He therefore argued that in order to continue the revolutionary struggle, it may be necessary to rebel against party bureaucracy, a rebellion to be led by Mao but to be carried out by those whose revolutionary consciousness had not yet been corrupted.[43]

The Question of Leadership within the Party

Central to the debate about who shoud lead the revolution and the Party was the so-called 'red vs. expert' dispute. While both the 'Liuists' and the 'Maoists' agreed that the Party should be the vanguard of the proletariat, dissent arose over the criteria by which leadership qualities should be defined. The former maintained that expertise should qualify for high leadership positions while the 'Maoists' emphasized that the right revolutionary spirit was at least as much a criterion as expertise.

After 1949 Zhou Enlai, Liu Shaoqi and Deng Xiaoping became aware that running a country is a far more complex task than struggling for revolution: it demands special skills which may be very different from those which helped the Communists to gain power.[44] During the early 1950s a new social group had emerged inside the party organization — the group of well-trained, experienced cadres who achieved their prominence by demonstrating their capability in developing the national economy.[45] Thus, social mobility and personal career seemed for a while to be dependent on competence and efficiency in certain fields.[46]

However, the need to have technical specialists leading the country toward modernization encompassed certain risks. Absorbed in the tasks of achieving results these cadres came to neglect what Mao considered the 'right revolutionary spirit' and, instead, led the country to 'change the colour' and follow the 'capitalist road'. From Mao's point of view, such an attitude obstructed the task of developing consciousness among the masses, and transforming their values so that they became consistent with Maoist goals.

When it became apparent that the country was drifting increasingly in an ideological direction unacceptable to Mao, he decided to reject Liu's approach completely and to lead the masses to 'bombard the headquarters'.[47] Furthermore he attempted to replace the existing party organization by the 'Commune' or so-called 'Revolutionary Committees'. These should be recruited from people of undisputed revolutionary spirit.[48]

The concept of Revolutionary Committee was supposed to change the process of recruitment to political office. In fact, it destroyed whatever had existed in terms of intra-party participation and institutionalized processes of conflict resolution. From now on the political will was to be established by direct consultation with the masses, with Mao Zedong having the power to interpret the expressions of the popular will.[49]

For all practical purposes this strengthened the leadership position of Mao Zedong. It also meant that Mao, as the ultimate arbiter for interpreting the correct line, would be in direct contact with the masses, bypassing the party bureaucracy. Mao had thus reached the peak of his power, a position which allowed him singlehandedly to choose his successors (Lin Biao in 1969, Hua Guofeng in 1975)[50] with the party bureaucracy denied any say on this issue.[51]

The Problem of Class Struggle

As in all Marxist debates on class struggle the relationship between base and superstructure had been central. But in China, Mao Zedong felt the necessity to reinterpret this relationship to fit Chinese conditions. As he put it:

> True, the productive forces, practice and economic base generally play the principal and decisive role; whoever denies this is not a materialist. But it must also be admitted that in certain conditions, such aspects as the relations of production, theory and the superstructure in turn manifest themselves in the principal and decisive role . . . When the superstructure (politics, culture, etc.) obstructs the development of the economic base, political and cultural changes become principal and decisive.[52]

In the controversy about the role and position of the Party as a part of the superstructure, this new interpretation of Marxist ideology played an important role. According to Deng Xiaoping the Party should be regarded principally as part of the superstructure. However, the expertise of some cadres, especially in the educational and research fields, makes them part of the productive forces which should be developed only in an evolutionary process. In one of the so-called 'Three poisonous weeds', namely the 'Outline Report on the Work of the Academy of Sciences' Deng and his followers had demanded: 'In science and technology, one should not talk about class struggle.'[53] This argument was rejected by the 'Maoists' who argued that it was exactly that bourgeois thinking or 'empiricism'[54] of the experts which hindered social development, and that the contradiction between that thinking and socialist goals could be resolved only by recognition of the supremacy of class struggle.

After pointing out the importance of the class struggle,[55] the 'Maoists' had to explain how class struggle and classes may exist in a society in which the means of production had been already nationalized and the conditions of production could no longer be called capitalist or feudalist. In their view, contradictions are not necessarily restricted to the relations of production but can also emerge within the existing superstructure or even in individuals.[56] In analyzing the actual situation in China, the revolutionaries detected 'bourgeois rights' and 'contradictions', which in the absence of capitalist conditions of production could only be caused by bourgeois or capitalistic thinking. This led them to the conclusion that, first, the superstructure plays the decisive role in the current situation and, secondly, that 'the correctness or incorrectness of the ideological or political line' depends on the class controlling the leadership.[57] While during the GPCR there had been only 'some elements taking the capitalist road', now they had become a class, which meant that there existed now in China a new class enemy.[58] In Mao Zedong's words: 'the class of bureaucratic officials (on the one hand) and the working class and poor and lower middle peasants (on the other hand) are two classes in sharp opposition'.[59] However, the term 'bureaucratic officials' was used not to include all party, state and army cadres but was limited rather inexplicably only to those who engaged solely in administrative work or to veterans.

After the purge of the Gang of Four the line of argument changed again.[60] The Gang was accused of being too 'idealistic' by 'overemphasizing subjective factors leading to wrong conclusions',[61] especially in analyzing the relation between base and superstructure. From now on the decisive role was to be played by the economic base, allowing for the modernization of the country as an evolutionary alternative to the revolutionary mainly political concept of Mao Zedong.[62]

2. Changes in the Composition of the Party Leadership

Whether the 'Liuist' or the 'Maoist' concept came into practice depended not only on the authority of the major proponents but also on how many people in the leadership organizations could be found supporting each concept. It seemed that none of these programmatic factions could achieve their objectives without making compromises.[63] Coalitions were formed on the basis of personal or institutional loyalties and/or specific issues.[64] In the 1950s when a relatively large number of non-communists were working within the bureaucracy,[65] the Party had been forced to grant a degree of autonomy to administrative organs. A decade later the situation had changed with the training of a sufficiently large number of politically reliable cadres who could both replace non-communist and military officers in the administration and extend party control over all organs including the military.[66] Not being compelled any more to sustain the working of the administration by making concessions to unloved technocrats the Party now could pursue its own policies. This however, required that the Party established what policies were to be followed, a decision-making process that caused large controversies within the Party, and was accompanied by reshuffles in the membership of its leadership organs.

One could expect that the end of the Cultural Revolution and the apparent victory of Mao would manifest itself in a clear majority of staunch Mao supporters in the newly constituted leadership organs.[67] But this was not the case.

Comparing the composition of the 8th and the 9th Central Committees it is obvious that the demand of the Maoists for a younger leadership had not been met, and the traditional domination of the Party by veteran cadres continued. The positions of the Central Committee that had become vacant as a result of the purge of Liuist 'capitalist roaders' from the Party had been filled not with dedicated Maoists but by the military.

The mass organizations, supposed to express the will of the revolutionary masses, were represented by only 17 per cent of all

Central Committee members while the regional military occupied 26 per cent of the seats.[68] This group, which in contrast to the central military command around Marshal Lin Biao had not supported the Maoist concept but had been more interested in rebuilding the administrative and economic structure, now formed a coalition with the party bureaucracy.

The dominance of the military in Chinese politics after the GPCR can be demonstrated more clearly by the background of party secretaries in the provinces.[69] While in 1965 only 10 per cent of the secretaries had had military background, in 1971 the percentage increased to 62 per cent; it declined after the reshuffle due to the Lin Biao incident, but with 48.6 per cent in 1973, was still very high. The take-over by the proponents of Mao Zedong's concept had failed, mainly because of the coalition of the party bureaucracy and regional military commanders.

The basic weakness of the Maoists did not change during the 1970s. In fact, one could argue that their position was further undermined by losing the few supporters they had in the military who were purged from the Central Committee or transferred out of Peking.[70] In addition, the representation of the masses by deputies from the mass organizations remained unchanged and low. Changes are obvious in the representation of the military and the party bureaucracy. By 1973 12 per cent of the former Central Committee members, mainly bureaucrats including Deng, had been rehabilitated. On the other hand military representation declined by approximately 10 per cent.[71] This trend accelerated with regard to the composition of the 11th Central Committee formed in 1977. More than one third of the members had been purged during the GPCR. Again, the military lost seats, whilst the party bureaucracy was able to form the largest group with more than 50 per cent of all members. Similar trends can be found in the provinces. Of the twenty-nine new First Secretaries in the provinces, autonomous regions and municipalities directly under the central government, twenty had been purged during the GPCR, and the percentage of those with military career background declined to 17.2 per cent.[72]

This shows clearly that the post-Mao leadership is mainly recruited from the ranks of the pre-cultural-revolutionary élite. Moreover, the rehabilitations in 1979 and 1980 indicate that the PRC may now be partially dominated by the political and economic élite of the pre-Great Leap era.[77]

The turnovers in the leadership during the GPCR and after

TABLE 1[73]

Composition of the Eighth, Ninth, Tenth and Eleventh Central Committees of the Chinese Communist Party

	8th CC, estab. in 1956, 97 members	9th CC, estab. in 1969, 170 members	10th CC, estab. in 1973, 195 members	11th CC, estab. in 1977, 201 members
I. Average age at time of formation	56.4	61.4	63.1	64.6
II. Birthplace:				
Administrated units (out of a total of 29)	17	21	25	23
South China (from here, all figs. in table are percentages)	70.6	72.8	67.5	65.5
Inland provinces	73.9	68.9	68	71.3
Hunan (birthplace of Mao Zedong and Liu Shaoqi)	29.3	19.9	17.7	16.6
Hupei (birthplace of Lin Biao)	10.9	17.2	10.1	12.1
III. Educational background				
higher education	73.2	76.2	74.5	64.4
universities	44.3	23.8	26.2	25.7
military academies	15.4	35.7	38.6	30.1

secondary schools	18.4	8.9	10.3	7.3
primary schools	17.1	8.3	11.9	6.2
IV. Extended Contact with foreigners	10.4	26.9	32.5	46.4
V. Party generations				
Entry before the end of the Long March	67.2	63.2	80.4	99
Entry before 1949	84.1	78.6	92.3	100
VI. Career background:				
People's Liberation Army	34.8	39.5	50	37.9
Party and civilian cadres	52.2	42.6	31.1	62.1
Mass organizations	11.9	17.9	17.7	—
Cadres purged during the GPCR	39	12	—	—
VII. Area of activity:				
civilian institutions				
central	25.4	22.7	20.4	46.1
regional	41.3	40.2	32	28.6
military forces				
central	16.4	13.8	21.0	23.1
regional	16.4	23.3	26.6	2.2
total central institutions	41.8	36.5	41.4	69.2
total regional institutions	57.7	63.5	58.6	30.8
total military	32.8	37.1	47.5	25.3

TABLE 2[74]

Career Background of the Provincial Party Secretaries (in percent)

	1965	1971	1973	1978[75]
People's Liberation Army	10.5	62	48.6	17.2
Civilian cadres	89.5	32.9	44.8	
Mass organizations	—	5.1	6.6	
Purged during the GPCR				69

Mao's death did not mean that a new and younger generation came to the fore, but that those of the first revolutionary generation who had opposed Mao's attempts at social transformation in the past have again taken over.[78]

3. The Role and the Function of the Party

The controversies within the CCP about the role and function of the Party can be regarded as a corollary to the debate about the state.

After the founding of the PRC, the Party needed a strong state administration as an instrument of control. Since the CCP could not provide enough personnel, and using Mao's interpretation that China had accomplished a bourgeois-democratic revolution leading to a New Democracy,[79] the first government was formed on the basis of a coalition consisting of the CCP and eight non-communist parties which the CCP had forged into a united front.[80] During the Hundred-Flowers-Campaign in 1957[81] these parties were considered to represent 'contradictions among the people'[82] under socialism. Yet, from July 1957, these contradictions were seen as having become antagonistic and, hence, most of their members were purged.[83] Ever since then, and at least until 1978, the CCP remained the only base for recruitment of leading cadres.

Mao's deep distrust of bureaucracy which was regarded as alienated from the masses led him — in 1956-58 as well as during the GPCR — to the question of how party policy could be translated into action without the help of state organizations.[84]

The difference between his concept and Liu's or Deng's approach lay in the different perceptions about bureaucratism. For Liu and Deng bureaucratism meant an excessive use of state power which could be reduced by a diversified and decentralized system of party and state control. For Mao, on the other hand, bureaucracy appeared as an evil by definition.[85] His criticism of the control structures built up in the 1950s focused on the point that bureaucracy, with its inherent tendency to become alienated from the masses, also represents a contradiction among the people in a socialist society.[86]

In his eyes, the Party, much closer to the masses than any state organization, should be used as the only instrument for implemen-

ting policy, thus replacing the state. Both attempts to put his concept into practice, however — in the Great Leap era as well as during the GPCR — failed. They either led to the excessive power of
inexperienced Party cadres (whom the masses regarded as acting ar-
bitrarily) and to bureaucratism within the Party, or they created a
vacuum in the operational sphere of policy implementation, viz. in
a lack of coordination or passivity, leading to organizational chaos.

After Mao Zedong's death, Deng obviously tried to re-install the
system of the 1950s. The non-communist parties as well as
economic control agencies reappeared which should now 'seek the
truth from facts',[87] no longer solely depending upon the Party's
will.

Although it is unlikely that the CCP and Deng Xiaoping will give
up the dictatorship of the proletariat executed by the CCP alone, it
seems that the role of the party will be newly defined. To implement the ambitious plan of the Four Modernizations,[88] Deng has to
look for a broad consensus in Chinese society. Hence, he regards
the non-communist parties as well as the former industrialists and
businessmen as 'political allies'.[89] This may indicate that the CCP
in his eyes, while remaining the only locus for policy formulation,
is no longer the only organization for policy implementation.

THE STATE

1. The Theory of the State

The CCP, like all Communist parties, regards the state as an instrument for the ruling class; that means in China for the proletariat and its vanguard — the Party. But unlike other communist
countries the 'state' is not understood as formed by the army, law
and bureaucracy. The constitution and the PLA, which was built
up as a Party-army, were instruments of the Party, sometimes even
in contradiction to any concept of the state. State in the Chinese interpretation means an infrastructure for the non-military command
and control of the Party-bureaucracy. Thus, the different constitutions reveal more about the theoretical debate inside the Party
over what the state, namely an appropriate control structure,
should be than about the actual distribution of power and rights in
the Chinese society.

TABLE 3
Percentage of Cadres Purged during the GPCR[76]

	Before Mao's death 1 Sept. 1976	After Mao's death
Leadership, total	19	36 (1 April 1978)
— Fullmembers, Central Committee	12 (1973)	39 (1977)
— Chairman, Vicechairman Provincial Revolutionary Committees	21.3	45 (1 April 1978)
— Ministers, Viceminister (Ministers only)	19.5	23.4 (1 April 1978) 57.6 (January 1980)

The constitution of 1954 was the first constitution of the People's Republic of China and reflected the Soviet model. But shortly thereafter in the 'Anti-rightist Movement' and during the Great Leap Forward it became clear that the alternative to ruling the country through mass mobilization had not disappeared. Although the Maoists had fiercely attacked any form of structured politics as it existed, they used their strength at the height of the Cultural Revolution to demand the abolition of the Constitution in what looked like a return to the traditional Chinese way of government without legal provisions. Somewhat surprisingly and paradoxically, at the Second Plenum of the 9th Central Committee meeting in 1970,[90] these same groupings set out to draft a new constitution, presumably one which would still incorporate Maoist thinking but also give the new-style politics an aura of legitimacy by having it officially promulgated. However, this plan seemed to have been abandoned at the 10th Party Congress in 1973 by which time Zhou Enlai had regained his position of strength.[91] But already by 1975 the Maoist group had become powerful enough to push through a new constitution. Only three years later, in 1978, another constitution was adopted by the 5th National People's Congress (henceforth: NPC). This last constitution assumed approximately a middle-of-the-road position between those of 1975 and 1954.

These frequent changes in the constitutional arrangements should, however, not simply be regarded as a manifestation of the ongoing power struggle which they doubtless were, but also reveal that the Chinese did not view the constitution as a set of lasting principles or legal frameworks but merely as an expression of current political concepts.

Mao Zedong's point of view that 'the Party commands the gun, and the gun must never be allowed to command the Party', as well as that 'the army is the chief component of state power',[92] is emphasized in article 2 of the 1975 Constitution: 'The Communist Party is the core of leadership of the whole Chinese People', and article 19 '. . . the Chinese People's Liberation Army is . . . led by the Communist Party of China'. Thus this Constitution seemed to lay down the relationship between Party and army.

Moreover, for the first time in the constitutional development of Communist China the Communist Party rated a mention in the Constitution. This is explained in the preamble by the fact that China is no longer a 'people's democratic state' governed by the united front of parties but is now a 'socialist state of the dictatorship of the proletariat', the ideology of which has been extended to everybody.[93] Consequently, the National People's Congress is the 'highest organ of power, under the leadership of the CCP' (article 16).

The 1975 Constitution differed from that of 1954 mainly by depriving the state organs, namely the National People's Congress and the government, of their role of functioning as institutions 'through which people exercise power'.[94] It also re-ordered the relationship between the Party and the military. In 1964 Mao had still urged the people to 'learn from the PLA', but after the Lin Biao 'coup' attempt of 1971 the need for the Party to domesticate the military had become so obvious that supreme command over the army was transferred from the Chairman of the PRC to the Chairman of the Party (article 15).[95]

The latest constitution (adopted by the 5th NPC on 5 March 1978)[96] seemed to be nearer to the constitution of 1954 than to that of 1975. It is characterized by the emphasis on socialist democracy,[97] and the expanding of the rights and prerogatives of the NPC (article 7). There is a reduced emphasis on the concept of the 'dictatorship of the proletariat', but the slogan of 'let a hundred flowers blossom and a hundred schools of thought contend' is raised as the guiding principle — and an article (article 14) in the constitution — for promoting sciences and cultural life.

While the functions of state organs were expanded, the rights of the PLA were further restricted. In 1975, the military was described not only as a combat force (article 19) but also as a force engaged in economic production and political tasks.[98] The provisions for the PLA in the new constitution have abandoned the latter ideas; the non-military functions of the army still contain the politically rather ambiguously worded task 'to safeguard the socialist revolution and socialist construction' (article 19).

As is the case in most communist countries, the state should not represent all people but is an instrument of the working class to exercise the dictatorship of the proletariat over the still 'unreformed landlords, rich peasants and reactionary capitalists' (article 18) who, consequently, are deprived of political and basic rights (article 44).[99] A further step toward more institutionalized decision-making and participation can be seen in the articles for the elections of the deputies to the NPCs. No longer should they emerge from a vaguely defined process of 'democratic consultation' but be elected 'by secret ballot' after such consultations (article 21).

2. Composition and Functions of the State

Mao's interpretation that the state is in fact no more than an administrative machine, and that bureaucracy has an inherent tendency towards alienation from the masses, made him attack not only the 'experts' and 'bureaucrats' in state agencies but the state institutions as a whole.[100]

The original concept of rural people's communes (developed during the Great Leap era), as well as the model of the Shanghai Commune in the GPCR, can be regarded as attempts to replace the state administration by a populist commune system, controlled directly by the masses.[101] Since the purge of the 'experts' and members of non-communist parties in the late 1950s, all functions usually reserved for state organs were taken over by the party or the PLA. The composition of state leadership became identical with the Party-leadership and need not be analyzed separately. This may also be the reason that all Maoist attacks on state bureaucratism sooner or later developed into an attack against party-bureaucratism.

While Liu Shaoqi and Deng Xiaoping viewed the establishment of a state apparatus as a means of control by qualified people, which sometimes may restrict the influence of the Party, Mao denied the advantages of all political institutions which would only hinder the 'permanent Revolution'. In his most radical criticism during the GPCR he argued that if party bureaucratism had replaced state bureaucratism, then the Party itself must be attacked from the outside.[102] In this sense, the populist movement, the establishing of new revolutionary mass organizations like the Red Guards, cannot be interpreted merely as an attempt to introduce more mass participation but as an instrument to control the Party from the outside. It seems that at this time the state was no longer seen as a control instrument of the Party but as the platform via which a highly mobilized population should permanently transform its society, led by the 'reds', no matter whether they were Party members or not.

Already between 1970 and early 1975, the institutions of the state machine had been re-established. It took the PRC almost three years after the death of Mao, however, to enact a new legal system which was finally put into practice on 1 January 1980.[103] Furthermore, state agencies for economic control[104] reappeared and have been ordered to exercise control by 'seeking the truth from the facts', not 'seeking the truth from ideology';[105] thus control by specialists has replaced control by the 'reds' of the Mao era. But — as the end of the 1978-79 Chinese Democracy Movement indicates — although a state and legal system has again been introduced in China it is still the Party which controls the state and claims the right to interpret the law according to its will. Thus, legal rights were not respected in the Wei Jingsheng trial and Democracy Wall was effectively closed.[106]

CONCLUSIONS

Unlike in other communist countries the role, function and position of the Chinese Communist Party was never clearly established. While some leaders in the CCP considered the Party to function primarily as a value-setting body, interpreting ideology and transforming ideology into practical rules, others were inclined to see in the CCP no more than one of several policy executing bodies without a claim to supremacy over the state bureaucracy or the army.

Ever since Lenin developed and implemented the concept of a tightly organized cadre-party, communist parties have been considered to have an advantage over other parties, due to their hierarchical and disciplined organizational format.[107] However, it has been argued that this was not the case in China. At least since the Great Proletarian Cultural Revolution it has become obvious that the so-called struggle between the two lines[108] was not only a debate on policy but also concerned the possible contribution the Party could make to political and social development. Instead of the orthodox opinion that the necessary changes toward communist goals could be achieved only by long-term stability in a political system guaranteed by the Party, Mao Zedong and his closest associates became convinced that the Party itself could obstruct the desired changes in the social system by turning into the new bourgeois class.

As has been demonstrated the coalitions necessary for implementing one of the two 'lines' were not only formed on the basis of subjective ideologies or personal loyalties. It seemed that another factor became important as well, viz. the corporate interest of functionally organized subsystems. The self-interest of these organizations led to ad hoc coalitions with other groupings inside the Party which sometimes turned out to be decisive in the intra-party struggle.[109]

The period of the First Five-Year-Plan, imitating the Soviet experience, had led to more institutional sophistication in China. The main political subsystems — state, party and army — were characterized by a relatively high degree of professionalization. The Party largely restricted itself to setting values, interpreting ideology and allowing state agencies to choose the means for implementing the socialist goals.[110] But even during this period the 'state' could not challenge the Party. Neither in communist ideology nor in traditional Chinese culture has the concept of the state a meaning of its own:[111] the state is understood to have no other function than to serve as an executive body of whoever is in power. Therefore, Party supremacy in the 1950s could not be questioned by the 'state', only by the non-communists still working in state agencies.

After 1954 the functions of Party and state became intermingled. What may have appeared to be a conflict about organizational principles between state agencies and the Party was in fact an ideological controversy about leadership concepts. Liu Shaoqi's concept of leadership by clearly institutionalized means tended to promote further organizational specialization, division of labour and enhanced the functional autonomy of bureaucratic agencies. Yet, bureaucracy was regarded as evil by Mao Zedong's concept of personal leadership.[112] Therefore, the conflicts about party, party bureaucracy and the establishment of state organs finally became a conflict between parts of the Party itself and Mao Zedong.

On a different plane the Maoist line came into conflict with parts of the PLA. Initially regarded as a model for the 'right' proletarian thinking, the army in general and Lin Biao in particular encroached increasingly upon the tasks of the Party — or Mao Zedong — including that of interpreting ideology. In the provinces, the military took over administrative responsibilities after the GPCR had created a power vacuum.[113] From that time onward, the Party apparatus and the PLA, rather than state organs, performed almost all the administrative functions.

At first sight, it appears that current PRC politics can be interpreted as a counter-cultural revolution and the triumph of concepts usually associated with Liu Shaoqi. But the policies now implemented are not just a repetition of those enacted between 1960 and 1965 when Liu had dominated the party's decision-making bodies. As the re-establishment of a more sophisticated state administrative system, the re-installation of a legal system, the reappearance of non-communist parties, the return of the experts of the 1950s to the political leadership, and the changes in the economic structure indicate, what is going on now is a counter Great Leap.

But it is as yet too early to formulate safe projections about what kind of leadership concept will be applied in the future. There may be more collective leadership at the top with a centralized and vertically sectorized administrative structure as in the USSR, or — what seems to be preferred by the economic élite — a more decentralized system with a socialist market system in some economic sectors, similar to the Yugoslav-Hungarian model. The question of participation and legal rights for the people, too, has not yet been solved.

But with the re-introduction of efficiency and productivity as criteria for economic and political decisions it seems that the party is newly defined as responsible only for supervising the ideological values of the 'superstructure' while the re-established state organs, mass organizations and non-communist parties are regarded as more efficient in implementing policy than the CCP in the (Maoist) past. China is now back to the stage of the New Democracy of the

1950s, accepting the contributions an effective state organization can make to the further political and economic development of the PRC. In such circumstances, it would be quite inappropriate to suggest that the Chinese state is withering.

NOTES

For critical comments and help, I would like to express my gratitude to Professor Dr Jürgen Domes, Dr Ulf Sundhaussen, and David S.G. Goodman.

1. See J.P. Harrison, *Der Lange Marsch zur Macht* (Stuttgart, Zürich: Belser, 1978), Engl. *The Long March to Power, 1917-1971* (New York: Praeger, 1972); L. Bianco, *Origins of the Chinese Revolution 1915-1949* (Stanford, Cal.: Indiana University Press, 1971); and R.C. Thornton, *China, The Struggle for Power 1917-1972* (Bloomington, Ind., 1973).
2. In the Opium War 1839-42; the Lorcha War 1856-58, and the war against Japan 1894-95.
3. The Taiping Rebellion 1852-64; the Mohammedan rebellions 1864-77, and the Boxer Rising 1900. For their history see for example W. Eberhard, *A History of China* (London: Routledge and Kegan Paul, 1977) (4th edition), 301-311.
4. On these debates see Bianco, op. cit., 2-21, P.J. Opitz (ed.), *Chinas Grosse Wandlung* (München: Beck, 1972), 7; Chow Tse-tsung, *The May Fourth Movement* (Harvard: Harvard University Press, 1960), 71, 215.
5. Thornton, op. cit., 3-6; Bianco, op. cit., 23.
6. Compare the resolutions of the 2nd World Congress of the Comintern, in J. Domes, *Vertagte Revolution* (Berlin: W. de Gruyter, 1969), 65, and Thornton, op. cit., 5-6.
7. Chow Tse-tsung, op. cit., 71; Bianco, op. cit., 41; J. Domes, *The Internal Politics of China* (henceforth: *Politics*) (London: C. Hurst & Co., 1973), 9.
8. Ibid., 10.
9. Declaration of Liu Renching at the 4th World Congress of the Comintern, quoted in Opitz, op. cit., 236.
10. J. Domes, *Die Kuomintang-Herrschaft in China* (Niedersächsische Landeszentrale für Politische Bildung, 1970), 17.
11. F. Schurmann, and O. Schell, 'Urban Revolution Begins and Rural Revolution Breaks Out Again', in Schurmann/Schell (eds.), *Republican China, China Readings 2* (Harmondsworth: Penguin, 1968), 111, 123.
12. Ibid., 105.
13. Eberhard, op. cit., 335; Domes, *Politics*, 12-13.
14. On the reasons for the failure of the Guomindang, see ibid., 14-16.
15. Thornton, op. cit., 24-48; Harrison, op. cit., 286.
16. Thornton, op. cit., 448.
17. Ibid., 470-480.
18. Byung-joon Ahn, 'The Cultural Revolution and China's Search for Political Order', in: *The China Quarterly* (hereafter: *CQ*), No. 58 (April 1974), 259.

19. J. Guillermaz, *The Chinese Communist Party in Power, 1949-1976* (Boulder Colorado: Westview Press, 1976), 75-161.

20. Ibid., 144; Domes, *Politics*, 67-69.

21. Ibid., 114-137; Guillermaz, op. cit., 247.

22. Ibid., 344; Domes, *Politics*, 130-139; Ahn, op. cit., 260; *People's Daily* (Renmin Ribao, hereafter: *RMRB*) 1 February 1964.

23. Domes, *Politics*, 175-184.

24. Ibid., 181-188.

25. J. Domes, 'China in 1976: Tremors in Transition', in *Asian Survey*, No. 1 (January 1977) (hereafter: *AS*77), 3.

26. J. Domes, *China nach der Kulturrevolution* (Munich: Fink, 1975), 111.

27. Ibid., 179, also in *AS* 77, 7; R.C. Thornton, 'Teng Hsiao-p'ing and Pekings's Current Political Crisis', in: *Issues and Studies* (hereafter: *IS*), No. 7 (July 1976), 53.

28. This became obvious with the official rehabilitation of Liu Shaoqi on 28 February 1980.

29. J.K. Kallgren, 'China 1979: The New Long March', in: *AS*, No. 1 (January 1979).

30. Liu Shaoqi, 'How To Be a Good Communist', in Liu Shaoqi, *Collected Works*, ed. by Union Research Institute URI (Hongkong: Union Research Institute, 1969), 155; Tang Tsou, 'The Cultural Revolution and the Chinese Political System', in: *CQ*, No. 38 (April 1969), 69.

31. Liu Shaoqi, op. cit., 181; also: 'It (the party) is not simply a grouping together of several hundred thousand party members, . . . it is the union of several hundred thousand party members in accordance with a definite organizational form and definite rules.' Liu Shaoqi, quoted from S. Schram, 'The Party in Chinese Communist Ideology', in: *CQ*, No. 38 (April 1969), 5.

32. L. Schapiro and J.W. Lewis, 'The Roles of the Monolithic Party under the Totalitarian Leader', in: *CQ*, No. 40 (October 1969), 50-51.

33. Mao Zedong, October 1939 in *The Communist*, quoted from S.R. Schram, *The Political Thought of Mao Tse-tung* (New York/Washington/London: Praeger, 1970), 37.

34. Mao Zedong, 'Stalin is our Commander', quoted from Schram, op. cit., 427.

35. Liu Shaoqi, 'Liquidate Menshevist Ideology within the Party', 1 July 1943, in *Collected Works*, 437.

36. Liu Shaoqi, quoted from Schram, op. cit., 6.

37. Wuchang jieji.

38. Schram, op. cit., 17.

39. Deng Xiaoping tended to minimize objective criteria of class origin by emphasizing the higher social mobility in socialist countries.

40. Schram, op. cit., 20.

41. Mao Zedong, 'On New Democracy', in *Selected Works*, Volume II, (hereafter: *SW* II) (Peking: Foreign Language Press, 1965), 348.

42. Schram, op. cit., 23.

43. 'Daring to rebel . . . is the fundamental principle of the proletarian party spirit', *RMRB* (24 August 1966); *Peking Review* (hereafter: *PR*) No. 37 (1966), and *Red Flag* (Hongqi, hereafter: *HQ*) No. 3 (1967).

44. J.M. Lindbeck, 'Transformations in the Chinese Communist Party', in D. Treadgold (ed.), *Soviet and Chinese Communism* (London and Seattle: University of Washington Press, 1967), 99.

45. Ahn, op. cit., 279.

46. See also the statistics in F. Schurmann, *Ideology and Organisation in Communist China* (Berkeley and London: University of California Press, 1966), 170.

47. 'Bombard the Headquarters', instruction used by Mao Zedong, 5 August 1966.

48. Guillermaz, op. cit., 399-431.

49. J.D. Seymour, *China. The Politics of Revolutionary Reintegration* (New York: Thomas Y. Crowell, 1976), 111.

50. Guillermaz, op. cit., 453; Domes, *Ära*, 181; J. Domes, 'The Gang of Four and Hua Kuo-feng', in *CQ*, No. 71 (September 1977), 473-497.

51. Hua Guofeng's legitimacy depends on the Mao 'instruction': 'With you in charge, I'm at ease' of 27 April 1976, quoted in *RMRB* (25 October 1976).

52. Mao Zedong, 'On Contradiction', in *SW* II, 336.

53. The term 'empiricism' was used by the Cultural Revolutionaries to describe the arrogance of cadres 'who relied only on their own experience to manage affairs', *Guangming Ribao* (12 December 1976).

54. On this point and the following controversial issues, see Zhang Chunchiao, 'On Exercising Dictatorship over the Bourgeoisie', in *HQ*, No. 4 (April 1975) and *PR* (14 April 1975): Deng Xiaoping, 'Outline Report on the Work of the Academy of Sciences', in *Study and Criticism* (Xuexi yu Pipan) (Shanghai), May 1978.

55. Mao Zedong, in *HQ*, No. 5 (May 1976), 1.

56. Zhang Chunchiao, op. cit.; it is in this sense that Mao Zedong's criticism of Deng Xiaoping should be seen: 'He does not understand Marxism/Leninism, he represents the capitalist class . . . he does not understand class struggle', Mao Zedong in *HQ*, No. 5 (1975), 1.

57. Zhang Chunchiao, op. cit., here quoted from Tang Tsou, op. cit., 522-523.

58. Ibid., 519; *Guangming Ribao* (9 May 1977), *HQ*, No. 7 (July 1976).

59. Mao Zedong, quoted from Tang Tsou, op. cit., 506.

60. Chi Hsin, *The Case of the Gang of Four* (Hong Kong: Cosmos Books, 1977), 1-50.

61. Ibid., 55.

62. Although Zhou Enlai had propagated the 'Four Modernizations' of agriculture, industry, national defence, and science and technology at the 10th Party Congress of the CCP in 1973, they did not come into practice until 1976-77.

63. The campaign for organizational reconstruction of the party in 1968 already indicated the failure to replace the party by revolutionary committees. Guillermaz, op. cit., 448.

64. On the problem of defining 'factions', see J. Domes, 'The Relationship Between Party, Army, and Government in Communist China', in *IS* (August 1976), 59, and in *AS* 77, 3.

65. J. Domes, *IS* (August 1976), 49.

66. Ibid., 50.

67. See Table 1.

68. See Table 1.

69. See Table 2.

70. The decrease of CC members with the same regional origin as Lin Biao is significant.

71. J. Domes, *Politische Soziologie Chinas* (Manuscript April 1979, Saarbrucken), 112, to be published in 1980.

72. Ibid., 172.

73. Domes, *Kulturrevolution*, 45-53, 241-249; 'China in 1978: Reversal of Verdicts', in: *AS*, No. 1 (January 1978), 8-9; *Politische Soziologie Chinas*, 184-192.

74. Domes, *Kulturrevolution*, 66; *Politische Soziologie Chinas*, 174.

75. For 1978 only data for the First Party Secretaries are available.

76. David Goodman, 'Changes in Leadership Personnel After September 1976', in J. Domes, *Chinese Politics after Mao* (Cardiff: University College Cardiff Press, 1979), Tables 2-5, 46-52, and own calculations.

77. 29 per cent of the members of the 8th Central Committee (1956) held the same posts in September 1978, W. Bartke, 'Das Schicksal der chinesischen Führung aus der Zeit vor der Kultur-revolution', *China Aktuell* (January 1979), 871. This can also be proved by the rehabilitation of Chen Yun, Bo Yibo, Wang Renzhong and Peng Zhen, *China News Analysis (CNA)*, 1146 (19 January 1979) and 1164 (28 September 1979).

78. Goodman, op. cit., 38-39.

79. Mao Zedong, 'On the People's Democratic Dictatorship', in *SW* IV, 411.

80. In the highest decision-making body, the Central Government Council of 1949, only thirty-two out of the Council's sixty-three members belonged to the CCP; in the Government Affairs Council ten out of twenty-one; also fifteen of the thirty-one ministers at this time were members of non-communist parties; Domes, *Politics*, 23-24.

81. Ibid., 58-59.

82. Mao Zedong, 'On the Correct Handling of Contradictions among the People', 27 February 1957, *SW* V, 434-478.

83. Guillermaz, op. cit., 144-145.

84. Schurmann, op. cit., 110-111.

85. Ibid., 111.

86. Mao Zedong: '. . . a certain bureaucratic style of work in our state organs is in contradiction to our socialist base', in *SW* V, 395.

87. This is the most often used slogan in the economic and technical field.

88. Compare note 62.

89. So, for example, in a newly-elected People's Congress in Beijing East District, only 62.64 per cent of members belong to the CCP. *Beijing Review*, No. 50 (14 December 1979). In a newly-established Trust responsible for all kinds of foreign trade and foreign investment more than half are members of the old capitalist class, namely of the All-China Federation of Industrialists and Businessmen, BBC's *Summary of World Broadcasts*, FE 6238 (6 October 1979) (hereafter *SWB*). All eight non-communist parties as well as the Federation of Industrialists and Businessmen held Party congresses in October 1979; *SWB*, FE 6257 (29 October 1979). Furthermore, it was said that the 'Central Committee has restored the tradition of holding consultations with leaders of democratic parties . . . about once every two months', *Beijing Review*, No. 50 (14 December 1979).

90. Ibid., 458.

91. Domes, *Kulturrevolution*, 233-235.

92. Mao Zedong, 'Problems of War and Strategy', in *SW* II, 224.

93. *CNA*, No. 1114, 3 March 1978, 6. Guillermaz, op. cit., 474; O. Weggel, 'Die neue Verfassung der VR China', Teil I, in *China Aktuell* (May 1978), 257.

94. Guillermaz, op. cit., 475.

95. The retirement of the commanders of eight Military Areas in December 1973 can be regarded as the first attack of the party against the regional military leaders who became too powerful after the GPCR. Domes, *AS* 77, 5.

96. *PR*, No. 11 (17 March 1978); Weggel, op. cit., 257.

97. Pointed out by Ye Jianying in his report. *PR*, No. 11 (3 March 1978); *CNA*, 1114, 6.

98. Weggel, op. cit., 257; *CNA*, 1114, 7.

99. Weggel, op. cit., 258.

100. See above.

101. Guillermaz, op. cit., 217-225. The Shanghai Commune seemed to have failed even before it had started, R. Hoffmann, *Der Kampf zweier Linien* (Stuttgart: Klett & Cotta, 1978), 95-98.

102. See above.

103. Seven laws have been enacted: An Organic Law for the Local People's Congresses and Local People's Government; an Electoral Law; an Organic Law for the People's Court; an Organic Law for the People's Procuratorate; a Criminal Law; a Law of Criminal Procedure; and a Law for Joint Chinese and Foreign Investment Enterprises. For an analysis see *CNA*, No. 1160 (3 August 1979).

104. R.F. Dernberger, and D. Fasenfest, 'China's Post-Mao Economic Future', in *Joint Economic Committee Congress of the United States*, Volume I (Washington: US Government Printing Office, 1978), 9-11.

105. *RMRB* (15 November 1978), Eng. in *BR* 50 (19 December 1978).

106. David Goodman, *Beijing Street Voices* (London: Marion Boyars, forthcoming).

107. L. Pye, quoted from Treadgold, op. cit., 39.

108. 'Struggle between the two lines' was a term used by the leadership during and after the GPCR to describe the struggle between the 'sinister line' of Liu Shaoqi and the 'correct line' of Mao Zedong. See, for example, Guillermaz, op. cit., 460.

109. Domes, *IS* (August 1976), 53.

110. Deng Xiaoping's remark about black or white cats should be regarded in this sense.

111. Schurmann, op. cit., 167.

112. Ibid., 176.

113. Domes, in: *CQ*, No. 44, 112-145.

4 Party and State in Post-1970 Cuba

Lourdes Casal
Rutgers University, Newark

Marifeli Pérez-Stable
SUNY, Old Westbury

INTRODUCTION

Profound changes have taken place in the Cuban Communist Party, in the Cuban state system and in the relationship between them since 1970.[1] The crisis which followed the failure to achieve the ten million ton sugar harvest in that year spurred Cuba to embark on an accelerated process of institutionalization.[2]

This process has been characterized by the development of new institutions, in particular the Organs of Popular Power (OPP), the elected representative institutions of the Cuban state; the strengthening of basic structures and internal processes in the Cuban Communist Party (CCP) and a membership drive; the reorganization of mass organizations, particularly the trade unions (CTC) and the Committees for the Defense of the Revolution (CDR); a conceptualization of mass organizations as special interest organizations; an effort to differentiate the party from the state system and to regulate their roles and relationship; a restructuring of the state's legal foundations and of the judicial system (new constitution in 1976, a new system of court organization in 1977 and a new penal code in 1979); an emphasis on 'socialist legality', and the rule of law; and the development of a new economic and management system.

Before 1970, the Council of Ministers was the crucial structure in the Cuban political system. According to the then existing constitution,[3] executive, legislative and juridical functions were concentrated in this council.

Although a constitutional and juridical affairs commission had existed in the party's Central Committee since 1965, the differentiation and decentralization of functions within the political system started in 1972 with the creation of the executive committee of the Council of Ministers. The nine deputy prime ministers began to share the coordination of the ministries with the prime minister.

But the most far reaching changes in the state system began with the Matanzas experiment in 1974. This was the first attempt to develop representative state organs, the Cuban version of the soviets.[4] After the evaluation, the Matanzas experiment was expanded to a fully-fledged national system in 1976 when national elections were held (10 and 17 October 1976). In those elections, 10,725 deputies to the municipal assemblies were elected who in turn elected the deputies to the provincial assemblies and the 481 deputies to the National Assembly.[5] The latter held its first meeting in December 1976.

Raúl Castro has summarized the leadership's explanation for the delay in developing representative institutions: in its first stage of fast, violent changes and internal and external aggression, the revolution needed a 'fast, operative state apparatus' to exercise the dictatorship in the name of the working masses. Furthermore, a lack of material resources, the limited development of the mass organizations, the absence of a strong party and a certain lack of understanding of the role of representative institutions among some leaders made the development of these institutions impossible until the 1970s.[6] An earlier attempt to establish 'poder local' (local power) in 1967 had failed because material and political conditions did not exist.

During the first stage of the transition period, the main tasks are those of dismantling the basic structures of the bourgeois state and of consolidating the revolutionary forces' hold on power. In Cuba, these tasks had to be performed in conditions of sharpened class struggle; a powerful internal counterrevolution was abetted by the United States which also carried out its own acts of aggression. Furthermore, the Cuban Revolution had not been led to power by an organized proletarian party but by the 26th of July Movement, an anti-imperialist, petit-bourgeois movement embodied primarily in the Rebel Army (sierra) and secondarily in its urban underground (llano). Thus the vanguard role had corresponded to the Rebel Army under Fidel's leadership. But there was no strong, unified, well-developed party.

During the first stage of the revolution, the Cuban Communist Party had to be forged from rather disparate forces: the 26th of July Movement, the DRE (Revolutionary Student Directorate) and the PSP (Popular Socialist Party, the former communist party). The process was complex and lengthy. In 1962, the ORI (Integrated Revolutionary Organizations) were created. They were followed by the PURS (United Party of the Socialist Revolution) and finally, in 1965, by the Cuban Communist Party.[7] The party, however, did not structure itself according to the model of most ruling communist parties until 1973. Its first congress was not held until 1975. Numerically, it was also rather weak before 1970. (See Table 1)

In the aftermath of the 1970 harvest failure, the Cuban leadership decided to revamp the party, to give the Cuban state a more elaborate institutional form, to reassess the party's role and party-state relations, to reconceptualize the role of unions during the transition period, to decentralize some administrative functions and to develop formal ways for popular participation in the decision-making process.

THE PARTY:
CHANGES SINCE 1970

In 1970, the Cuban Communist Party was numerically and structurally weak (less than 100,000 members in a population of eight and a half million). Although, since 1965, the party had been organized with a one-hundred member Central Committee, an eight-member Political Bureau, a six-member Secretariat and the subsequent provincial, regional and local structures, its institutions, particularly at the top, did not function regularly. Fidel Castro pointed out that 'the political bureau considered the most important political questions, but did no strictly systematic work . . . in the direction of party and state' and while most of the party's energies were devoted to structuring and developing the base, 'the apparatus of the central committee virtually did not exist.'[8]

Since 1970, there have been major changes. In order to lead the institutionalization process, the party had to solve the many problems which had affected its functioning during the preceding period. It had to increase its membership so that there would be enough militants to perform its various political tasks and improve its membership composition by increasing female and worker participation. The general educational and politico-ideological level of the membership had to be raised. Functional internal institutions were needed to strengthen democratic processes within the party. Finally, the party had to emphasize its proper guiding role by extricating itself from overinvolvement with administrative tasks.[9]

Numerical Growth

The party had grown from 50,000 members in 1965 to 202,807 on the eve of its first congress in 1975. Compared to other ruling communist parties, the Cuban party remains relatively small, encompassing roughly 2.5 per cent of the population in 1979 (total population nearly ten million). However, the party has grown fivefold in the fourteen years since its first Central Committee was announced.

TABLE 1
Communist Party of Cuba: Numerical Growth

Year	Members and candidates
1965	50,000
1970	100,000
1971	101,000
1972	122,000
1973	153,000
1974	186,995
1975	202,807
1979 (estimate)	250,000

Sources: Fidel Castro, *Informe Central al Primer Congreso del Partido Comunista de Cuba* (Havana: Departamento de Orientación Revolucionaria, 1975), 205; Carmelo Mesa-Lago, *Cuba in the 1970s* (Albuquerque: University of New Mexico Press, 1978), 71.

Since its foundation, the Cuban Communist Party has used a rather rigorous and unique method for selection of members.[10] Most members are selected from amongst the vanguard workers elected by workers' assemblies. Party candidates thus have to be chosen from those elected by their fellow workers. This method ensures party members' high quality and prestige among fellow workers. It also promotes their working class origins, although it has probably contributed to the low representation of women in the party (see below).

The statutes of the Cuban Communist Party, approved in 1975, establish the method of selecting candidates for party membership from among vanguard workers in article 6. Young candidates can have access to the party through the UJC (Union of Young Communists) according to article 4.

The 1975 statutes also establish the possibility of individual applications between workers' assemblies (article 6b) and of direct selection to membership by the Central Committee, the Secretariat and the Political Bureau in cases of 'extraordinary merits' where security considerations prevent following normal procedures. Except in this last instance, candidates must always be subjected to 'consultation with the masses' (article 3c) and to the approval of the corresponding party cell and of the next highest party level (articles 3c and 3d).

Domínguez[11] has interpreted these provisions in the statutes as suggesting that the vanguard worker path to party membership is being de-emphasized and that the 'autonomy of the party from the population has been increased and the adaptability and responsiveness of the exemplary worker method are lost.'[12] However, there is no independent evidence that the vanguard worker method is being de-emphasized. The 1975 statutes do not contain profound innovations in party practices. They are rather a systematization and formalization of previous experience and of common practices in other ruling communist parties. The newly formalized procedures may, as Domínguez points out,[13] help to improve female representation in the party since admission can be obtained through activities in mass organizations and not just workers' assemblies. In fact, interviews conducted by Lourdes Casal during 1977 and 1978 suggest an increased effort in recruiting party members in work centres due to the drive to improve the party's working class composition (see below).

Composition of the Party

The strategy of increasing party membership (without transforming it into a mass party) responded to the need to separate the party from the state and to the emphasis on its re-proletarianization. Given its membership selection method, there was no question of the working class or peasant origins of the majority of its militants. However, precisely because the party was numerically small, many members tended to be drafted into positions of political leadership or administrative responsibility. In the central report to the first congress, Fidel outlined the problem:

> On many occasions, concern has been expressed over the fact that because the party is formed by workers with the highest prestige among the masses, with great authority and most outstanding achievements in labor, they are always the first to be chosen to hold any administrative post . . . But it is obvious that as a result of these constant extractions, the relatively low cultural level of our masses and a certain lack of development, the party is not numerically strong enough in important sectors like the sugar industry and other fundamental industries, the farms and agricultural stations, construction, transportation, education . . .
>
> The party must grow without detriment to the permanent effort to assure the quality of its ranks, preferably in these sectors, and also and above all, among the workers directly engaged in industrial and agricultural production, construction and services, to be able to complement in the party composition the necessary and active presence of thousands of communists . . . who hold leading state or political posts, with the entrance into the party of a sufficiently high number of workers who guarantee their active presence within the fundamental working class centers.[14]

Although there has been an effort to increase workers' representation in the party since 1970, progress has been limited and the leadership is pushing for further improvements. Table 2 summarizes the relevant information.

Although the proportion of industrial, construction and service workers has increased somewhat in the last five years, the end result is still not satisfactory. The transfer of party members to administrative positions is still being reflected.

Another problem in party composition frequently discussed by the leadership is female representation. Although female percentage among party members increased from 10 per cent in 1967 to 15 per cent in 1975 and to 17.5 per cent in 1979,[15] it is still small when compared to the proportion of women in the population at large (49 per cent) or even in the labour force (18 per cent in 1975 and 31 per cent in 1980). The 1975 party congress established that the pro-

TABLE 2

Comparative Analysis of the Composition of Party Membership and of New Members, December 1974-June 1975 and of Party Membership in 1979 (figures given in percentages)

	Total Membership December 1974	New Members January-June 1975	Total Membership June 1975	Total Membership 1979
Workers in industry, agriculture, construction and services	36.5	38.7	35.9	44.9
Professional and technical workers	9.2	19.8	9.2	13.5
Administrative cadres	33.5	24.0	33.4	26.2
Political cadres	9.1	4.6	8.7	4.8
Workers in administrative functions	4.0	6.8	4.1	4.8
Peasants	1.9	1.3	1.8	1.3
Others	5.8	4.8	6.9	4.8

Sources: Departamento de Orientación Revolucionaria, *Tesis y resoluciones: primer congreso del Partido Comunista de Cuba,* (Havana, 1976), 23 and Isidro Gómez, 'El Partido Comunista de Cuba,' paper presented at the seminar on Cuba sponsored by the Institute for Cuban Studies at the American University, Washington, D.C., 13-17 August 1979, 28.

Note: The categories are taken from Cuban sources which do not distinguish in the first groupings among service and production workers. 'Administrative cadres' means persons in managerial positions. 'Workers in administrative functions' are office and clerical staff.

portion of female party members should approach their labour force participation by 1980.[16]

Female representation in the party national and provincial leadership is even lower. Although the number of female full members of the Central Committee did not show any gains at the 1975 congress, almost half of its new alternate members (5 out of 12) were women. The leadership's commitment to increasing female representation in the decision-making process is also evident in the drive to elect more women to the different levels of Popular Power.

Given the social origins of its members and cadres, the Cuban party has had to struggle with improving their educational levels. Table 3 summarizes the information concerning changes in these levels for the period 1967-79.

Although there have been marked improvements in the educational levels of party militants, the majority could only boast a sixth grade education on the eve of the party congress. The congress in fact established the goal of achieving an eighth grade education for a majority of the membership by 1980.[17]

In sum, we have a party whose militants are clearly working class or peasant in origin and it is thus affected by educational handicaps which make it difficult to exercise the complex role of a ruling communist party.

It is hard to say that there has been a re-proletarianization of the Central Committee since differences in the composition of the first (1965) and the second (1975) are minimal. Ten of the one hundred members of the 1965 Central Committee had either died or been expelled before the 1975 congress. Of the remaining 90 members, 13 were removed in 1975 and 35 were added for a new total of 112 full members. Twelve alternate members were also selected.

In an attempt to assess continuity and change in the Cuban political elite, Leogrande[18] compared the composition of the ORI national directorate (1962) and the CCPs first and second Central Committees. He emphasizes the military's weight in the 1965 Central Committee (57 per cent) and its reduction (to 29.8 per cent) in 1975. However, as Leogrande himself points out, the reduction is due primarily to the transfer of military members to civilian positions, not to an actual change in composition.

If we consider the history of the Cuban Revolution and the fact that the Rebel Army played the role of the vanguard party during the struggle, the military's weight in the 1965 Central Committee is not surprising. During the first years of the revolution, the small group of guerrilla leaders which headed the military and political fight against Batista became the political and military leaders of the revolution. These men changed from military to civilian positions (and vice versa) as needed. Hence, Dominguez's concept of the 'civic soldier.'[19] Furthermore, the weight of the military was also

TABLE 3
Educational Composition of CCP Membership (in percentages)

	1967	1968	1969	1970	1971	1972	1973	1974	1975	1979
Less than 6th grade	44.2	38.4	34.9	33.6	31.0	28.9	25.9	19.5	18.1	11.4
6th grade	36.2	42.2	44.0	44.6	46.0	46.7	47.6	44.7	42.2	40.5
Total Elementary Education	80.4	80.8	78.9	78.2	77.0	75.8	73.5	64.2	60.3	51.9
Junior High School	11.9	10.1	11.9	12.1	13.0	14.0	15.0	22.4	25.7	29.0
High School	4.8	5.7	6.3	6.9	7.0	7.5	8.4	9.9	10.2	12.9
Higher Education	2.9	3.8	2.9	2.8	3.0	2.9	3.1	3.5	3.8	6.2
TOTAL	100.0	100.0	100.0	100.0	100.0	100.0	100.0	100.0	100.0	100.0

Sources: Departamento de Orientación Revolucionaria, *Tesis y Resoluciones: Primer Congreso del PCC*, (Havana, 1976), 34-35 and Isidro Gómez, 'El Partido Comunista de Cuba', paper presented at the seminar on Cuba sponsored by the Institute for Cuban Studies at the American University, Washington, D.C., 13-17 August 1979, 29.

enhanced by the fact that in 1965 Cuba was still the target of foreign-supported attacks. Counterrevolutionary bands in the Escambray mountains and other areas of the country were still active.

Leogrande[20] also notes the increased participation of the party apparatus in the 1975 Central Committee as a reflection of its growing organization and institutionalization. He criticizes factional models for analyzing Cuban political elites and finds no evidence to support the existence of a 'fidelista-raulista' cleavage (i.e. factions consisting of those who fought with Fidel and Raúl respectively during the revolutionary war).[21] Moreover, Leogrande finds evidence (removal of old PSP members most opposed to the 26th of July, a reduction of policy differences between the two groups and the passage of time) that by 1975 the 'cleavage' between the 'old communists' and the 'new communists' had subsided. The party, therefore, seemed reasonably free of factional struggle and hostility. Leogrande nevertheless neglects to mention the most important factor contributing to the present unity: the unity-building action of Fidel Castro himself.

There are no indications that the new members of the 1975 Central Committee are different in social class origins from the 1965 members. In his closing speech at the 1975 congress, Fidel emphasized that election to the Central Committee could be attained several ways. Among the new members were an internationalist fighter, a scientist, a writer and four workers.[22] He seemed to be emphasizing new members of working class background who had not participated in the revolutionary war.

The relationship of party membership and cadre composition (and particularly of Central Committee composition) to the 'dictatorship of the proletariat' is a serious theoretical and practical question which can only briefly be touched upon. The fundamental questions about the transition to socialism are political in nature. The central question is who wields state power.[23] But, it is not easy to answer the inquiry 'how do we know that the proletariat is in power?' The party, the state system and the mass organizations must be examined. But the answer lies in an exhaustive analysis of how the entire system, including the economy, functions. The dominating class is ultimately that which determines how the societal surplus is allocated and/or the class to whom this surplus goes.[24] This analysis must also encompass a discussion of society's class structure, an analysis of party ideology and programme and an understanding of the mechanisms of political direction of the party, the state, the government, the unions and the other mass organizations. Thus, although the social origins of party members and cadres and their present function and position (i.e. the jobs they do) are important indicators, they are not the only parameters which must be looked at in the global analysis of how working class ideology and interests are promoted in the transition to socialism.

Changes in the Theory of the Party's Role[25]

During the late 1960s, the party's role was not clearly delineated. The basic political decisions were made by the Council of Ministers, since, as has been pointed out before, party structures, particularly at the national level, were not activated. Furthermore, the party's guidance and supervisory functions were obstructed by its limited membership, an undeveloped state system and an overlap in political and administrative cadres.

Since 1970 a concerted effort has been made to clarify the party's role. The 1975 constitution establishes (article 5) that the Communist Party is the 'highest leading force of the society and the state, which organizes the common effort toward the goals of the construction of socialism and the progress towards a communist future.'

The party, then, establishes policy directions in the economy and for the state and mass organizations, but is not directly involved in their implementation. Domínguez[26] has argued that, given the number of overlaps at the top and the responsibility political cadres have for production, confusion between party and administrative functions is inevitable. He suggests that this confusion will persist until party responsibility for production and the politicization of promotion policies ends. But the party cannot relinquish responsibility for production, since one of its major roles during the transition period is to lead the construction of the technical and material base of communist society (preamble to the 1975 party statutes).

Although party-state relations are still more clearly defined in theory than in practice, progress has been made in delineating their respective roles and responsibilities. In 1965, virtually all ministers were Central Committee members. In 1975, only 27 of the 45 members of the Council of Ministers were Central Committee members. This is an indicator of the increased differentiation between party and government. In keeping with the intra-elite conflict suggested by Kautsky,[27] Leogrande points out an emerging division between revolutionary and managerial modernizers.[28]

Leogrande, however, mentions the crucial factor without expanding on its implications and significance: the party's Central Committee still reflects the leadership of the revolutionary struggle against Batista. As the regime has institutionalized new structures and processes, the revolutionary generation has retained control of the party's political leadership. Nevertheless, the regime has also recruited new elites through the regular party mechanisms, promotion in mass organizations, the administrative bureaucracy or the army and by election to Organs of Popular Power.

Many 1976 ministers were recruited into the elite through the above-mentioned routes. Their absence from the Central Committee reflects the increased differentiation of party-state structures, the recruitment of new leaders for state and government positions and the conceptualization of the party's primary role as political. It is clear that the ultimate political authorities, however, are still the leaders of the revolutionary war and their associates. Mechanisms to incorporate new members to this 'elite of elites' are not yet developed.

Cuba will soon have to face other problems in the circulation of elites: remotion of members (unless the Central Committee keeps expanding) and incorporation of second generation cadres (persons who did not participate in the revolutionary war) to the top of the elite. Power transition problems have plagued both the Soviet Union and China. The Cuban leadership may well have a better chance to solve these problems successfully. They may take heed of the experience of other socialist revolutions. Also, their revolutionary generation was younger when it came to power, giving them significant lead time to develop differentiated institutional structures and mechanisms for elite recruitment and promotion.

In Cuba, Raúl Castro has made the major theoretical contributions on the party's role, the state's functions and their differentiations.[29] Adhering to Leninist principles, Raúl points out that the dictatorship of the proletariat is exercised by the vanguard organized in the party. But the dictatorship of the proletariat cannot be constrained to the party. 'The dictatorship of the proletariat is not the dictatorship of the communist party,' states Raúl.[30] The party is the leading force within that dictatorship, but the state is its most direct instrument. While state laws are binding for all citizens, party rules and statutes lack this juridical character. They must be followed only by the party membership. The party does not have a coercive apparatus. Its power rests on its moral authority while that of the state stems from its material authority and its coercive apparatus.

Raúl further states that harmful consequences follow confusion between party and state. 'In the first place, damage to the tasks of ideological and political persuasion of the masses, tasks which must be performed by the party and which only the party can fulfill and furthermore, harm to the activities of the state because its functionaries cease to be responsible for their decisions and activities.'[31] The party must fulfill its guiding function with respect to the state and the mass organizations without substituting for them or becoming confused with them. It must rely on persuasion, not coercion, for the political education of the masses.

The party guides the state through the elaboration and supervision of the general party programme for the economic, social, political and cultural development of the country, its role in the selection of the state's top leadership (some of whom have dual roles in party and state) and the activities of party militants in state structures.

Besides Raúl's speeches, other key documents on party-state relations are the Political Bureau's *Document on the Structure, Mechanisms of Functioning and Tools which the Party has to Exercise the Direction and Control of the State and Society* and the *Communique of the Secretariat of the Central Committee of the CCP about the Relationships between the Central Committee Apparatus and the Central Organisms of the State.*[32] The latter document states that the Council of Ministers is primarily an executive and administrative institution. It is, therefore, charged with 'the tasks of planning the implementation, implementing and administering the policies and general directives approved by the superior organs of the party with respect to the different sectors of economic and social activity.' On the other hand, the Secretariat's communique emphasizes that the Central Committee departments 'must help in the formulation of such policies and general directives and later supervise and aid in their implementation.'[33]

Changes in Party Structure

Major changes have taken place in party structure since 1970. The Secretariat was reorganized and expanded (1973). Existing departments were revamped and new ones created in the Central Committee apparatus (1973).[34] At the first party congress in 1975, the Political Bureau and the Central Committee were expanded. The national control and revision commission of the party was organized in 1979. The leadership currently emphasizes the importance of collective decision making and the adequate internal functioning of the party so as to prevent costly mistakes.

Again, Raúl Castro provides the most elaborate descriptions of party structures and functions outside the statutes (see footnote 28),

> The party congress is its supreme organ. . .It is followed by the central committee and its plenary meetings, whose directives are valid for all other organisms, but which must follow the congress' directives. . .After this, we find the political bureau which guides the activities of the party, state and mass organizations but must do so within the framework established by the congress and the plenary meetings of the central committee. . .The specific activities of the party apparatus are directed, at a national level, by the secretariat of the central committee.[35]

The first step in preparation for the party congress was the strengthening of the Secretariat and the party apparatus. The expanded apparatus was organized by departments. A labour affairs department was revamped; the department of foreign affairs was divided into a general department and area departments; a general affairs department was organized; the economic commission was superseded by several specialized departments; the departments of revolutionary orientation, of science, culture and educational institutions, of party affairs, of mass organizations and of the Organs of Popular Power were also added. Institutes under Central Committee supervision, such as the Institute for the History of the Communist Movement and the Socialist Revolution in Cuba, were likewise created.

In sum, the party is both expanding and restricting its activities. The increased differentiation in the organization of the state, the effort to separate state and party are minimizing party-administration confusion and overlap. There is a concomitant emphasis on the party's political role, in its guiding and controlling (supervisory) functions. The party is, in sum, undergoing significant organizational growth in the development of new structures, institutionalized operational mechanisms and increased internal differentiation.

THE STATE:
CHANGES SINCE 1970

After the 1974 Matanzas experiment, the Organs of Popular Power were structured nationally in 1976. A number of modifications resulted from the Matanzas experience, the most significant one being the elimination of the regional level to streamline functioning and reduce the bureaucracy. A new political-administrative division of the country was adopted: six provinces were broken up into fourteen and the special municipal district of the Isle of Youth. Furthermore, the previous 407 municipalities were reduced to 169. Each municipality was divided into various 'circunscripciones', the basic electoral units. In 1976, 10,725 municipal deputies were elected who in turn elected the 1,084 to the provincial level and the 481 deputies to the National Assembly. The functions of the Organs of Popular Power are regulated in the 1975 constitution (articles 66-120). Municipal OPP elect their executive committees and appoint administrative departments as needed. The provincial OPP are structured similarly.

At each level, the administration of productive and service units serving the community is under the aegis of the OPP. Thus, the administration of schools, polyclinics, grocery stores, garbage collection, maintenance shops, movie theatres and small local industries, for example, has been transferred to the corresponding OPP levels. There are, however, cases of double subordination. A movie theatre is a case in point. On the one hand, it is dependent on the OPP for programme fulfillment, the appointment of its administrator and general maintenance. But, on the other, its film programme comes from the National Film Institute.

The National Assembly of Popular Power, the supreme organ of state power, is invested with constituent and legislative authority. It elects (from its ranks) the Council of State whose president is also the head of government. The National Assembly appoints the members of the Council of Ministers at the initiative of the president of the Council of State. It also exercises general supervision over the Council of Ministers and the local organs of popular power. Thus, although not directly vested with executive authority, the National Assembly is the organ to which the executive units respond since it also appoints executive personnel.

Domínguez[36] takes a rather dim view of the significance of the National Assembly and the structure of popular power. They do not even rank a separate chapter in his otherwise encyclopaedic book. He distinguishes between formalization and institutionalization of the state and argues that although the former has advanced considerably, judgement must be reserved about the latter. He sees the National Assembly as a pro forma affair, although he concedes that it makes some contributions to policy making such as responding to constituents on special issues, improving the technical quality of legislation, passing a few amendments and strengthening links among local leaders.

A study currently in progress by Lourdes Casal on the proceedings of five meetings of the National Assembly (December 1976, June and December 1977, and June and December 1978) demands considerable correction of Domínguez' views. Domínguez simply transposes to Cuba what mainstream North American political scientists believe about assemblies and parliaments in socialist countries. It is true that deputies to the National Assembly serve only part time, and that its meetings are held twice a year for three days each time. But, an analysis of the activities of the Assembly must be placed in the context of the Cuban legislative system — the work of the standing commissions of the National Assembly and the method whereby draft laws are discussed by the party, the mass organizations and the people before the laws come up in the Assembly. An analysis of the trends in the five meetings under study suggests an increasing participation in the debates by the deputies, particularly those who are not members of the Council of State, an increased amount of spontaneous participation from the floor (more than ninety per cent of all interventions are spontaneous), and a discussion of substantive issues, not only modifications of draft laws. Although a majority of decisions are taken by unanimous vote, by no means all are. In the December 1978 session, for example, there were 70 decisions requiring a vote; 62 were unanimous, eight were decided by a plurality. Of these 70 decisions, ten represented *rejections* of proposed amendments.

The National Assembly meetings are not rubber stamp or cosmetic affairs. They also function as the last resort whereby a deputy may try to introduce a modification (which may be a mandate from his constituency) not included by the corresponding commission in the draft law.

Composition of the OPP: Local and National

Of the 10,725 deputies to municipal assemblies, 856 are women (8 per cent), 6,310 are party members (58.8 per cent), 1,760 belong to the Communist Youth Organization (16.4 per cent) and 3,042 were black or mulatto (28.4 per cent). The largest age category among deputies is 31-40 years (39.1 per cent) and the majority had no less than a junior high school educational level (nearly 69 per cent). Thus, municipal assemblies are a predominantly male, middle-aged group of above-average education composed largely of party or communist youth members (although a quarter do not belong to either the party or the young communists).[37] 267 deputies (55.5 per cent) to the National Assembly were elected in their municipalities. Table 4 summarizes the available information on the deputies.

Thus, in comparison with the municipal deputies, national deputies are older, better educated, more homogeneous in party militancy and more representative of national and local leaders. Female representation increased markedly from the municipal (8 per cent) to the national (22 per cent) level. This increase is against the common trend in Western and most Eastern European societies where female representation decreases as we move up the hierarchical scale in elected bodies. It responds to an explicit policy decision by the Cuban leadership. Black representation is also more significant at the national level (38 per cent) than at the municipal (28.4 per cent).[38] However, the leadership has not addressed itself to redressing mechanisms for blacks as it has for women. It could be that, even in the absence of an explicit reference, such a policy does in fact exist.

Changes in the Theory of the Role of the State

The main outlines of the theory of the role of the state have been presented earlier. The state has undergone major changes in programmatic statements and in actual practices since 1974. From a relatively simple, highly centralized system which vested legislative,

TABLE 4
Cuban National Assembly — 1976 Composition
(N = 481)

	Number	Percentage
Sex:		
Male	376	78.0
Female	105	22.0
Age Distribution:		
18-30	51	10.6
31-40	196	40.8
41-50	158	32.8
51 or more	76	15.8
Occupational Distribution:		
Workers in production, services & education	144	29.9
Peasants	7	1.5
Technicians	38	7.9
National Leaders	59	12.3
Other leadership positions	140	29.1
Defense	35	7.3
Others	58	12.0
Militancy:		
CCP members & candidates	441	91.7
Young communists	24	5.0
Non-militants	16	3.3
Educational level:		
Basic	57	11.8
Intermediate	287	59.7
Higher	137	28.5

Sources: Granma Weekly Review, 12 December 1976 and interview with José Arañaburu, secretary of the National Assembly, in December 1978.

judicial and executive powers in the Council of Ministers, the Cuban state is evolving to a highly complex and differentiated structure with elected representative bodies, a National Assembly and a Council of State.

Once again, Raúl Castro has elaborated in most detail the relationship between the party and the elected state organs.[39] The party can (and has to) attempt to influence (primarily through the activities of its militants) the decisions of the state, but it must do so within clearly specified limits. If the party fails to influence the state at the municipal level, for instance, it must refer the matter in question to the party's provincial level so that it can be discussed with the corresponding Popular Power level. In the most complex cases, the disagreement may reach the Political Bureau and the Council of Ministers, but it is very unlikely that this would happen because, as was pointed out earlier, as we move up the elected state structures, the proportion of party members increases significantly. But the basic principle is that if persuasion does not work, the party cannot force a decision upon a Popular Power organ at the same level, but rather it must argue the case at superior levels and wait until the orientation reaches the local popular power organ through its own hierarchy.

CONCLUDING REMARKS

No description of the Cuban political system is complete without a discussion of the mass organizations. However, it would carry us too far from the central concerns of this paper. Suffice it to say that the role of mass organizations within the Cuban system is one of its most interesting and innovative aspects. Article 7 of the constitution establishes that mass organizations 'gather in their midst the various sectors of the population, represent specific interests of the same and incorporate them to the tasks of edification, consolidation and defence of the socialist society.' Mass organizations are thus recognized as representatives of specific popular interests.

The Federation of Cuban Women (FMC) is a case in point. In 1976, the ministry of labour passed a resolution banning women from certain jobs on alleged safety grounds. That resolution was in sharp conflict with the party thesis on the equality of women and the activist stance the Federation had taken in incorporating women into the labour force. Although the resolution has not been repealed, it has not been strictly enforced. The Federation 'lobbied' against it and at its third congress, in March 1980, Fidel Castro noted the commitment to maintain the current (31 per cent) proportion of female participation in the labour force.[40]

Conflict of interests, albeit non-antagonistic, are therefore present in societies undergoing the transition to socialism. An analysis of how these conflicts are expressed, resolved or stunted is also essential for understanding the dynamics of the dictatorship of the proletariat.

It is still too early to determine whether the Cuban state is in fact 'withering away.' Since 1970, relations between party and state have been delineated and differentiated. The party has simultaneously expanded its apparatus and restricted its direct involvement in administrative affairs. The establishment of the Organs of Popular Power has been the most significant development in the Cuban state system in the past decade. Mass participation and internal party democracy are two of the key elements in socialist democracy. The Cuban state will begin to 'wither away' to the extent that both are further institutionalized and consolidated in the 1980s.

NOTES

1. The literature on the changes in the Cuban political system is neither abundant nor satisfactory. See for instance: Carmelo Mesa-Lago, *Cuba in the 1970s: Pragmatism and Institutionalization* (Albuquerque: University of New Mexico Press, 1978); Jorge I. Domínguez, *Cuba: Order and Revolution* (Cambridge, Mass: Harvard University Press, 1978); Ronald Radosh, *The New Cuba: Paradoxes and Potentials* (New York: William Morrow and Co., 1976).

2. Several leftist critics of the revolutions had pointed out the need to develop a more responsive political system in which the masses could systematically participate in the decision-making processes. See Leo Huberman and Paul Sweezy, *Socialism in Cuba* (New York: Monthly Review Press, 1969); Rene Dumont, *Cuba: est-il Socialiste?* (Paris: Editions du Seuil, 1970); K. S. Karol, *Guerrillas in Power: The Course of the Cuban Revolution* (New York: Hill and Wang, 1970).

3. The *Ley Fundamental de la República de Cuba,* promulgated 7 February 1959, was a modified version of the 1940 constitution. See Leonel de la Cuesta (ed.), *Constituciones Cubanas* (New York: Ediciones Exilio, 1974), 400-464.

4. Carollee Bengelsdorf, 'A Large School of Government', *Cuba Review,* Vol. 6, No. 3, 3-18; Lourdes Casal, 'On Popular Power: The Organization of the Cuban State during the Period of Transition', *Latin American Perspectives,* Vol. 2, No. 4, 78-88.

5. Comité Central del Partido Comunista de Cuba, *Informe sobre el desarrollo*

del trabajo de constitución de los órganos del poder popular (Havana: Talleres del Comité Central, 1976).

6. Raúl Castro, 'Discurso en la clausaura del seminario a los delegados del poder popular en Matanzas', *Granma Resumen Semanal,* 9 September 1974. Quotes are from Fidel Castro and Raúl Castro, *Selección de discursos acerca del Partido* (Havana: Editorial Ciencias Sociales, 1975), 193-242.

7. Literature about the Cuban party and its history is scarce. There is no adequate history of the present party or of the first communist party founded in 1925. See Fidel Castro, *Informe central al primer congreso del Partido Comunista de Cuba* (Havana: Departamento de Orientación Revolucionaria, 1975); Fidel Castro and Raúl Castro, op. cit. For contrasting views on the present party in US literature, see Lourdes Casal, 'Cuban Communist Party: The Best among the Good', *Cuba Review,* Vol. 6, No. 3, 23-30; Domínguez, op. cit., 306-340; Hanz Magnus Enzensberger, 'Portrait of a Party: Prehistory, Structure and Ideology of the CCP', in Radosh, op. cit., 102-137, which was originally published in German in *Kursbuch* in 1969, is a scathing attack on the pre-1970 party. It includes a somewhat cavalier, careless history of the PSP and of PSP-26th of July relations. The latter is the central topic of Andrés Suárez, *Cuba: Castroism and Communism,* 1959-1966 (Cambridge: The MIT Press, 1967). Suarez' ideological perspective introduces serious distortions in his analysis: over-emphasis of the Castroism-Communism rift, underplay of the PSP's role in the revolutionary struggle and minimizing the masses' role in the revolution which he characterizes as an 'administrative' revolution. A history of the PSP by two exiled authors is: Jorge García Montes and Aurelio Alvarez, *Historia del Partido Comunista de Cuba* (Miami: Ediciones Universal, 1970). Several articles in Cuban publications are the best sources for the early history of the PSP—Fabio Grobart, 'El cincentenario de la fundación del primer Partido Comunista de Cuba', *El Militante Comunista* (August 1975), 9-44 and Fabio Grobart, 'Preguntas y respuestas sobre los años 30', *Universidad de La Habana,* 200, 1973, 128-157.

8. F. Castro, op. cit., 108.

9. For a discussion of these problems, refer to F. Castro, ibid; 'Tesis y resolución sobre la vida interna del Partido', in *Tesis y Resoluciones: Primer Congreso del Partido Comunista de Cuba* (Havana: Departamento de Orientación Revolucionaria, 1976), 15-54; R. Castro, op. cit., 228 and ff.

10. The system had been instituted in the PURS in 1963.

11. Domínguez, op. cit., 315-316.

12. Ibid., 315.

13. Ibid., 316.

14. F. Castro, op. cit., 207.

15. *Tesis y Resoluciones,* op. cit., 28. The 1979 female party militancy will be found in Isidro Gómez, 'El Partido Comunista de Cuba', paper presented at the seminar on Cuba sponsored by the Institute for Cuban Studies at the American University, Washington, D. C., 13-17 August 1979, 28.

16. *Tesis y Resoluciones,* op. cit., 29.

17. Ibid., 36.

18. William Leogrande, 'Continuity and Change in the Cuban Political Elite', *Cuban Studies/Estudios Cubanos,* Vol. 8, No. 2 (July 1978), 1-31.

19. Domínguez, op. cit., Chapter 9.

20. Leogrande, op. cit., 14.

21. The alleged 'Fidelista-Raulista' cleavage has been a favourite of factional model analysts such as Andrés Suárez and Edward González.

22. Fidel Castro's closing speech at the first party congress in *Unity Gave Us Victory* (Havana: Department of Revolutionary Orientation, 1977), 392.

23. Refer particularly to V. I. Lenin, 'The State and Revolution' in *Collected Works,* Vol. 25 (Moscow: Progress Publishers, 1964), 385-497. For a contemporary controversy about the transition period, see Paul Sweezy and Charles Bettelheim, *On the Transition to Socialism* (New York: Monthly Review Press, 1971).

24. 'Control' and 'for the benefit of' are not the same. Under capitalism although office holders may come from classes other than the bourgeoisie, there is no question that the latter reaps most of the benefits from the extracted surplus. In the transition to socialism, particularly in the early stages, power may be exercised by a small vanguard group in the name of the proletarian masses. Such a regime can be profoundly democratic in allocating surplus to the large masses without the latter actually exercising direct control of the state. However, transitional regimes must also develop effective forms for mass participation and mechanisms for internal party democracy which ensure workers' interests and ideology. Advanced socialism will probably evolve a variety of political instructions, but it will still have to pursue mass participation and internal party democracy.

25. The bourgeois state is institutionalized upon the conceptions of 'separation of powers' (executive, legislative, judicial) and 'checks and balances'. The transitional state, on the other hand, refines and differentiates the functions and interrelations of the vanguard party, the state (in Cuba's case, Organs of Popular Power) and its government (the ministries).

26. Domínguez, op. cit., 326-328.

27. J. H. Kautsky, 'Revolutionary and Managerial Elites in Modernizing Regions', *Comparative Politics,* Vol. 1 (July 1969), 441-467.

28. Leogrande, op. cit., 23.

29. There are two key speeches by Raúl Castro: to the central committee cadre on 4 May 1973 and to the seminar on the Matanzas experiment on 22 August 1974. Both are published in *Organos del Poder Popular* (Havana: Editorial Orbe, 1974), 127-143 and 145-168.

30. Ibid., 130.

31. Ibid., 130.

32. Ibid., 146-160.

33. Ibid., 153.

34. In the 1965 structure, there were five commissions: revolutionary armed forces and state security, economy, constitutional studies, education and foreign affairs. See *Cuba Socialista,* Vol. 5, No. 51, 11-12.

35. R. Castro, 4 May 1973 speech in *Organos de Poder Popular,* 141.

36. Domínguez, op. cit., 243-249.

37. *Informe sobre el trabajo del desarrollo de la constitución del poder popular,* op. cit.

38. Lourdes Casal, 'Ethnic Composition of the Cuban Elected Popular Power Organs: A Mini-Report', forthcoming in *Latin American Research Review.*

39. R. Castro, 22 August 1974 speech in *Organos del Poder Popular,* 45-68.

40. The issue is complex because it is largely related to the rationalization of the labour force in the reforms under the new economic and management system. In the 1960s, Cuba eliminated unemployment through underemployment throughout the

economy. Labour productivity consequently suffered. In the 1970s and into the eighties, economic rationality and improved labour productivity are top priorities. Cuba is therefore experiencing low levels of unemployment. The 1976 resolution valued male employment more highly than that of females. The female proportion of the labour force continued to increase nevertheless to 31 percent in 1980. Female employment moreover requires investments in daycare centres and other services supportive of child and house care. For Fidel's 8 March 1980 speech see *Granma Weekly Review,* 16 March 1980. For mass organizations in Cuba, see Max Azicri, 'The Governing Strategies of Mass Mobilization: The Foundations of Cuban Revolutionary Politics', *Latin American Monograph Series*, No. 2 (Erie, Pa.: Northwestern Pennsylvania Institute for Latin American Studies, 1977).

5 The Restoration of the Party-State in Czechoslovakia Since 1968

Jacques Rupnik
Institut d'Etudes Politiques de Paris and
British Broadcasting Corporation, UK

INTRODUCTION: THE LEGACIES OF 1968

The drastic changes in the role of the Communist Party and the State after the fall of Alexander Dubček in April 1969 were proportional to those undertaken by the party during the Czechoslovak reform movement of 1968. Indeed, if one had to sum up in one sentence the basic orientation of the policies of Dubček's successor, Dr Gustáv Husák, one could describe it as the systematic eradication of the reforms of 1968 (as well as of those in the party who had promoted and supported them) and the re-establishment of tight party control over all spheres of social life. In Hungary, five years after 1956, Janos Kádár could declare that 'he who is not against us is with us' and embark on a more flexible and pragmatic course. To understand why the 'kadarization' of Czechoslovakia did not take place — why it took more than a decade to eradicate one year — one has to recall some of the differences between these two offspring of destalinization. The impetus for the largely spontaneous and radical Hungarian revolt came from outside the Communist Party, while the Czechoslovak reform movement, more gradual in character and spread over a longer period was started 'from above', by the Communist Party itself, after the election of Alexander Dubček as First Secretary in January 1968. Because the Czechoslovak Communist Party under A. Novotný refused, after 1956, to undertake any serious step towards dismantling the Stalinist model of the party-state, the crisis of the 1960s which culminated during the Prague Spring of 1968 was simultaneously that of the Party, that of the command economy and of the state structure (with regard to the relationship between Czechs and Slovaks).[1] Though carried out by the party, the reform could not limit itself to cosmetic changes, but questioned the very nature of the party's place in the state.

The proposed changes in the political system were outlined in the April 1968 Action Programme of the Czechoslovak Communist Party (KSČ), which stressed the need both for a greater separation of the party from the state and a wider scope for pluralism within the limits of the system. 'The Party policy', said the programme, 'is based on the principle that no undue concentration of power must occur, throughout the state machinery, in one sector, one body or in a single individual'.[2] The document said more specifically that this principle was 'infringed mainly by undue concentration of duties in the existing Ministry of the Interior'. The Central Committtee of the KSČ, the text went on, 'deems it necessary to change the organization of the security force and to split it into two mutually independent parts — the State Security and Public Security'.[3] The dismantling of the secret police control over the party apparatus was a necessary pre-condition for the project of separation of powers and the resurgence of pluralism both within and outside the party.[4] Similarly, the National Assembly was defined as a 'socialist Parliament with all the scope of activities the parliament of a democratic republic must have. . . a National Assembly which actually decides on laws and important political issues, and not only approves proposals submitted'.[5] Another aspect of this trend in party-state relations was the emphasis on greater decentralization and on local self-government. 'It is the national committees that make the backbone of the whole network of representative bodies in our country as democratic organs of state power. It must be in the national committees that the state policy is formed, especially in districts and regions'.[6] Clearly the reform of the state structure, as much as that of the functioning of the party itself, was central to the 1968 development of pluralistic trends within the Czechoslovak political system.

From the point of view of the KSČ's attitude towards the traditionally dominant pluralistic political culture of the country, the Prague Spring of 1968 was for the party also an occasion to rediscover its own indigenous roots in the Czech labour movement. The KSČ, the product of a majority split in the social-democratic movement, was in the interwar period the only mass party in Eastern Europe, the only one to have a long experience of parliamentary democracy and which obtained nearly 40 per cent of the vote in the last free elections in 1946. In this perspective 1968 and the 'normalization' that followed represent a third main period of conflict between an attempt by the KSČ to shape its policies in accordance with the country's dominant political culture and the imperatives of conforming to the norms of Soviet communism. There is clearly a great deal of continuity between the policies pursued in the 1920s under B. Šmeral's leadership, in the period 1945-47, and again in 1968 on the two main issues of inner democracy and independence from Moscow.[7] On the other hand, the 'normalization' of the party of the early 1970s is in many ways reminiscent of the 'bolshevization' of the party in the late 1920s (the purge that followed Gottwald's seizure of power at the 5th Congress in 1929) or again the Stalinist purges of 1949-54.[8] Czechoslovakia turned out to be, paradoxically, a fertile ground not only for a brand of communism reconciling the libertarian dimension of Marxism with the national and democratic political tradition of the country, but also for the most solidly entrenched kind of Stalinism.

There are at least two aspects of the Czechoslovak Communist Party's dramatic conflict with the Soviet leadership in 1968 which help explain some of the features (and obsessions) of the 'normalization'. The first is the question as to whether or not Dubček was really aware of the threat the KSČ reform policies in 1968 posed to the legitimacy of Communist rule in the whole of the Soviet bloc. The very fact that the Warsaw Pact invasion took place on the eve of the planned 14th Congress of the KSČ leaves little doubt that it was the transformation of the role and the function of the communist party, as much as the uncontrolled activity outside the party (the media, an embryonic social-democratic party, and generally the pressure of the public opinion) — not to mention alleged Western influences — that was perceived as the prime threat by the Soviet Party leadership.[9]

The invasion only crystallized fundamental differences between Soviet and Czechoslovak positions. The clandestine Party Congress of August 1968 held in a factory (ČKD Vysočany) in occupied Prague represented a radical break of the umbilical cord with Russian Communism that nobody, even the most outspoken reformers, could have envisaged. More generally, it can be said that despite Dubček's compromises in Moscow, many of the trends emerging during the Spring continued, were even reinforced, after the invasion: for instance the workers' councils movement took off really only in September 1968 and was disbanded only in the late Spring of 1969, after Gustáv Husák took over the Party leadership from Dubček.[10] Political mobilization had been accelerated by the invasion but declined with the impossibility (or sometimes reluctance) of the 1968 Party leadership to remain a national focus of identification.

Thus, paradoxically, the first task of the 'normalization' was to deal at once with the reformist legacy of 1968 and the direct consequences of the invasion. This duality is to be found in most Central Committee statements between April and September 1969. Thus, for instance, the September 1969 Central Committee resolution cancels *its* decision of July 1968 not to take part in the Warsaw meeting of Communist parties; it then procedes to cancel the party leadership statement of 21 August 1968 condemning the invasion and declares 'non-valid' the documents of the 14th (Vysočany) Party Congress as the product of 'fractionist activities of certain members of the Central Committee'. The next step is to invalidate the mandates of the (for the first time) democratically-elected delegates to the Congress.[11] But besides restoration there is still ambivalence in the new party leadership's search for legitimacy — at times presenting itself as the only plausible continuator of the course inaugurated in January 1968 (merely introducing changes in the application), at other times as the purifying force after the 1968 'counter-revolution', thus implicitly recognizing the Warsaw Pact invasion as the real source of its power.[12]

THE PARTY

Changes in the Theory of the Party's Role

The replacement of A. Dubček by Dr Gustáv Husák as the First Secretary of the Party clearly began a radically new period in the history of the KSČ which brought significant changes both in the party's conception of its role, its internal life and its relationship with the state. 1968 provided the 'normalizers' with the anti-model of what they claimed the party should become. It is thus not surprising to find the first comprehensive outline of what the precise role of the Communist Party should be in a document entitled 'Lessons from the Crisis Development in the Party and Society since the 13th Congress of the Communist Party of Czechoslovakia', adopted at the Central Committee meeting of December 1970.[13]

The first 'cardinal sin' of the party in 1968 was, according to the document, that it 'gradually ceased to be the "leading centre" of the socialist social system' which was curiously attributed to Dubček's having 'monopolised' decision-making in the party leadership at the expense of the Central Committee and thus helped the emergence within the Party of the so-called 'second centre'[14] (rooted mainly in the Prague party organization), described as the driving force of the counter-revolution. Hence the prime feature of the Party's role is to re-establish its 'leading role' in society, which in turn requires it 'to defeat the right wing ideologically and organizationally'; in short, *normalize first the party in order to normalize the society* as a whole.

The second 'lesson' concerns the 'disintegration of socialist power' which refers to state institutions in general and more particularly to the Party's control over State Security, the Army, and Justice.[15]

The third task was to re-establish the Party's leading role in the National Front; in other words, to reintroduce the 'transmission belt' relationship between the KSČ and other parties (socialist, populist) and the trade unions who were accused of have gained excessive autonomy during 1968.

Fourthly, the Party was to restore its 'leading role in the economy' which meant the liquidation of Professor O. Šik's economic reform combining market socialism and self-management along lines not too dissimilar to the Yugoslav model. Central planning of the economy is considered by the December 1970 Central Committee document as a necessary corollary of the consolidation of the Party's monopoly of political power.

The fifth aim is absolute ideological monolithism; concretely the 'ideological struggle' is to be conducted through the party's total control over the media.[16]

The final reference is to the Party's role as the guarantor of the 'basic foreign political orientation of the State'. The document concludes on this subject that the 'Central Committee of the KSČ rejects the abstract concept of sovereignty of the socialist state'. Thus there is the return to 'true internationalism', of which the first step is the endorsement of the Brezhnev doctrine of limited sovereignty and the proclamation of the August 1968 invasion as an act of 'fraternal assistance'.

All these basic features of the restoration of Party control over state and society were reasserted at the 'remake' of the 14th Party Congress held in May 1971. They were also reflected in the new party statutes adopted there. In contrast to the amendments of these statutes put forward in 1968 (and which were to introduce the right for a minority to disagree with majority policies — a right that disappeared in the communist movement in 1921 with Lenin's decision to ban 'fractions' within the party), the 1971 version of the statutes provides a legal framework for a permanent purge: not only individual members, but also entire basic organizations which do not toe the party line, or are merely considered 'completely passive', can be disbanded from above. Party control in the economy and the civil service is to be strengthened through increased powers of the factory or office party organization (in contrast to the 1966 statutes, there is no mention of co-operation with the trade unions in personnel policies). All these measures, confirmed without significant changes at the 15th Party Congress in 1976, were merely the legalization postfactum of the most drastic, though by no means theoretical, change in the development of the Communist Party in Czechoslovakia — the great purge of 1970.

Changes in the Structure and Functions of the Party

The Great Purge

The 'normalization' of Czechoslovakia started with the greatest party purge in the post-war history of the communist movement in Europe, and has no equivalent except perhaps the Chinese 'cultural revolution'. It implied a substantial reshuffle in the Party's leading organs and a massive purge of the membership.

At least formally it was the same Central Committee elected under Novotny in 1966 which supported Dubček in 1968 and then Husák. However, a closer look at the Central Committee Praesidium and the Central Committee gives a somewhat different picture. Considering first the Central Committee: the clandestine Vysočany Congress of August 1968 re-elected only 25 of the 108 incumbent members elected at the 13th Congress in 1966. At the opposite end of the purge, the 14th Congress of 1971 curiously also re-elected only 26 of those entering the Central Committee at the 1966 Congress: the proportion is the same but they were obviously different people. Only nine of those elected at the Vysočany Congress (and 34 of those composing the modified Central Committee at the end of August 1968) survived into the Central Committee at the 14th Congress in 1971. Between September 1969 and May 1971 the dismissals of reformers and the co-optation of 'realists' were carried out at a steady pace. 1969-70 was a perfect demonstration of the way the Party leadership can reshape — against the norms of the Party statutes which prohibit co-optation of more than 10 per cent of the Central Committee members — the composition of the theoretically supreme body of the Party according to the needs of the power struggle at the top.

In the Praesidium the reshuffle proceeded along similar lines. In the team that received the imprimatur of the 1971 14th Party Congress, four were old-type Stalinists and opponents of the Prague Spring — Bilak, Indra, Hoffmann, Kapek. Štrougal, Colotka and to some extent Lenart were remarkably skilled survivors.[17] Gustáv Husák was the only prominent reformer not just to survive, but to become General Secretary of the Party and later (in 1975) the President of the Republic.[18] Separation of the two functions in January 1968 marked the beginning of the Prague Spring; their merger again confirmed symbolically its end.

The rise of Gustáv Husák, a victim of the Stalinist purges in the 1950s, the most prominent Slovak reformer in the 1960s and under whose leadership was conducted the 'normalization' of the 1970s deserves to be recalled in greater detail. In 1968 Husák believed that the reform process under Dubček was not advancing fast enough in Slovakia because of the obstruction of the Slovak Party leadership chaired by hardliners such as V.Bilak, his present-day colleague. On the eve of the invasion he declared in a factory at Ziar nad Hronom,

> There are here tendencies to slow down the democratization process and to close the door; even on the eve of the Congress of the Slovak Communist Party one can observe busy efforts of various well-placed people in order to preserve their posts, in order to preserve power in one way or another. I am firmly convinced that the new course represented by comrade Alexander Dubček is so strong

among the Czech and Slovak people that there is no longer any force able to close the door, to bring us back and block our future development.[19]

During the Prague Spring Husák was deputy-Prime Minister in the Černík government though he held no position in the Slovak Communist Party still run by Bilak. Interestingly it was the Soviet invasion which provided Husák with the opportunity to topple Bilak and take over the Slovak Party. Bilak — who hoped the invasion would give him the leadership of the Czechoslovak Party — was even forced to quit the leadership of the Slovak Party, leaving the road open for the ascension of the great hope of the liberals, Gustáv Husák.[20] As the new boss of the Slovak Communists, Husák attended the Moscow negotiations. On his return from Moscow he attended the extraordinary congress of the Slovak Party where he dismissed the Soviet justification for the invasion and declared his total support for Dubček.

The question is the following: either give firm support to Dubček and the others or have no confidence in them. There is no third way. I stand firmly behind Dubček's conception. I was its co-author and I will support him entirely; *either I will stay with him or I will leave with him.*[21]

Husák did not leave with Dubček. In fact he did everything to make him go and formed an alliance with Bilak which has constituted the political base for the normalization policies of the 1970s.

To understand this complete turnabout one must not see Husák as a genuine representative of the reform movement gone astray or suddenly converted by the persuasiveness of the Soviet arguments, but rather as a politician whose main ambition had always been power. As a victim of the Stalinist purges he had no other way available for a comeback into the forefront of the political arena than to support the reformist trend of the 1960s. Brought to the leadership of the Slovak Party on the reformist tide and as an opponent of the Soviet-led invasion he then proceeded to use the Slovak card to invalidate the clandestine Vysočany Congress of the KSČ under the pretext of insufficient Slovak representation at the Congress. As the boss of the Slovak Party he earned in Moscow a reputation as an able 'normaliser' and was thus entrusted in April 1969 with the task of suppressing revisionism in the Czechoslovak Communist Party. In Slovakia his task had been made incomparably easier than in Prague because under Bilak's leadership the reform process in the Slovak Party in 1968 lagged far behind the developments in the Czech lands. So in a way there was greater continuity in the Communist Party in Slovakia between the pre-August policies of Bilak and the post-August transition to fully-fledged normalization under Husák. Husák and Bilak followed two radically different itineraries — one was a 'reformer', the other a Stalinist; one was opposed to the invasion, while the other helped the Russians prepare it. The two have been throughout the 1970s the most powerful men in the Communist Party of Czechoslovakia.

There is therefore both continuity and change in the ruling elite from the Prague Spring to the 'normalization', which reflects not only the degree of continuity in the political system but also in the party bureaucracy as a social group, with monopoly over political power and the social privileges that come with it. However, there are no consistent patterns as to how 'Stalinists' become 'reformers', nor how reformers turn into 'realists' and then 'hardliners' (Husák, Štrougal) or, on the contrary, remain faithful to the reformist cause and join the opposition movement (Kriegel, Dubček).[22] Here personality more than previous political experience can make all the difference between a Moscow trained apparatchik like Alexander Dubček and a victim of Stalinist repression like Gustáv Husák.

Evolution of the Membership and of the Social Composition of the Party

The reshuffle at the top was also accompanied by a purge of the membership, conducted on an unprecedented scale by means of the 1970 'exchange of party cards' (provĕrka). According to an interview with Bilak some 70,934 people were expelled from the party and 390,817 were 'struck off' the lists which gives a total of 461,751.[23] In other words, nearly half a million members (i.e. nearly a third of the total membership) left the party.

Beyond the obvious political aim of the post-1968 purge it deserves at least two remarks regarding the place of the party in the society. First, if one adds up the expellees from previous purges (about 600,000 between 1946-1950) and the people who departed because of political pressures (approximately 300,000 during the purge trials of the early 1950s),[24] one must conclude that, although an exact figure is hard to reach, a significant proportion of the adult population (perhaps as much as a quarter) had, at one point or another, been members of the party. The ideologically motivated hard core of the party is easier to estimate: there were 235,272 organisers chosen to run the screening commissions during the 1970 purge.[25] The 'party of the expelled' is therefore by far the largest party in the country. Though by no means a homogeneous group, the half a million communists expelled in 1970 constituted a de facto base for a 'Eurocommunist' type opposition to the 'normalized' party.[26]

The second, less speculative, remark concerns Bilak's admission in his interview that some 30 per cent of those who did not pass the party screening successfully also lost their jobs. Even if we consider this to be the understatement of the decade, it is an open acknowledgement of political victimization in the professional sphere which points to an essential feature of party policies in Czechoslovakia in the 1970s — the reintroduction of the Leninist concept of 'partijnost' in all spheres of social and economic life. Indeed the guidelines for personnel policies issued first on 6 November 1970, confirmed at the 14th Party Congress in 1971, and brought out again more recently in *Rudé Právo* define professional competence with criteria such as 'political maturity', 'class consciousness' etc. Among the essential components of professional qualification are 'political attitudes, faithfulness to socialism, to the Marxist-Leninist policies of the Party and of the State, friendship towards the Soviet Union'.[27] The statement could not be more explicit. In 1968 the abolition of the *nomenklatura* (a detailed list of posts throughout the state machinery and society generally, which can be filled only by politically reliable people) had been one of the most 'revolutionary' (in Skilling's sense of the word) measures altering the modus operandi of the Communist Party. Since 1970 it has been reintroduced with an unprecedented rigour. Thus, in contrast to policies pursued by Gierek in Poland or Kadar in Hungary (relying on the support of the technocratic strata), Husák still seems to maintain the primacy of ideological loyalty over technical competence, though recent debates about economic management (since December 1978) suggest that not everybody shares this approach in the face of growing economic difficulties.[28]

Almost a decade after the post-1968 purge of the party, a new exchange of party cards has taken place in the second half of 1979. Though the results are not yet known and thus prevent a proper assessment, the guidelines for the exercise give us some indications about its basic orientation. At least formally, it is presented in similar language, though with less vehemence, as ten years ago. The December 1978 Central Committee resolution insists on the need for the Party to 'part with those who . . . do not exercise required activity, avoid duties . . . violate norms of Party life, Party and State discipline and continue in their mistakes'.[29] However, instead of the struggle against 'revisionism', this time the economy seems, according to *Rudé Právo*, to be the main battle ground.[30] The exchange of party cards is this time linked to the crisis of economic management and the 'need for a better cadre policy'. 'Some comrades', says an editorial in the party paper, 'have misunderstood the policy of cadre stability and believe that irrespective of the results their jobs are guaranteed . . . . Other comrades think that their past merits will safely protect them against any kind of criticism . . . in cases where they have slackened off, become too arrogant or simply are no longer capable of coping with greater and more intricate tasks'.[31] The editorial declares unfit for a managerial position those who 'lagged behind the needs of the times, who impair communist morale and even enrich themselves at the cost of the society . . . and who create around them, sometimes by pressure, unjustifiably, uncritically, an aura of infallibility and untouchability. We would be naive to think that such people do not exist in our country. Not everybody will meet our hopes, not everybody will pass a serious test.'[32] This suggests that this time the exchange of party cards will be accompanied by sweeping changes in the industrial management and perhaps even in the ministries in order to reverse the slow-down of the economy. After a decade of ideological purification the 1980s are likely in Czechoslovakia to see the economic issues back at the centre of the political debate in the Communist Party leadership.

While the new exchange of party cards is being completed the KSČ has almost recovered the level of membership it had in 1968.

Evolution of the Membership of the KSČ[33]

1 April 1969	1,650,587
28 August 1971	1,200,000
29 May 1974	1,360,000
April 1976	1,382,860
1 January 1978	1,473,112
17 November 1978	1,500,000

Simultaneously with the increased level of membership of the party the social composition has also changed in the 1970s; the trend has been clearly towards the lowering of the average age and a greater proportion of workers in the rank and file.[34] It was announced at the 15th Party Congress in 1976 that 62 per cent of the new recruits were workers and 8 per cent peasants — and that there were 34.8 per cent of workers in the total party membership. The trend has apparently continued since at the same pace; some 117,000 workers have joined the party since the 15th Congress, i.e. 62 per cent of the candidates for membership.[35] Thus the total proportion of workers has increased to 45 per cent, which means that after twenty years of steady decline of the proportion of workers in the Party the trend has been reversed.[36] The return to ideological orthodoxy has been accompanied by a rather voluntaristic 're-proletarianization' of the party.

Proportion of Workers in the KSČ membership (percentage of total)[37]

1946	57	1971	25
1956	36	1976	35
1960	33	1978	45

The increased level of membership and the younger and more working class composition of the party are not in themselves significant criteria of increased popular political participation. The overall context described above and the forceful reintroduction of the *nomenklatura* principle account for the fact that the party card in the 1970s was more than ever primarily a 'work permit'. Political participation has thus been reduced to its formal aspects, breeding conformism rather than consensus.[38]

The official concept of participation remains primarily to promote and supervise the implementation (mainly in the economic sphere) of decisions imposed from above. Thus a clear distinction is to be made between this merely 'apparent' or official participation and a new kind of political participation introduced by the opposition and which is best represented by the Charter 77 human rights movement.[39] The new opposition of the 1970s no longer strives for reform from within the Communist Party in the name of an amended version of the official ideology, but has tried (without much success so far) to establish a minimal, but genuine, dialogue with the authorities on issues such as political victimization in the job market, schooling, the condition of women in the labour force, the status of national minorities (Hungarians, gypsies), 'zhdanovism' in cultural life, etc. — all of which pose the fundamental question of the role of law in a state subjected to the leading role of the Communist Party.

THE STATE

Changes in the Theory of the State

For almost a decade after 1960, when Czechoslovakia became, according to the new Constitution, a 'socialist state' the dominant official theory had been that fundamental class conflicts in the society had been overcome and the role of the state was to change accordingly. Along the lines suggested by the Khrushchevian concept of the 'state of the whole people' (as opposed to the previous phase of the 'dictatorship of the proletariat') the party ideologists predicted that the construction of communism would gradually also bring about the decline (if not quite the 'withering away') of the centralistic and coercive features of the state. In Czechoslovakia the main proponents of the new theory of the state were Mlynář and Lakatoš whose team at the Academy of Sciences outlined the political systemic reforms of 1968. The project aimed at the institutionalization of pluralistic trends within a state where the Communist Party would retain its 'leading role'.[40] This concept was repudiated after the fall of Dubček. The 1970 Central Committee document 'Lessons from the crisis . . .' emphasized again the key role of the state as the instrument of the dictatorship of the proletariat. Parallel with that of the Party a massive purge swept the state apparatus.

The federalization of the Czechoslovak state is the only major visible remnant of the reforms of 1968. Since the 1950s the official theory of the solution of the Slovak question had been that it would automatically emerge from economic and cultural development in that area. Rejecting this theory, the reformers of the mid-1960s (and particularly in 1968) claimed a political answer had to be found, and put forward constitutional changes which were implemented only after the Soviet-led invasion of August 1968.[41]

Changes in the Structure and the Functions of the State

Though being an integral part of the 1968 reforms the federalization of the state was considered by the Slovaks to have priority over all the rest of the reform programme while for the Czechs democcratization of the system had priority over federalization.[42] Though obviously a simplification this dichotomy is essential for an understanding of Husák's political strategy behind the reforms of the structure of the state.

On 28 October 1968 (the 50th anniversary of the foundation of the Czechoslovak state) President L. Svoboda signed the federalization bill passed by the National Assembly and as of 1 January 1969 Czechoslovakia became a federal and binational state of Czechs and Slovaks. The Slovak Communists had earlier rejected both the 'tripartite' or regional proposal (Bohemia, Moravia, Slovakia) as well as the 'asymmetric' proposal made by some of the Prague reformers (i.e. autonomy, which implied giving the Slovaks a national minority status). [43] Finally the law drafted in July and passed in October 1968 made the distinction between the two nations considered as the two pillars of the federal state and the national minorities. According to the law the Czechs and Slovaks share power on an equal basis which is reflected in the bicameral Parliament. The Federal Assembly is composed of the House of the People with 200 deputies of which two thirds are Czechs and one third Slovaks (reflecting the numerical balance between the two nations) and the House of the Nations made up to 150 deputies on the basis of parity : 75 Czechs and 75 Slovaks. The legislative bodies in the Czech lands and Slovakia are respectively the Czech National Council and the Slovak National Council. At the top of this structure there is the Federal Government with the two provincial governments. The seven federal ministries were to have exclusive powers in areas such as defence, foreign affairs, federal state material reserves, protection of federal legislation and administration, interior, labour, social affairs. Seven, more specialized, federal committees were created on parity basis (mainly economic matters). The specifically Czech government had seventeen ministers and the Slovak fifteen.

Party and State

A product of the 1968 reform movement, the federalization was implemented in a political context marked by the overwhelming priority given to re-establishing central and unitary controls of the Communist Party. Little over a year after the federalization was introduced an amendment was passed designed to 'strengthen the functions and the integrating role of the federal bodies, to solidify the management of a unified Czechoslovak economy, and to fortify the control functions of the federal centre'.[44] The number of the federal ministries was increased from seven to thirteen and the state planning commission's economic plan became mandatory for both republics.

The dominant factor in the re-centralization of the state was the centralistic nature of the Communist Party policies and organizational structure.[45] In the initial Prague Spring version the federalization of the state had to be accompanied by that of the Party. A Czech Communist Party and a Slovak Communist Party were to become the 'national-territorial' organizations of a unified Communist Party of Czechoslovakia. However, the Czech bureau, which had been created in 1968 as the first step in that direction, disappeared as soon as Husák took over. Already in May 1969, merely a month after the fall of Dubček, Husák declared at a Central Committee meeting : 'The party is not federalized; on the contrary, it is unified and we are responsible for the work of Communists at all levels, federal as well as national.'[46] In fact Husák, who had throughout his career been the leading advocate in the KSČ of Slovak autonomy, was ironically entrusted with the task of restoring Prague centralism.This is how he outlined the relationship between the Party and the State at the January 1970 Central Committee meeting:

As a unifying and integrating force, the Communist Party of Czechoslovakia must play an important role as a unitary party led by a Central Committee, with a united programme and objective. Certain elements of the federalization have got into the party, with the national elements, the Czech bureau and the Slovak Central Committee playing their part vis-à-vis the old leadership. These questions too will have to be put in order in the new conditions; the various controlling elements of the party will have to be harmonised with the unified principles of our programme, but also, specifically, in action, as this will considerably enhance the strength of the party as a whole. [47]

Husák had merely used the Slovak Party in the second half of 1968 as a springboard for the conquest of the leadership of the Czechoslovak Party; once this aim had been achieved, the logic of the new function required bringing the Slovak party back to its position as a mere territorial organization of the KSČ and to water-down considerably the political content of the 1968 federalization of the state institutions. Logically this meant putting greater emphasis on the economic aspects of a 'Slovak policy': investment, production and income distribution grew at a much faster pace in Slovakia in the 1970s than in the Czech lands. [48]

There are, however, other reasons as well why it can be said that despite the restoration of the centralized party-state the federalization has benefitted the Slovaks — on a symbolic level (not unimportant in any nationality problem), Bratislava became the 'capital' of Slovakia, the seat of the Slovak government. The federalization also meant the creation of a new bureaucratic structure in Slovakia, thus opening prospects of social mobility for the Slovak intelligentsia. Finally, the Slovaks have not only kept with Husák the leadership of the KSČ, they have also penetrated the new federal apparatus in Prague where they are considerably over-represented considering they account for less than a third of the fifteen million strong population: of eight Deputy-Premiers four are Slovaks; of sixteen full members of the government, eight are Slovaks. They also hold key ministries, such as Defence (Dzùr), Foreign Affairs (Chňoupek), Foreign Trade (Barčák). If one adds to this that, on the whole, political repression has been throughout the 1970s rather milder in Slovakia, Husák's political strategy emerges more clearly: unable to win even a minimum of political consensus (the régime still relies primarily on coercion) Husák's skillful use of the Slovak card is primarily an attempt to compensate for this failure by providing at least a minority social base for the régime.

CONCLUSIONS

So the main trend of the post-1968 decade has been the re-establishing of a rigidly centralized Party-State. The apparatus has grown considerably due primarily to its federalization and has been strictly subordinated to the Party in quest of 'normalization'. At present, therefore, there is no sign at all of the state or party withering away! However, the Party-State is becoming torn between the increasingly contradictory roles it tends to play: as an instrument of economic management and a control organ over all spheres of social and cultural life. Indeed the immobilism imposed by Husák and the delicate political balance in the Party leadership (Bilak-Husák-Štrougal) is now being questioned (though very cautiously) by those in charge of economic management. After a decade of Party-State merger, change is to be expected primarily from the pressure of state organs in charge of the economy. At the end of March 1979 Prime Minister Lubomír Štrougal told the Czechoslovak National Assembly that the Government had rejected draft proposals for the next five year plan and that industries would have to submit new proposals. [49] His call for a change in the obsolete methods of planning was echoed by Vice-Premier V. Hůla, and the Finance Minister Leopold Lér, who is in charge of the so-called 'complex experiment of effectiveness and control' introduced in January 1978 for a period of three years in 150 plants with almost half a million employees. Although nobody dares pronounce the word 'reform', it seems that the more pragmatic faction in the party leadership (Štrougal) is pressing hard for a complete overhaul of the system of economic management. In many ways the present economic debate in the KSČ's leadership on the role of the Party and the State is reminiscent of that of the early 1960s. It is not clear yet whether the impact of the present world economic turmoil will produce similar repercussions to those of the economic fiasco caused by using the Stalinist model in the late 1950s and early 1960s in Czechoslovakia. The world energy crisis might in fact help to keep the KSČ closer in the Soviet orbit. The question for the 1980s remains; after a decade of 'normalization' will the Husák leadership of the Communist Party be prepared to let economic experimentation also bring greater flexibility in the political sphere?

NOTES

1. On 1968 see H.G. Skilling, *The Interrupted Revolution* (Princeton: University Press, 1976); V.V. Kusin, *Political Groupings in the Czechoslovak Reform Movement* (London: Macmillan, 1972); Z. Mlynář, *Československý Pokus o Reformu 1968* (Cologne: Index, 1975). Z. Mlynář, former Party Praesidium member now in

Vienna, is the director of a vast research project on 'The experiences of the Prague Spring 1968'.

2. *The Action Programme of the Communist Party of Czechoslovakia* (Notingham: The Bertrand Russell Foundation, 1970), 12.

3. Ibid.

4. At the clandestine Party Congress of August 1968 the National Front was described as a 'pluralistic platform within but with monopoly political power outside' in J. Pelikán (ed), *XIV Mimořádný Sjezd KSČ* (Wien: Europa Verlag, 1970), 220; for French edition see *Le Congres Clandestin* (Paris: Seuil, 1971).

5. *Action Programme*, op. cit., 11-12.

6. Ibid.

7. Jacques Rupnik, *Histoire du Parti Communiste Tchécoslovaque* (Paris: Presses de la Fondation National des Sciences Politiques, 1980); A. Brown and G. Wightman 'Czechoslovakia: Revival and Retreat' in A. Brown and J. Gray, *Political Culture and Political Change in Communist States* (London: Macmillan, 1977), 159-196.

8. The parallel between the 'bolshevization' and 'normalization' is made by the most official of Czechoslovak historians today, V. Král, in his introduction to *Cesta k Leninismu* (Prague: Academia, 1971). See also K. Doudera's article in *Rudé Právo*, 20 July 1977; on the relation of the Stalinism of the 1950s and of the 1970s to the Czechoslovak political culture see H. G. Skilling, 'Stalinism and Czechoslovak Political Culture' in R.C. Tucker (ed.), *Stalinism: Essays in Historical Interpretation* (New York: Norton, 1977), 257-280; and Skilling, '1968 in Historical Perspective' in the special issue entitled 'Prague 1968: The Aftermath' in the *International Journal* (Toronto) No. 4, 1978, 678-701.

9. See the documents prepared for the Congress and published in Pelikan, op. cit. (the English edition is published by Macdonald, London).

10. V.C. Fisera (ed.), *The Workers' Councils in Czechoslovakia 1968-69* (London: Alison and Busby, 1978); on Dubček's own attempts at a milder version of the 'normalization' see P. Tigrid, *Why Dubcek Fell* (London: Macdonald, 1970).

11. Central Committee Meeting of 25-26 September 1969, *Sbornik Studijních Dokumentù k Dějinám KSC, obdobi* 1960-72 (Prague: Vysoká Škola Politická, 1975), 30-34.

12. Guidelines of 3 June 69, ibid.

13. *Rudé Právo*, 14 January 1971; in English supplement to *Moscow News*, No. 4, 1971.

14. An echo of the terminology used during the trial of the Party leader R. Slánský and others in 1952. This time nobody was executed; the Stalinism of the 1970s was unquestionably much more 'civilized' than that of the 1950s.

15. Dubcek's dismantlement of the so-called 'Eighth Department' also cut off Soviet security control over the KSČ apparat.

16. 'There was emerging a new structure of the political system which was naturally restoring the situation before February 1948', *Moscow News*, No. 4 (1971), 18. 'The Communist Party must control all the instruments for attaining their political class aims. The mass media, the press, the television and film are an important instrument of power and mass political education which must never get out of the direction and control of the Marxist-Leninist elements in the Party and the socialist state', ibid., 19.

17. For a detailed break-down of the composition of the leading organs cf. V.V. Kusin, *From Dubcek to Charter 77* (Edinburgh: Q Press, 1978), 70-74.

18. Husák replaced as President General Ludvik Svoboda who died in September 1979; for a profile of Svoboda see J. Rupnik, *Encyclopedia Universalis' Survey of 1979* (Paris: Encyclopedia Universalis, 1980).

19. *Pravda* (Bratislava), 21 August 1968.

20. The Slovak Central Committee, under the Chairmanship of Bilak's deputy Hruškovič, at first supported a resolution approving the invasion, but it had to cancel it as soon as it learned that Bilak had been defeated in Prague, where the KSČ Praesidium supported a resolution condemning the invasion.

21. *Mimoriadny Zjazd Komunistickej Strany Slovenska — Podla Stenografickeho Zaznamu* (Bratislava: Vydavatelstvo Politickej Literatury, 1968), 14.

22. Kriegel, the only member of the KSČ leadership who refused to sign the Moscow document in August 1968, became an active member of the Charter 77 human rights movement until his death at the end of 1979. Alexander Dubček refused to recant. An employee of the Ministry of Forestry under constant police surveillance, he published in the Spring of 1975 a devastating attack on the state of the Communist Party and the whole country since Husák came to power.

> Corruption inevitably spreads in a party deprived of the possibility of open discussion and of regular and effective control of even its highest offices. Fear for their means of existence leads a great number of Party members to endorse decisions they do not agree with. Two-facedness becomes general: people act one way at the meetings and differently at home, in private, among friends. Instead of open attitudes in the Party, the Trade Unions, the Youth movement, the Women's movement and other organizations, and also in the press, apathy creeps in amongst the people: an atmosphere of suspicion, fear, hypocrisy and police informing is created. In that kind of situation it is impossible to obtain a *democratic majority* in the Party and therefore it must lack drive towards a progressive development. The whole life of our country is festooned with webs, and those who spin them need sustenance and sanction. I cannot call this other than by its real name: it is misuse of power and a violation of socialist principles and party principles. It is a violation of human rights. (Full text in the *New York Times*, 13 April 1975)

23. *Rudé Právo*, 13 September 1975.

24. G. Wightman and A. Brown, 'Changes in the Levels of Membership and Social Composition of the Communist Party of Czechoslovakia 1945-73', *Soviet Studies*, Vol XXVII, No. 3 (July 1975), 405.

25. V. Kusin, *From Dubcek to Charter 77*, 88.

26. The emergence of the Charter 77 and the general erosion of 'revisionist' marxism in Eastern Europe account for the diminishing influence of the Czech 'Eurocommunist' opposition in the late 1970s. See V.V. Kusín, 'Challenge to Normalcy: Political Opposition in Czechoslovakia, 1968-77' in R.L. Tökés (ed.), *Opposition in Eastern Europe* (London: Macmillan, 1979), 26-59.

27. M. Honzik, 'Angazovanost je součást kvalifikace', *Rudé Právo*, 24 February 1978.

28. On the XIIth session of the Central Committee of the KSČ see *Rudé Právo*, 4-8 December 1978: P. Lendvai, 'Economic Fears Break Through', *Financial Times*, 29 March 1979.

29. Full text in BBC *Summary of World Broadcast* EE/5988/C/15, 7 December 1978.

30. *Rudé Právo*, 10 September 1979.

31. *Rudé Právo*, 11 August 1979.

32. Ibid.

33. Membership figures in: *Život Strany*, No. 20, 1969; *Rudé Právo*, 28 August 1971; *Rudé Právo*, 29 May 1974; Documents of the 15th Party Congress, April 1976; *Rudé Právo*, 11 January 1978; *Život Strany*, 17 November 1978. The Party membership in Slovakia is 328, 000 — *Pravda* (Bratislava), 20 February 1979.

34. Between the XIIIth Congress of the KSČ in 1966 and the XIVth Congress of 1971 the average age went up from 45 to 49 years. Wightman and Brown, 415. Since the XVth Congress of 1976 90 per cent of the new recruits are allegedly under 35. At the end of 1978 about a third of KSČ members were under 35. *Život Strany*, 17 November 1978.

35. Ibid.

36. The social composition of the population evolved in the following way (in percentages)

	1947	1975
Workers	53.3	61.3
Employees	16.0	29.0
Peasants	16.6	9.6

F. Charvát, J. Linhart, J. Večerník, *Socialně-třídní struktura Ceskoslovenska*, (Prague: Horizont, 1978) 74.

37. For figures on workers in the KSČ membership see J. Rupnik, 'La classe ouvrière tchécoslovaque 1945-1978' in J. Rupnik and G. Mink, *Transformations de le Classe Ouvrière en Europe de l'Est* (Paris: La Documentation Française, 1979); *Život Strany*, 17 November 1978.

38. For an analysis of pseudo-participation in the KSČ see Irenée Levier, 'La Tchécoslovaquie normalisée: le militantisme apparent' in *Après-demain* (Paris), April 1980; Milan Šimečka, *Le Rétablissement de l'Ordre* (Paris: Maspéro, 1979), Ch. 4.

39. Cf. *The White Paper on Czechoslovakia* (published by the International Committee in Support of the Charter 77; Paris, 1977); V. Prečan (ed), *Kniha o Chartě*, (Cologne: Index, 1979) — the most complete collection of Charter 77 documents.

40. For a comprehensive analysis of the theory of the changes in the political system in 1968 see Mlynář's paper introducing the collective research project on '*The experiences of the Prague Spring*' to be published in 1981 by the revue *Dialectique* (Paris: Editions Maspero).

41. For a survey of the evolution of the Slovak question since 1945 see Zd. Jicinský, '25 let socialistického vývoje státoprávnich vztahu Ceského a Slovenského národa', *Právnik*, No. 5, 1970.

42. H. G. Skilling, *The Interrupted Revolution*, op. cit., 451-492.

43. Vice-Premier K. Laco, 'Ceskoslovenska socialisticka Federacia . . . ' in UV KSČ (ed.), *K 60 Vyroci Vzniku Ceskoslovenska* (Prague, 1978).

44. V. Plevza in *Nové Slovo*, 22 October 1976.

45. S. J. Kirschbaum, 'Federalism in Slovak Communist Politics' in *Canadian Slavonic Papers*, Vol. XIX (1977), No. 4, 463-464.

46. *Rudé Právo*, 2 June 1969.

47. G. Husák, *Projevy a Stati, Duben 1969-Leden 1970* (Prague: KSČ, 1970), 388.

48. For detailed statistics see K. Laco, art. cit., 73-76.

49. *Financial Times*, 29 March 1979.

6 The GDR: 'Real Socialism' or 'Computer Stalinism'?

Leslie Holmes
University of Kent at Canterbury, UK

INTRODUCTION

It is important to include the German Democratic Republic (GDR) in any comparative study of the party and state under communism. On the one hand, of all the communist states, only the GDR and Czechoslovakia had a social structure at the time of the communist takeover in which the industrial proletariat constituted the largest component. Thus although these two states were clearly not fully ripe for socialist revolution in the 1940s,[1] they were the countries nearest to the level of development Marx considered necessary for a successful socialist revolution. On the other hand, the GDR has remained the most industrialized state — and in the late 1960s, to the USSR's disapproval, even claimed that its development pattern could be used as a model for the less advanced communist states.[2]

Despite this, much of this chapter will demonstrate that there are no signs at present to suggest a withering away of either the party or the state. As in Czechoslovakia, the 1970s witnessed, under a new leadership, a strengthening and centralization of the party and state and, in the latter part of the decade, increased repression. This can be seen both in the stricter penal code and the harsher treatment of

The author wishes to acknowledge his indebtedness to Drs. G-J Glaessner and G. Neugebauer of the Free University of Berlin for both informational and inspirational assistance in the writing of this chapter; of particular value were two papers based on their presentations at the 1979 ECPR conference in Brussels — Glaessner's 'Institutional and Personnel Aspects of the Dominating Rule of the Party in Contemporary Socialism' and Neugebauer's 'Party Control over the State Machinery: The Practice of the Sozialistische Einheitspartei Deutschlands (SED)'.

dissidents (all of them Marxists) since the autumn of 1976,[3] as well as in the continued development of what might be called the bureaucratic-technocratic complex, which appears to have led to a further decline in participation by workers in the running of their industries. It was these sorts of developments which led one of the best known of the dissidents, Wolfgang Biermann, to criticize the 'Computer Stalinism' in the GDR.[4]

The GDR formally came into existence on 7 October 1949, largely as a result of the worsening relations between the victorious Allies and their different attitudes towards Germany as a whole.[5] Another outcome of this dispute was the establishment of the Federal Republic of Germany (FRG) in the summer of 1949; the existence of this other German state has given the East German authorities problems not experienced in quite the same way by other advanced communist countries.[6] First, although East German successes have been considerable in terms of economic and social development (and sport!), the higher standards of living and greater freedom of the West Germans cannot be denied by the East German authorities; this problem has been exacerbated in the late 1970s, as the ramifications of the oil crisis spread to Eastern Europe and worsened their economic situations.[7] Second, the Soviet Union/Russia has traditionally feared and disliked Germany. As a result, the Soviets have a far greater military presence in the GDR than in any other East European state — primarily to protect the communist block from possible West German aggression but also, one suspects, to ensure loyalty from the East Germans. The GDR authorities, in turn, are constantly expressing their loyalty and gratitude to the USSR — which displeases many East Germans, and hence adds to the regime's legitimacy problems.[8]

The East German leadership has been placing somewhat less emphasis on economic performance as a basis for regime legitimacy in the late 1970s, for instance by encouraging the development of a new East German national identity. Following the improvement in relations between the FRG and the GDR in the early 1970s and their admission to the UN in September 1973, the GDR mounted a major campaign to emphasize the separateness of the two German states, and to counter West German claims that the whole of Germany still constituted one nation. Having established that the two states were quite separate, there is now a policy of developing East German national identity, primarily through association with Prussia.[9] Nevertheless, the East German authorities have in the past emphasized the importance of economic growth to such an extent that the moves towards other legitimacy bases are unlikely to be very successful in the short run; for instance, the present constitution (the 1974 modification of the 1968 constitution) states very early on that:

> The further raising of the material and cultural living-standard of the people on the basis of a high rate of development of socialist production, the raising of efficiency, scientific-technical progress and the growth of labour productivity is the decisive task of developed socialist society.[10]

Since expectations are therefore presently being frustrated, it seems feasible that in the short-run, at least, the repressive aspects of the East German state will be further strengthened.

THE PARTY

Changes in the Theory of its Role

The present East German communist party is called the SED (from the German for Socialist Unity Party); this relates to its origins. The SED was founded in April 1946 on the basis of a merger of the former socialist party (SPD) and the communist party (KPD) in the Soviet Zone. It was established as a working-class party aimed at ridding Germany of the vestiges of Nazism and establishing the basis for socialism. At that time, many believed that it was to be closer to the German social-democratic tradition than to communism, and even the communists had seemed to favour a peculiarly German road to socialism.[11] However, with the development of the Cold War, and the dispute between Yugoslavia and the USSR, the former communists within the SED felt that the time had come to change the nature of the party. By September 1948, the SED had become a Marxist-Leninist type party, organized on the principles of democratic centralism, and overtly loyal to the USSR. Over the next few years, the Soviet occupying authorities transferred ever more power to the new East German state, which in turn meant an increased role for the party. At the Second Party Conference (July 1952) the General Secretary of the SED, Walter Ulbricht, declared that the GDR had now completed the anti-fascist democratic phase so that the building of socialism could proceed in earnest. The SED's role in this construction was to be further enhanced. However, the new phase got off to a bad start. A major collectivization drive in 1952 led many peasants to flee to the West, which meant that by the spring of 1953 there were shortages of agricultural produce. At the same time, the party attempted to force industrial workers to produce more for no more reward. Finally, the whole of Eastern Europe fell into confusion and/or a state of expectancy of change following Stalin's death in March 1953. In these circumstances, it is not surprising that a strike by construction-workers in East Berlin soon became a nationwide uprising in June 1953. Although the authorities, with the aid of the Soviet army, were able to contain this spontaneous, mass protest, the reputation of the SED and of its leader, Ulbricht, was seriously tarnished.[12]

Five years later, the leadership inaugurated an economic programme to develop industry more rapidly; one of the professed aims was to bring the GDR up to at least the FRG's levels of productivity and consumption. By 1961, the programme was failing dismally, and the sensitivity of the party leadership to this failure must undoubtedly be considered as one of the reasons for the erection of the Berlin Wall in August 1961. The GDR was no longer prepared to lose its most skilled citizens to the FRG every time there were problems in the economy — in 1961, this was partially as a result of the renewed collectivization drive of 1960 — so that the SED decided to take a firmer line with the population. But Ulbricht also decided that the party would have to play a more positive role in the running of the economy. Although he did not push this as far as Khrushchev did in the USSR, the SED leader started calling for better economic training for party functionaries, and increased party control in industry. In addition, via the party's Central Committees and the Council of Ministers, he organized conferences to discuss ways for improving the economy. Finally, leading economists were promoted to leading positions within the SED. All this led to the announcement in January 1963 of the New Economic System which not only led to changes in the state, but also further institutionalized the party's greater involvement in the economy.[13] At about the same time, the party leadership — and especially Ulbricht himself — started emphasizing the importance of the 'Scientific-Technical Revolution' (STR) to the development of East German society; party cadres were expected to propagate the importance of this and to understand it better themselves. In sum, the

1960s witnessed a changed emphasis in the party's role. From being primarily the political vanguard in a class struggle, its leading role was now in terms of understanding and spreading the ideology of cybernetics, etc. The de-emphasizing of its class-vanguard role emerged most clearly in 1967. In September of that year, the traditional interpretation of socialism and communism — ie. that they are different, but that the former is constantly developing towards the latter — was essentially abandoned. Ulbricht announced that socialism was not a 'short, transitional phase' but a 'relatively autonomous socio-economic formation in the historical era of transition from socialism to communism'. Ulbricht was aware that the analysis of the class nature of East German society would have to be altered to fit this new approach to socialism, so that the homogeneity of society was emphasized. There was now a stress on the 'socialist community' (sozialistische Menschengemeinschaft), and the party's main role from the time of the Seventh Congress (April 1967) was the construction and strengthening of the 'developed social system of socialism'. The essentially conservative nature of this reconceptualization was endorsed by the kind of terminology that accompanied the changes. The concepts of dialectical and historical materialism (which imply change) were played down, whilst concepts and terms from Western systems analysis — which emphasizes accommodation and stability — appeared increasingly in SED analyses of society.[14]

The changed role of the SED, reflective of an alleged change in the social structure, was formally embodied in the 1968 Constitution, which replaced the original one of 1949. There was no reference to the SED in the first Constitution, at a time when the SED was only the vanguard of the working class. By 1968, the SED warranted a reference in the Constitution; it was still formally the party of the working class, but now also led *all* working people in town and country. The party's theoreticians were beginning to experience problems in conceptualizing the party's role, since the concept of the dictatorship of the proletariat itself was becoming blurred.[15]

Honecker replaced Ulbricht as General Secretary in May 1971, and a process of reassessment of the party's role which had begun whilst Ulbricht was still in power accelerated — even if it was not always conducted very openly. Honecker and other party leaders had become increasingly unhappy with what they considered to be the trends towards technocratization and de-ideologization of the party and a blurring of its role vis-à-vis the state in the late 1960s, and already in 1970, the leading exponent of cybernetics and systems theory in the GDR (Georg Klaus) had had to acknowledge the difficulties and incorrectness of attempting to develop a systems theory for GDR society. In April 1971, the concept of the 'developed social system of socialism' was abandoned, and was replaced by the new goal of 'the formation of developed socialist society'. The GDR's leading ideologist, Kurt Hager, criticized systems theory and called for a return to Marxism-Leninism in the party and the reassertion of concepts such as dialectical materialism.[16]

However, it would be erroneous to argue that there has been a rejection of all of Ulbricht's ideas on the role and position of the party. For instance, the distinction between Ulbricht's view of the stage of socialism reached in the GDR and the present leadership's is a subtle one, and to a considerable extent reflects the present leadership's greater public loyalty to the USSR rather than a major ideological change. Thus the currently-valid official SED view of the GDR is that it is forming developed socialism — which implies that it is close behind rather than ahead of the USSR in terms of societal development. The rejection of Ulbricht's description is largely because it was linked in people's minds to his 'model' of socialism, which was seen by both the Soviets and the East German leaders as an affront to the USSR's leading role in the world communist movement.[17] Moreover, although the 'socialist community' concept has been replaced in the 1970s by a re-emphasis on the dictatorship of the proletariat, the official analyses of the role and position of the SED in the East German society reveal an identical class analysis and an *implied* community of interests. Thus in the introduction to the latest party statute adopted by the 9th Congress in 1976, the SED is defined as:

> . . . the leading force of socialist society, of all organizations of the working class (Arbeiterklasse) and of the working people (Werktaetigen), of state and social organizations.

and has to do everything:

> . . . for the interests of the working class, for the good of all the people.[18]

The SED's long-term aim, according to the party programme also adopted at the 9th Congress, is the construction of a communist society. This is to be achieved through the formation of the developed socialist society, so that the basic preconditions for the gradual transfer to communism will be created. Although the programme is unclear on the operation of the party's role under communism, there is no such ambiguity about the party's *present* role — it is to grow as society becomes more complex.[19] This has been reflected in a changed analysis of the party's relationship with various social organizations and the state in the 1970s. Primarily, the right of control or supervision (Kontrolle) by party organizations has been extended considerably. Thus in 1971, this right of control was extended to the management (Leitungen) of educational and medical institutions, whilst in 1976, ministries and other central state bodies were for the first time subjected to such control; this change is considered later in the chapter.

Although the present leadership has attempted to delineate the party's role more clearly, and in particular to distinguish it from the state, current developments in the GDR suggest the possibility of at least a partial return to the situation of the 1960s. Economic difficulties in the late 1970s have led the party leadership to reassess Ulbricht's New Economic System — which was largely abandoned in the early 1970s — and several moves taken in the last three or four years represent a return to some aspects of it.[20] Although it is not yet clear that this *will* lead to similar reassessments of the party's role, there is a strong possibility that the 1980s will witness the further blurring of the technical and political functions of the party at all levels. If this does happen and the present official class analysis continues to emphasize the essentially homogeneous nature of East German society, the separation of the party from the state will become increasingly difficult to justify. This is particularly true given the 1970s emphasis on 'real' socialism. When Honecker came to power, he emphasized that politics, economics and social development must proceed in line with real possibilities; implicitly criticizing Ulbricht, he argued that it was not the SED's role to raise citizens' expectations way above the achievements that could realistically be envisaged. Yet this emphasis on pragmatism to some extent undermines the leading role of the party. This emerges clearly from a recent, typical analysis of 'real socialism' by the head of the Central Committee's Academy of Social Sciences:

> Real socialism means above all that the communist parties of the socialist countries are led in their policies by the laws of social development and their objective requirements. It is not idealistic hopes (Wunschvorstellungen) which determine

developments in the economy, in politics, in the social and spiritual-cultural life, but the objective necessities confirmed by historical experience (Praxis).[21]

If the party is to be guided by 'objective necessities' rather than ideals, if it merely reflects rather than moulds social developments, then it has to a considerable degree rejected the Leninist, voluntaristic, vanguard interpretation of its own role. With the transformation from a teleological to an incremental approach to politics and development generally, plus the increasing emphasis on state representative bodies for controlling the state executive organs, the raison d'être of the party becomes seriously undermined. There will still be a need for macro-policy formulation and for ensuring that important positions throughout society are filled by the most suitable persons. But with the emphasis on realism rather than idealism, it is far from obvious that the state will not be increasingly able to fulfil these functions itself. In fact, current developments suggest that the most fundamental re-appraisal to date of the party's role could shortly have to be undertaken.

There is no shortage of indigenous criticism of the SED; but since most of this criticism is aimed both at the party and the state apparatus, it is more appropriate to consider it later in this chapter.

Changes in Structure and Functions

During the 1960s, in line with the party's increased involvement in the economy, the SED underwent certain structural changes. The most important of these occurred in 1963 when, though still organized on the 'territorial-production principle', the stress shifted markedly from the first to the second of these components both at the level of the base (or primary) organization and at higher levels.[22] Despite marginal changes in the 1970s, this basic production orientation has been retained.

Another change connected with the constant attempts to improve production relates to the development of combines since the late 1960s. Combines are groupings of enterprises, and several were formed from 1967-70. The present leadership was initially loath to create more, but has since 1977 substantially changed its policy on these bodies, so that by late 1979 they accounted for approximately ninety per cent of production from all centrally-managed industry. As in other East European states, this concentration of production and centralization of administration has had important ramifications for the structure and activities of the base organizations of the party. Most importantly, it has led to a centralization of party decision-making at the level of production units, which must have led to even less opportunities for rank-and-file members to participate in decision-making.[23]

An important upgrading of the role of the base organization in the state administrative organs occurred in 1976. Until then, the party organs did not have the same rights as they did, for instance, in the industrial enterprise, where the base organization had the right of control over management activities. In the state executive organs, the base organization had merely had to use its influence to improve the state machinery's work, and to report mistakes and deficiencies to leading cadres in the state machinery or to the responsible higher party organs; reports and proposals could be sent direct to the Central Committee. This restricted right of control was due to the distinctive character of the state machinery's work. The work of industrial management is generally restricted to a certain area (the plant) and a specific issue (the economic plan). All relations between the enterprise and its partners are determined by the plan, which generally contains strictly-defined responsibilities. The activities of an institution of the state machinery, on the other hand, influences activities in other areas both within and outside the institution itself. If the party organization in a state organ were (indirectly) to control the activities in mass organizations, economic or cultural institutions, or anywhere else, it would be interfering with responsibilities of other party organizations. This could be seen as leading to the violation of democratic centralism, which demands that all activities in an organization depend on *central* (SED) decisions.[24]

The new control regulations extended the rights of the party organizations in the state machinery as follows:

> The party organizations in the ministries, the other central and regional state organs and institutions have the right to exercise control over the activity of the apparatus in the realisation of the decisions of the party and government and in the observance of socialist legal norms.[25]

Furthermore they are obliged to exert influence on the effective organization of work, to examine shortcomings and mistakes, and to report proposals to the responsible party cadres or to the Central Committee. The extension of the control rights also means an extension of the control tasks; more work is to be done by the party organization. Yet there is a dilemma here. On the one hand, there are often warnings against the danger that the party organization might do the work of the state machinery;[26] this could promote a situation in which there would no longer be a difference between party and state apparatus (i.e. the loss of the party's specific political leading role). On the other, the regulations demand control down to the smallest detail, although it is supposed to be restricted to essentials.[27] The party member in the state machinery is not allowed to decide whether a certain aspect is essential or not. The higher party organs want theoretically to receive reports only on the political aspects of an issue, but the close connection between 'political' and 'professional' aspects of a task demands the control of both of them. The merging of political and professional/technical is clear; the distinction between party and state at this level is ever less so.

There have been no significant structural changes at the central levels of the SED in the 1970s. Contrary to some expectations, the new party statute of 1976 still provided for the convening of party conferences — extraordinary gatherings of party members brought together to discuss 'urgent questions of the policy and tactics of the party' — even though there has not been one since 1956.[28] Otherwise, the Politburo — created in 1949 to replace the less powerful and less Soviet-like Central Secretariat — is the most important body within the party and still awaits a detailed, official analysis of its functions. However, the composition and perhaps the role of the Politburo has changed. When Honecker took power, he immediately emphasized the importance of collective leadership in the party. One aspect of this has been a conscious move to include more representatives of key functional groups (including the military and the secret police) on the Politburo; on the other hand, the policy of relative over-representation of economic functionaries typical of Ulbricht's later years has been reversed.[29] As for the Politburo's role, some commentators have argued that Ulbricht developed the State Council to the most important policy-making body in the 1960s, at the expense of the Politburo.[30] In the 1970s, there is no doubt that the Politburo has once again become the senior political organ in the GDR. It has also been argued by some that the Central Committee has lost influence to the Politburo; although there are some indications that this might be so, they are too few to enable us to draw any firm conclusions.[31] The frequency of Party Congresses — officially the highest organ of the party on the rare occasions when it meets — has marginally declined in the 1970s, from once every four years in the 1960s to once every five in the 1970s.[32] However, the Congress was and is in fact an almost powerless organ anyway, so that this change is not important. One indication of the predominantly ceremonial as opposed to discussive (let alone policy-making) role of the Congress is reflected in the fact that the 9th Congress (1976) adopted the new SED programme and statute without any discussion whatsoever.

Composition

Membership of the SED as a proportion of the population is amongst the highest in the communist world. In May 1980, there were 2,130,671 full and candidate members of the party; expressed another way, approximately one sixth of the adult population belongs to the SED.[33] The leadership appears to be more content than it has ever been with the quality of party members, since a 'cleansing of the ranks' early in 1980 led to the smallest number ever (less than four thousand) losing their membership.[34] However, it is also true that the rate of growth has declined in the 1970s in comparison with the 1960s, which can be interpreted as a sign that the SED is being more selective in its admissions policy.[35]

A process of reproletarianization — of increasing the number of industrial worker members of the party — began in the 1960s and peaked in 1971, since when the proportion of worker members has remained virtually constant.[36] Nevertheless, the SED is one of the few communist parties in which the industrial workers actually constitute an absolute majority of members.[37] However, whilst the number of industrial workers has remained constant since the reproletarianization drive of the 1960s, the percentage of intellectuals within the SED's ranks increased from seventeen to approximately twenty-two percent in the period 1971-80; in 1961, the intelligentsia accounted for less than nine per cent of membership.[38] This is a function both of the SED's attempts to recruit more of the people it perceives as vital to the tasks of economic development, and of professional and technical personnel learning to live with and take advantage of the system; until 1961, many professional people who disliked the East German regime could 'vote with their feet' by fleeing to West Germany, whereas since the building of the Wall, both the party and the intelligentsia have had to learn to accommodate each other.

Although workers constitute the majority of membership, they are poorly represented at the top of the party. No workers sit on the Politburo, and despite the reproletarianization policy, the proportion of party and state apparatchiki on the Central Committee has increased from less than 58 per cent in 1963 to almost 66 per cent of the Committee elected by the last Congress (1976).[39] Given that most of the other members are industrial managers, professional people, etc., it is quite clear that ordinary workers are severely under-represented at the senior levels of their 'own' party. In this sense, the GDR is still at best a dictatorship on behalf of the industrial workers rather than a society run by them.

Other Parties

In 1972, the SED launched another major nationalization drive, as a result of which industry is almost totally state-owned in the GDR. As noted above, the 1970s have also witnessed an attempt by the East German authorities to replace the notion of one German nation with the concept of two. Collectivization was completed in 1960, since when the amount of private, small-scale farming in collectives has decreased markedly.[40] The 1970s also witnessed a (not invariably successful) attempt by the SED to improve relations with the churches and to integrate them better with the dominant party-state complex.[41] Despite all these changes — and other, long-term social developments — there has been no attempt by the SED to argue that the four minor parties in the GDR — the Liberal Democrats (LDPD), the National Democratic Party (NDPD), the Farmers' Party (DBD) or the Christian Democratic Union (CDU) — should be abolished or even significantly downgraded. On the contrary, recent statements by leading SED spokesmen have assured the more than 350,000 members of these parties that the communists appreciate the important role played by their organizations.[42]

However, it would be erroneous to suppose that the minor parties play any meaningful role in the GDR. They formally accept the SED's leading role in the polity, and only once has any of them voted against the SED in the East German parliament.[43] Even the number of seats they have within this parliament is fixed and determined by the SED rather than freely by the electorate.[44] A typical communist view of them was contained in a 1974 article by leading

SED-functionary Horst Dohlus, in which he rejected completely the notion of 'new models of socialism' which would include 'political pluralism' (ie. where political forces would be permitted to compete with each other).[45]

There was a marginal, implicit downgrading of the minor parties in October 1976, when the office of the President of the Volkskammer (parliament) was occupied for the first time by a SED-member rather than a member of one of the minor parties. However, little importance should be attached to this, since it was more a reflection of politics within the SED, and has now partially been redressed.[46] Overall, the position of the minor parties has remained fairly static in the 1970s, and there are no signs at present to suggest their imminent abolition.

THE STATE

Theory of its Role

As in other communist countries, the primary role of the state was and is to implement party policy, represent the people in international affairs and defend them, and provide channels through which the citizens can exert some influence over the executive. But this is not to deny the possibility of change in its theoretical role.

Following the rejection of Ulbricht's essentially static model of socialism by the present leadership (see above), a more dynamic theory of the role of the state has now returned to East German official analyses; the state's role must change as society and the economy develops. However, 'change' is not to be equated with 'withering'; the 1976 SED-programme refers explicitly to the 'all-round strengthening of the socialist state',[47] whilst a recent authoritative article by Kurt Hager deals directly with the concept of the state's withering:

> The 'left' doctrinaires continue to emphasize the necessity of the immediate withering away (Absterben) of the state. In fact, Marxist-Leninist state theories have never separated the question of withering from the level of maturity (Reife) of social relations and from the international class-struggle. The dialectic of the

development of the socialist state lies precisely in the fact that only through its all-round strengthening are the conditions for the comprehensive development of socialism secured.[48]

At present, therefore, official East German theory is calling for a strengthening rather than a withering of the state.

However, the current class analysis also means that the state is no longer *clearly* an instrument of class domination. Although the state constitutes a form of the dictatorship of the proletariat, it also represents the interests of all working people in the towns and the countryside — an awkward theoretical standpoint which illustrates the problems of trying to apply classical Marxist and Leninist analysis to many contemporary, established communist states.[49]

One other feature of the 1970s has been the increasing codification of the state and its subdivisions. Although the East Germans have always favoured clear and detailed legislation on the state and its functioning, attempts to integrate legislation on the component parts have intensified in the past decade. One example of this was that, in introducing the 1974 constitutional modifications, Honecker explicitly stated that the roles and relationships of certain state organs needed clearer delineation.[50] Another is that the position of the VVBs was never formally specified in the 1960s; within about two years of Honecker taking office, a decree on the VVBs had been ratified. Whilst some criticize the idea of basing an allegedly socialist state on such formal conceptions of law — the 'Sozialistischer Rechtsstaat' — East German theoreticians have sought to overcome this problem by distinguishing clearly between 'bourgeois' and 'socialist' laws and legal concepts.[51]

Changes in Structure and Functions

Throughout most of the 1950s, the East German state structure became increasingly centralized. In 1952, the traditional provinces (Länder) — which still form the basis of the West German federal system — were abolished; six years later, the second parliamentary chamber (which had been based on the Länder) suffered a similar fate, and the East German parliament (Volkskammer) has been unicameral ever since. There was also increasing centralization within the executive, symbolised by the creation in 1954 of an inner cabinet (Präsidium) of the Council of Ministers (which had been established in 1950). However, towards the end of the 1950s —

largely in an effort to increase efficiency but also in partial emulation of changes in the USSR — the administration of the economy
was marginally decentralized. The industrial ministries in Berlin
were abolished, and enterprises subordinated to the more
numerous and geographically dispersed 'VVBs' (associations of
nationally-owned enterprises). However, the powers of these
bodies were severely circumscribed, and not until the economic
crisis of the early 1960s did they become relatively autonomous.
However, ministries were reintroduced in 1965, and by the beginning of the 1970s were acquiring ever more powers. This recentralization of economic administration typified the early- and mid-
1970s. In the late-1970s, increasing economic problems have led to
a decentralization of powers from the ministries to the combines.[52]
Although in some ways this represents a greater level of decen-
talization and deconcentration than the earlier policy of creating
VVBs, it is more than countered by the centralization of powers
from the individual enterprise to the combine. On balance,
therefore, state administration of the economy has become more
centralized — certainly from the viewpoint of the production
workers — in the 1970s.[53] Moreover, the East German authorities
have persistently criticized many aspects of the Yugoslav concept of
self-management, and were highly critical of the 'Prague Spring'
proposals for enterprise autonomy and worker-participation.[54]

Apart from these developments, most of the major structural
and functional changes in the East German state in the 1970s have
been of a horizontal rather than vertical nature. The most important of these has been the reassessment of the roles and relationships of the State Council and the Council of Ministers.
Throughout the 1960s, the powers of the State Council — established in 1960 to replace the deceased President Pieck — were increased
both formally and in practice, particularly at the expense of the
Council of Ministers.[55] When Ulbricht lost the General
Secretaryship of the SED in May 1971, he retained his chairmanship of the State Council. But within less than two years, laws had
been passed which curtailed the powers of this body, transferring
many of them to the Council of Ministers. Since this could be interpreted as a predictable attempt to minimize Ulbricht's influence
within the polity, the formalization of the roles of the two councils
in the 1974 constitutional modifications (i.e. after Ulbricht's death)
is more significant. The downgraded role of the State Council was
retained; since 1974, its role has been primarily that of head of state

(i.e. in foreign relations, for ceremonial purposes, etc.), whilst the Council of Ministers was defined as 'the government'.[56]

The role of the Volkskammer — the central representative and officially sole legislative organ of the state — has not undergone any major changes in recent years. There are constantly calls to upgrade its significance, but little practical change to endorse these. However, there does appear to have been an upgrading of the Volkskammer's committees (Ausschüsse) — both de jure and de facto — since 1971, largely as a result of the declining role of the State Council; but despite this upgrading, it is still not clear that they play the decisive role in the legislative process.[57]

What of the coercive/defensive branches of the state? The East German military — the NVA — formally came into existence in 1956, though its origins can be traced back at least to June 1948.[58] It is divided into ranks, and the traditional military distinction between officers and men has been retained. Its position within the GDR is subject to two major constraints. The first is the communist party itself — of the five political parties, only the SED may organize cells in the military, whilst overall control of the military has been the task of the National Defence Council, established in 1960, and headed ever since by the General Secretary of the SED. Finally, the head of the military has been included in the Politburo since 1973, which helps the SED to assess the military mood at least as much as it gives the military access to the highest policy-making body. The second constraint is the USSR and the Warsaw Treaty Organization.[59] These two factors for the present ensure that the military is not becoming a 'state within a state' — even though the status of the military has been enhanced in the 1970s by the GDR's greater involvement in revolutionary movements abroad (e.g. Angola) and by the general militarization of society (notably the spread of military training to the schools — see the references in note 41). In the 1970s the police, too, is well under party control and has also been represented at Politburo-level, for the first time since the 1950s.[60] And whilst judges in the GDR are elected/appointed by the representative organs of the state, they require approval by the party because of the nomenclature system.

Mass Political Participation

According to the constitution, East German citizens have the right to participate in the political life of socialist society and the socialist state in line with the maxim of 'work with, plan with, rule with' (Article 21); what this means in practice is the subject of this section.

Despite several changes in electoral law in the past twenty years or so, the East German electorate still cannot choose between alternative party programmes, and enjoys only a highly formal right to choose between different candidates. In reality, elections are very much under the control of the SED.[61] However, as in many other communist states, the East German authorities place more emphasis on the pre-election stage than on the election itself, arguing that the population plays a really important role in and enjoys plenty of opportunities to influence the candidate-nomination stage. Although there is evidence that ordinary citizens do play some role at the nomination stage, this is encouraged by the party largely for feedback and legitimation purposes, and citizens cannot secure the nomination of a candidate of whom the SED disapproves.[62] The East German authorities also occasionally organize referenda, particularly before the adoption of a new constitution; there have been no significant changes in this recently, however, and referenda are never held on really contentious issues.[63]

But in talking of mass democracy, the East Germans themselves place even more emphasis on participation in discussions and policy-implementation than on elections or referenda. However, this emphasis is very much more on the quantitative rather than qualitative aspects of participation.[64] There are numerous examples of new laws etc. being discussed by thousands or even millions of people — though the number of constructive suggestions for alterations (as distinct from mere endorsement) of the draft proposals relative to the total number of comments is low.[65] What is not clear is the extent of deviation from official drafts that is tolerated, or how the decision to incorporate particular suggestions is reached.[66] Similarly, although there can be no doubt that the various 'mass organizations' in the GDR — the trade unions (FDGB), the youth movement (FDJ), the women's league (DFD) etc. — do involve an enormous number of citizens in various forms of 'state activity', such activity includes officially-organized marches on public holidays, teach-ins on new policies or legislation, etc. In other words, participation is typically of a guided rather than self-motivated nature.

What of worker-participation in the factories? In addition to the problems of party-member participation already discussed, official sources acknowledge that attempts in the 1960s to increase the role of ordinary workers in discussions and decision-making were not very successful.[67] However, legislation on the VVBs, combines and enterprises in the 1970s has further limited even the formal channels for participation, and the role of the individual manager/director vis-à-vis the workforce has been strengthened.[68] This has been justified in terms of greater efficiency — which is argued to be in the interests of all in a socialist state.[69] The right of individual groups of workers to strike was guaranteed in the 1949 Constitution, but was not mentioned in either the Labour Code of 1961, or the 1968/1974 Constitution. In sum, although the East German communists often criticize the shallowness of the West German concept of co-determination (Mitbestimmung), workers in the GDR appear to have even less direct say in the running of their industry than their counterparts in the FRG.[70] Moreover, current CMEA policies of further concentration and integration of industry — of which the SED has been one of the most ardent supporters — would suggest ever less opportunities for meaningful worker-participation.

CONCLUSIONS

Both in theory and in practice, the party and state in the GDR are becoming stronger and more repressive at present rather than withering away. At the same time, the SED is facing a growing crisis of identity. In the early days of the new republic, the party played a major role in transforming the economy, producing the blueprints for a future society, etc. By the 1960s, the new state had been consolidated, and the party's role began to be less obvious; Ulbricht responded by 'co-opting' leading state functionaries and academics into the central party organs, to some extent in an attempt to ensure that they did not develop their own group identities and thus challenge the party. The present leadership partially rejected this notion, and has striven to distinguish clearly, once again, between the roles of the party and the state. Partly in an endeavour to strengthen the ideological, innovative role of the party, old concepts have received far greater emphasis than before (e.g. socialist integration), and new concepts have been developed (e.g. the idea of an East German nation). But the party's increasing dependence on the technical expertise of those who are to implement its policies could not be overcome by Honecker any more than by Ulbricht. The party has attempted to increase its control of the state, but in doing so becomes more entangled with it. The nomenclature/cadres system is part of this control mechanism, yet whilst attempting to ensure that all key 'technical' posts in the state are filled by specialists who also have the correct political perspective, party officials are encouraged to improve their technical knowledge in order to increase their authority for control.[71] The kind of personnel overlap at the apex of the political system — in the Politburo — reflects the mutual interdependence of both state and party at all levels.[72]

However, to highlight these problems of identity is not to argue that there exist *fundamental* differences between the party and state apparatuses; both have a mutual interest in maintaining their elite position within society as what Glaessner calls the 'power-knowledge complex', and attempt to legitimate their right to direct society (the party in terms of strategy, the state in terms of tactics) by reference, inter alia, to their superior education in special, exclusive institutions.[73] Hence indigenous criticism of these apparatuses frequently treats both party and state as essentially one organization. Rudolf Bahro, for instance, sees the humanization of existing socialist systems (including the GDR) as possible only by overcoming the power-knowledge complex.[74] Robert Havemann, too, often treats the party and state bureaucracies as one; in addition to making specific proposals for change (e.g. the right to strike, genuine choice at elections)[75] he has argued that the most fundamental problem in the GDR is that the party-state does not place any confidence in the people.[76] This is a familiar theme in much of the East German dissident writing, which suggests that the present party-state is playing a restrictive, conservative role. Indeed Bahro argues that the refusal by many East European states, especially the GDR, to allow the mass of the population any meaningful political role has led these masses to become irresponsible and over-concerned with narrow economic issues. It is this official emphasis on the importance of technical knowledge (even if this is put more in terms of Marxism-Leninism than systems theory in the

1970s) plus the lack of faith in the masses that have led to the charges of 'computer Stalinism' in the GDR.[77] Despite this, none of the leading dissidents advocates a society without a party or state. Bahro wants a new, less corrupt communist party subject to proper control in the form of a legalised opposition and with less correlation between knowledge and power; Havemann believes that reform must come from above, within the party ranks; whilst Wolfgang Harich argued in the mid 1970s that it is mere anarchistic utopianism to suggest that societies can be run without an organized state machinery in an age of limited natural resources, environmental pollution, etc.[78]

The East German people seem to have accepted many basic aspects of socialism in the economic and social fields, such as social ownership of the means of production and full employment. But considerable political change is needed in the GDR before the sort of socialism many Marxists wish to see is achieved. At present, as has been argued, even the official description of society as 'real socialist' recognizes a wide range of limitations and reflects a highly pragmatic system rather than enthusiastically building a classless society. Moreover, any attempt to democratize the GDR will require Soviet approval — all the world witnessed in August 1968 what can happen if the Soviets disapprove of a 'new model' of socialism. It is an irony of history that where once Russia's chances of progressing to socialism and communism were seen to be dependent upon change in the leading states of Western Europe — notably Germany — any moves now nearer to communism in the GDR will depend on similar moves in the 'developed socialist' USSR.

NOTES

1. Primarily in terms of socialist revolutionary consciousness. Many Germans were politically apathetic after the war, whilst even amongst the socialists and communists there were significant differences of opinion and suspicion. See J.P. Nettl, *The Eastern Zone and Soviet Policy in Germany 1945-50* (London: Oxford U.P., 1951), esp. 12-14 and H. Krisch, *German Politics under Soviet Occupation* (New York: Columbia U.P., 1974).

2. See Z.K. Brzezinski, 'The Soviet Past and Future', *Encounter,* Vol. 34, No. 3 (1970), 13-15. The most important exposition of the model is in *Politische Okonomie des Sozialismus und ihre Anwendung in der DDR* (Berlin: Dietz Verlag, 1969).

3. E.g. Wolfgang Biermann was expelled from the GDR in November 1976; Robert Havemann was under house arrest for two and a half years from the same date; Rudolf Bahro was imprisoned in June 1978 and expelled late in 1979. The new penal code has been translated into English and will appear in B. Szajkowski (ed.), *Documents in Communist Affairs—1980* (London: Macmillan, forthcoming), 280-298.

4. Cited by G. Minnerup in 'Why was Biermann expelled?', *Labour Focus on Eastern Europe,* Vol. 1, No. 1 (March-April 1977), 16.

5. An invaluable introduction to this early period is A. Grosser, *Germany in Our Time* (Harmondsworth: Penguin, 1974), 37-118.

6. Some of the less economically developed communist states have experienced somewhat similar problems — i.e. North Vietnam, North Korea.

7. The situation does not look like improving in the early 1980s—for an analysis of current SED awareness of the problem see H.D. Schulz, 'Die SED will eine Wende erzwingen', *Deutschland Archiv* (hereafter: *DA*), Vol. 13, No. 1 (January 1980), 1-6.

8. Ulbricht played down the regime's devotion to the USSR—which was probably one of the reasons why the Soviets were anxious to have him replaced. On the Soviet involvement in Ulbricht's fall see H. Lippmann, *Honecker and the New Politics of Europe* (New York: Macmillan, 1972), 214-216.

9. See 'Aufruf zum 30. Jahrestag der Deutschen Demokratischen Republik', *Neues Deutschland,* 18 November 1977, 1, and H. Bartel, I. Mittenzwei and W. Schmidt, 'Preussen und die deutsche Geschichte', *Einheit,* Vol. 34, No. 6 (1979), 637-646.

10. *Verfassung der Deutschen Demokratischen Republik* (Berlin: Staatsverlag der DDR, 1975), 9-10 (Article 2).

11. For details see Krisch, op. cit., 174-199.

12. The standard work on the 1953 events is A. Baring's *Uprising in East Germany* (Ithaca and London: Cornell U.P., 1972). Although the GDR was not the first East European country to experience worker riots against the communist regime after the Second World War — Czechoslovakia and Bulgaria, for instance, had troubles in 1952 and early 1953 — the GDR was the first to have nationwide riots on a massive scale.
Throughout this chapter, we refer to the holder of the senior office in the SED as the General Secretary, merely to avoid confusion; in fact the position was re-named the First Secretaryship in 1953, but reverted to General Secretaryship in 1976.

13. For details see P.C. Ludz, *The Changing Party Elite in East Germany* (Cambridge, Mass: MIT Press, 1972), passim but esp. 89-120.

14. Ibid., 325-407 and H. Zimmermann, 'The GDR in the 1970s', *Problems of Communism,* Vol. 27, No. 2 (March-April 1978), 8-9.

15. The East Germans use the term 'proletariat' to refer explicitly to the industrial (manual) workers. See W. Böhme et al. (eds.), *Kleines Politisches Wörterbuch* (Berlin: Dietz Verlag, 1973), 54-56 and 684.

16. Zimmermann, op. cit., 17-18 and M. McCauley, *Marxism-Leninism in the German Democratic Republic* (London: Macmillan, 1979), 182-184.

17. The fact that some Western commentators see the phase of forming developed

socialism as dating from 1961 endorses the argument that there is a higher degree of continuity between the official analyses of the 1960s and 1970s than is sometimes recognized — see R. Rilling (ed.), *Sozialismus in der DDR: Dokumente und Materialien* (Cologne: Paul Rugenstein, 1979), esp. Vol. 2. Honecker himself, as late as June 1970, was talking very positively about the 'developed social system of socialism'—see *The Implementation of Lenin's Theory of the Leading Role of the Party by the Socialist Unity Party of Germany in the German Democratic Republic* (Berlin, 1970), esp. 25-29. For the difficulties in distinguishing the different stages in the development of socialism in the GDR see A. Fischer and H. Weber, 'Periodisierungsprobleme der Geschichte der DDR', *DA*, Sonderheft 1979, 17-26.

18. *Statut der Sozialistischen Einheitspartei Deutschlands* (Berlin: Dietz Verlag, 1976), 5.

19. *Programm der Sozialistischen Einheitspartei Deutschlands* (Berlin: Dietz Verlag, 1976), 5, 20, 37, 65-71, 75.

20. The New Economic System was renamed the Economic System of Socialism in 1967, though most Western commentators call the whole phenomenon by its original title; for an early argument that NES was returning see H.D. Schulz, 'Fortsetzung des NOeSPL in Sicht?', *DA*, Vol. 11, No. 2 (February 1978), 117-121; indeed several commentators saw the October 1976 reshuffle of senior party and state personnel as possibly indicating the return to real power of such architects of the New Economic System as Günter Mittag.

21. O. Reinhold, 'Der reale und der unreale Sozialismus', *Einheit*, Vol. 34, No. 9/10 (1979), 1011. For a critique of 'real socialism' see R. Damus, *Der Reale Sozialismus als Herrschaftssystem am Beispiel der DDR* (Giessen: Focus-Verlag, 1978) and R. Bahro, *Die Alternative: Zur Kritik des Real Existierenden Sozialismus* (Cologne: Europäische Verlagsanstalt, 1977). Bahro's book has been translated into English as *The Alternative in Eastern Europe* (London: NLB, 1978).

22. See note 13.

23. The recent renewed interest in combines culminated in the issuance of a new decree on them in November 1979—see *Gesetzblatt der Deutschen Demokratischen Republik,* Pt. 1, No. 30 (13 November 1979), 355-366. One aspect of the centralization is the creation of 'Councils of Party Secretaries', which discuss the party business and take joint decisions on behalf of all the workers in the component enterprises of a combine.

24. On democratic centralism see L.T. Holmes, 'Democratic Centralism in the GDR' (European Consortium for Political Research Conference Paper, 1975) and K. Hanf, 'The State in Developed Socialist Society' in L.H. Legters (ed.), *The German Democratic Republic* (Boulder, Colorado: Westview Press, 1978), 17-59.

25. *Statut,* op. cit., 25 (Article 63).

26. See G. Neugebauer, *Partei- und Staatsapparat in der DDR* (Opladen: Westdeutscher Verlag, 1978), 204, fn. 26.

27. W. Meinke, 'Gegenstand und Methoden der Parteikontrolle im Staatsapparat', *Neuer Weg*, No. 20 (1978), 775.

28. There have only been three SED-conferences — in January 1949, July 1952 and March 1956.

29. For details of changes in the Politburo as well as biographies of Politburo-members see McCauley, op. cit., passim. The reversal of the dominance of economic functionaries has been more noticeable at the Central Committee level.

30. E.g. Zimmermann, op. cit., 16. There were various reasons for this. First, it

was easier for Ulbricht to dominate the State Council than the Politburo because far fewer leading SED-politicians sat on it (the State Council includes representatives of all five political parties and some of the mass organizations); indeed, whereas the dominant position of the General Secretary within the party hierarchy is so only by tradition, the chairman of the State Council is and was constitutionally obliged to direct the council's work. Finally, Ulbricht placed so much emphasis on the New Economic System in the 1960s that the body which oversaw the implementation of this was almost bound to be more important than the more general Politburo. However, its very downgrading since 1971 testifies to the ultimately more powerful position of the Politburo.

31. See e.g. J. Kuppe, 'Zum 12. ZK-Plenum der SED', *DA*, Vol. 13, No. 7 (July 1980), 677-678.

32. Betwen congresses, the Central Committee is officially the highest organ. According to the first SED-statute, congresses were to have been held 'as a rule annually', but they became approximately quadrennial by 1950.

33. E. Honecker, 'Das Beste zum X. Parteitag! Alles zum Wohle des Volkes!', *Neues Deutschland,* 22 May 1980, 3.

34. For an historical overview of the four official SED purges see K.W. Fricke, 'Die SED nach der Uberprüfung', *DA*, Vol. 13, No. 7 (July 1980), 680-683.

35. See McCauley, op. cit., 140 and 215.

36. Ibid., 140 and 215. The latest figure on the proportion of industrial workers in the SED is 56.9 per cent — see Honecker, 'Das Beste . . .', 3.

37. Even in the USSR, the proportion of manual workers in the party is well below 50 per cent.

38. McCauley, op. cit., 140 and Honecker, op. cit., 3.

39. Calculated on the basis of figures in McCauley, op. cit., 145-146 and 213.

40. For a detailed, up-to-date analysis of the organization of East German agriculture see V. Freeman, 'From Collectivisation to Cooperation: A Study of Recent Trends in East German Agriculture', *GDR Monitor*, Vol. 1, No. 1 (Summer 1979), 39-49.

41. On this see e.g. G. Helwig, 'Zeichen der Hoffnung', *DA*, Vol. 11, No. 4 (April 1978), 351-353; H.J. Röder, 'Fragwürdige Friedenspolitik', ibid., No. 8 (August 1978), 800-805; K. Richter, 'Kirchen und Wehrdienstverweigerung in der DDR', ibid., Vol. 12, No. 1 (January 1979), 39-46; G. Minnerup, 'Government Retreats on Military Education', *Labour Focus on Eastern Europe*, Vol. 3, No. 1 (March-April 1979), 3.

42. *Programm,* op. cit., 44 and K. Hager, 'Unser Staat — unser Stolz', *Einheit,* Vol. 34, No. 8 (1979), 803.

43. In 1972, some of the CDU-deputies voted against a bill on abortion.

44. The number of seats allocated to the minor parties has remained constant and equal (52 seats or 10.4 per cent of the membership of parliament each) since 1963 — see *Statistisches Jahrbuch der Deutschen Demokratischen Republik 1979* (Berlin: Staatsverlag der DDR, 1979), 385 and P.J. Lapp, *Die Volkskammer der DDR* (Opladen: Westdeutscher Verlag, 1975), 115. Although the total number of deputies from the four parties is greater than the number of SED-deputies, it should be borne in mind that the East German legislature includes representatives of the mass organizations (e.g. the trade unions) as well as the political parties; the overwhelming majority of these representatives are also members of the SED, so that the communists have a majority in the Volkskammer — for details see ibid., 124-131.

45. H. Dohlus, 'Demokratischer Zentralismus im Zeichen wachsender Anforderungen an die Partei', *Einheit*, Vol. 29, No. 11 (1974), 1234. See too W. Bernet, 'Antikommunismus in westdeutschen Publikationen über die Verfassung der DDR', *Staat und Recht,* Vol. 20, No. 12 (1971), 1912.

46. In October 1976, Horst Sindermann was replaced as Prime Minister by Willi Stoph; he then became President of the Volkskammer (i.e. as a sop), replacing Gerald Götting of the CDU. Götting was appointed Deputy-President of the Volkskammer in July 1980 (details in *Neues Deutschland*, 4 July 1980, 2).

47. *Programm*, op. cit., 40.

48. Hager, op. cit., 800. For a Western analysis of the state see Hanf, op. cit., passim; for a thorough East German analysis see G. Schulz et al. (eds.), *Sozialistischer Staat und Staatliche Leitung* (Berlin: Staatsverlag der DDR, 1976).

49. Article 1 of the Constitution.

50. E. Honecker, *Statement in Support of the Law Amending the Constitution of the GDR* (Berlin: Panorama DDR, n.d.), 11.

51. See e.g. U. Kensy, 'Wissenschaftliche Arbeitsberatung zu Rechtsfragen der Kombinate bei der Durchführung der Beschlüsse des VIII. Parteitages der SED', *Wirtschaftsrecht*, 1971, No. 6, 361-362. For a brief introductory argument that the concept of the 'Socialistischer Rechtsstaat' is incompatible with Marxism see W. Seiffert's review, 'Die DDR — ein Rechtsstaat?', *DA*, Vol. 13, No. 7 (July 1980), 765-66. VVBs are administrative organs in industry, between the ministries and the production units.

52. Official acknowledgement of the change is summarised nicely in the following quotation from Honecker, made in December 1979, 'A rise in economic output cannot be organized nowadays on the basis of the means and methods of the beginning of the 1970s' — cited in Schulz 'Die SED. . .', 1.

53. Western analysts are divided as to whether the recent moves represent centralization or decentralization — see K. Belwe, 'Tagungsberichte — 5. Symposium der Forschungsstelle für gesamtdeutsche wirtschaftliche und soziale Fragen', *DA*, Vol. 13, No. 1 (January 1980), 88-89; we are arguing here that it is both.

54. See the various speeches from the ninth plenum of the Central Committee published in *Neues Deutschland*, 25-30 October 1968.

55. For instance, the Council of Ministers was formally subordinated to the State Council in 1963. For a highly detailed analysis of the work of the State Council to 1971 see P.J. Lapp, *Der Staatsrat im Politischen System der DDR* (Opladen: Westdeutscher Verlag, 1972).

56. Articles 66-80 of the Constitution.

57. See Lapp, *Die Volkskammer*, 149-155 and 256-264.

58. T.M. Forster, *The East German Army* (London: George Allen and Unwin, 1967), 19.

59. For an argument that the SED is currently attempting further to strengthen its control over the military see K.W. Fricke, 'NVA — Revirement politisch motiviert', *DA*, Vol. 12, No. 2 (February 1979), 118-120. Even allowing for the moderate troop withdrawal since late 1979, the Red (Soviet) Army still has considerably more divisions in the GDR than in any other East European state.

60. For an introductory analysis of the role of the state security forces by their director see E. Mielke, 'Verantwortungsbewusst für die Gewährleistung der staatlichen Sicherheit', *Einheit*, Vol. 35, No. 2 (1980), 151-158.

61. For a listing and some analysis of the changes in electoral law (primarily for local elections) see K.W. Fricke, 'Zur Geschichte der Kommunalwahlen in der DDR',

DA, Vol. 12, No. 5 (May 1979), 454-459. On the latest (June 1979) changes see W. Seiffert, 'Anmerkungen zur Anderung des Gesetzes über die Wahlen zu den Volksvertretungen der DDR', ibid, No. 8 (August 1979), 792-793. As in other communist states, electoral turnout and endorsement of the official list is never far short of one hundred per cent. For an analysis of why this should be so — including a reference to the fact that elections in German-speaking countries traditionally enjoy very high turnouts — see D. Childs, *East Germany* (New York: Praeger, 1969), 90-96.

62. Ibid., 94-95. See too J.M. Starrels and A.M. Mallinckrodt, *Politics in the German Democratic Republic* (New York: Praeger, 1975), 154-156.

63. This is probably why the 1974 constitutional changes — one of the most important of which was the abandonment of the concept of one German nation — were not subject to a referendum.

64. See e.g. 'Die Volksvertretungen in der DDR', *Einheit*, Vol. 31, No. 9 (1976), 1058-1060.

65. For details of the discussion of three major laws in recent years (Labour Code, Youth Law, Civil Code) see H. Sindermann, 'Sozialistische Demokratie — ihre Entwicklung und Vervollkommung', *Einheit,* Vol. 34, No. 9/10 (1979), 920.

66. According to Kurt Hager, in recent years every important law and every essential state decision is prepared and discussed with working people in enterprises and institutions and with representatives of social organizations ('Unser Staat', 803-804); this is in line with Article 65 of the Constitution. However, he does not explicitly state that working people have much scope for making changes to such laws. It is instructive to note in this connection that Honecker criticized party-organizations for letting the discussion of the draft party programme get out of hand in February 1976 (McCauley, op. cit., 216) and that the major changes to the constitution were introduced in 1974 without any public discussion. Discussing the GDR of the late 1960s, T. Baylis has pointed out that the more emphasis there was on centralized planning, the more there was on participatory democracy — largely for legitimizing purposes; the same is probably true of the 1970s. See his *The Technical Intelligentsia and the East German Elite* (Berkeley: University of California Press, 1974), 254.

67. This was acknowledged at the 13th plenum of the Central Committee in June 1970 (speeches from this were published in *Neues Deutschland*, 11-13 June 1970). See too K. Heuer and G. Klinger, 'Einige Fragen der Verordnung über die Aufgaben, Rechte und Pflichten der volkseigenen Betriebe, Kombinate und VVB', *Staat und Recht*, No. 7 (1973), 1073-1074.

68. In emulation of the Soviet concept of one-man management (edinonachalie), East German industry is run on the lines of 'Einzelleitung'; on the origin and development of the Soviet concept see J. Azrael, *Managerial Power and Soviet Politics* (Cambridge, Mass: Harvard U.P., 1966) 42-46, 52-53 and 91-93. On the East German concept and the very limited possibilities for workers to participate in industrial decision-making see K. Belwe, *Mitwirkung im Industriebetrieb der DDR* (Opladen: Westdeutscher Verlag, 1979).

69. Heuer and Klinger, op. cit., 1073-1074.

70. J. Klug, 'Arbeiterinteressen — unvereinbar mit Bernsteinschem Reformismus', *Einheit,* Vol. 29, No. 11 (1974), 1304. For the approved East German version of 'Mitbestimmung' see Article 21 of the Constitution. Evidence of worker unrest or opposition to the regime is scarce. However, we know that in September 1977 eight young workers from Jena and Leipzig were deported for openly supporting Wolfgang Biermann; they have subsequently published the details of their ac-

tivities in the GDR and the authorities' reactions — see *Labour Focus on Eastern Europe*, Vol. 2, No. 1 (March-April 1978), 9-11 and No. 2 (May-June 1978), 14-15.

71. The most detailed study of this is G.J. Glaessner's *Herrschaft durch Kader* (Opladen: Westdeutscher Verlag, 1977), esp. 218-256. See too R. Herber and H. Jung, *Kaderarbeit im System Sozialistischer Führungstätigkeit* (Berlin: Staatsverlag der DDR, 1968).

72. Details on the overlap between the Politburo and leading state organs (as of 1978) can be found in H. Wassmund, 'The German Democratic Republic', in B. Szajkowski (ed.), *Marxist Governments — A World Survey*, Vol. 2 (London: Macmillan, 1981), 337-338.

73. For details see Glaessner, op. cit., esp. 256-341; also G.J. Glaessner and I. Rudolph, *Macht durch Wissen* (Opladen: Westdeutscher Verlag, 1978) and Neugebauer, op. cit., 87. The intelligentsia — and therefore to a large extent the party and state apparatuses — was reproducing its social position in the 1960s according to a recent East German sociological work — see *Grundlagen der Marxistisch-Leninistischen Soziologie* (Berlin: 1977), 179.

74. Bahro, op. cit., passim and esp. 361-414. In this book Bahro draws a comparison between the current position of the bureaucracies in Eastern Europe and the political-social-economic system described by Marx as the 'Asiatic mode of production'.

75. R. Havemann, *Berliner Schriften* (Berlin: Verlag Europäische Ideen, 1978), esp. 122-134.

76. Ibid., and R. Havemann, 'Die Regierung soll dem eigenen Volk Vertrauen Schenken', *DA*, Vol. 7, No. 1 (January 1974), 46-49.

77. It must, however, be emphasized that several major aspects of Stalinism — particularly the apparent arbitrariness — are not typically characteristic of the contemporary GDR.

78. W. Harich, *Kommunismus ohne Wachstum?* (Reinbek: Rowohlt, 1975).

7 Hungary — Quiet Progress?

Mária Huber
University of Tübingen, FRG

Hans-Georg Heinrich
University of Vienna, Austria

INTRODUCTION

Throughout most of its recent history, the organization of political power in Hungary has shown a marked tendency toward a 'strong state' model. Intense social and international conflict stimulated the creation of a system that was monopolized by small groups and was essentially stability-oriented. Social and political change was usually the result of outbursts of violence, such as wars and revolutions. The collapse of the Dual Monarchy further aggravated Hungary's precarious situation, mainly because of the dramatic increase in her dependence on foreign markets and raw material supplies. The land reform combined with the impact of economic crisis turned the landed aristocracy and the gentry into an aristocratic middle class, for which the state had to provide adequate occupational facilities through a rapid expansion of the civil service.[1] The value system of the political elites reflected their fear of losing traditional privileges to the newcomers. As a result, industrialization and social change were delayed rather effectively until the beginning of the Second World War. Hungary's inclusion in the Soviet defence system after the War marked the end of attempts to insulate society against the impact of social and economic development. The Hungarian Communists were committed to a course of fast and large-scale socio-economic transformation. However, the immediate consequences of this process together with the structural weaknesses of a still traditional society makes the present leadership face a set of serious problems that considerably restrict the chances for the realization of the ambitious Communist programme.

THE PARTY

While the basic goals of the Hungarian Communists (HSWP) have
not changed significantly, the methods of Party leadership had to
be restyled completely following the collapse of Stalinism in 1956.

The Hungarian Communists, driven underground or exiled in
the interwar years, were haunted by the ghosts of their unsuccessful
revolutionary experiment in 1919. After the war, they were clearly
handicapped by being identified with Soviet Communism. Their
actual power was small but there was a potential for winning
broader support for their policies, as was shown in the 1945 elections.[2] The value system of the Party leadership was based on the
conviction that the application of the Soviet model was the only
way to reach a higher historical stage of development. This theory
gave perfect rationalization for the challenges that the policy-
makers were facing: economic recovery from wartime destruction
was the most urgent goal. No opposition party could deny its
necessity. Soviet strategic interests were met (around fifty per cent
of total investments during the first five-year plan went towards
military expenditure).[3] The power base of the Communist Party
could be enlarged most rapidly by creating an industrial proletariat
and transforming the peasantry from independent small-holders to
state or collective employees.[4]

The leading role of the party under Rákosi meant an absolute
and unconditional monopoly for the party devising and executing
policies, the only limitation being Soviet interests. Party cadres
were, by and large, assigned the task of 'fighting the class enemy',
of unmasking saboteurs and kulaks, thus devoting all their attention to the establishment and maintenance of the dictatorship of
the proletariat.[5] The crash industrialization programme actually
resulted in lower living standards, caused grave disproportions in
economic development[6] and drew severe criticism from within the
Party itself.[7] However, the Party leadership was in a position to
devise active strategies, selecting from among the available options.
The existence of intra-party opposition (e.g. I. Nagy's 'right wing')
demonstrates the awareness of the existence of developmental alternatives within the Party.

Changes in the Theory of the Party's Role

Official criticism of Stalinist policies and the liberal course pursued by the HSWP leadership after 1957 tend to obscure the fact that there is a great deal of continuity in the basic value system of the Hungarian communists. The present leadership still identifies with the basic idea underlying industrialization in Hungary: the fact that 'distortions occurred does not alter the fact that socialism was being built in our country.'[8] Although the social power base is considered to be solid and reliable, the leaders are very well aware of the social and political implications of industrialization —

> The economic policy of the party has two mutually connected goals — to ensure the *construction of the Socialist society* and the steady growth of the living standards of workers through the development of productive forces (emphasis added).[9]

The commitment to transform Hungary into a developed industrial society remains the key political value for the party elite.

However, since 1956, a genuine change of the theory, style and methods of leadership has taken place. First Secretary J. Kádár's dictum 'whoever is not against us is with us' is not only the central slogan of the 'alliance policy', but also a fairly realistic assessment of Party attitudes. The HSWP has shown a gradually increasing flexibility and responsiveness to the demands of social groups during the last twenty years. Kádár's statement at the XIth Party Congress (1975) that the policy of the HSWP 'represents not only narrow party interests, but expresses the interests of the working class, of our whole working people' can claim a certain degree of truth; it is an example of 'honest Marxist thought'.[10] But it also reflects the desire of the Party leaders to draw the picture of a new, entirely democratic party that is free from past errors and distortions. This is obvious in Kádár's explanation of the leading role of the Party:

> Based on the lessons of the past, the leading role of the Party is realized . . . by the Party taking the initiative and formulating the main guidelines of the work of construction, convincing non-party citizens of the correctness of the decisions, mobilizing and controlling their implementation. The Party bodies can pass binding decisions only for the Party, for Party members.[11]

The logical supplement of this type of leadership theory is a view of society which recognizes the existence of conflicting interests: 'Beside the interests of the whole society, there exist also various group and invididual interests. The Party recognizes them and considers their realization, within the limits of the primary social interests to be its obligation.'[12] Although this is not stated explicitly, the classical dichotomy of 'antagonistic' versus 'non-antagonistic' conflicts is rendered more or less useless by the wide range of conflicting interests that are to be integrated in Hungary's socialist society. In a statement by a typical representative of the younger Party generation, the Minister of Culture and former department head in the Agitprop Department of the Central Committee, Imre Pozsgay, conflict is explicitly welcomed:

> Amidst present socio-political conditions the HSWP, in addition to developing its organizing abilities, can fulfil its interest-integrating functions only if the different group interests can manifest themselves openly and come into conflict with one another . . . I admit that open, politically conscious possibilities of selection and classification of interests must be enhanced, that is, socialist democracy must be strengthened.[13]

Politburo member Valéria Benke displayed realistic insights into the political culture of the Hungarians stating that,

> One cannot speak of the realization of an ideological unity of our society. In various scientific fields as well as in cardinal questions there are influential non-Marxist positions; in public discussions views emerge that are far from the Marxist-Leninist concepts of society and from the dialectical method.[14]

The Guidelines for the XIIth Congress of the HSWP mention trade unions, non-Marxists, religious believers and national minorities among groups whose interests are officially recognized.

However, the central Marxist-Leninist tenet of Party leadership never seems jeopardized, even in the most 'liberal' statements. Thus, I. Pozsgay hastens to add that socialism is still the realm of necessity and not yet that of freedom; the main political decision-mechanism must invariably be 'the authoritative solution of the interest conflicts for the sake of the whole of society with priority for the interests of the working class.'[15] The pragmatic approach to Party leadership is still genuinely Marxist-Leninist. The classical argumentative pattern of the 'basic correctness of the Party line' is never omitted when the problem of incorrect Party decisions is discussed, as in the following statement by István Katona, the former editor of the Party newspaper *Népszabadság:*

> Our Party does not claim that the past twenty years were free from faults and errors . . . Nor does it promise a lack of disappointments for the future, because

> Socialism is not a structure that can be subjected to experiments in a test-tube, but a developing society that grows out of work, that progresses over many obstacles . . . The Party is not in possession of the philosophers' stone . . . In the main question the Party was not wrong: in the determination of the principal political direction.[16]

The last sentence is not just lip-service to the party-line but reveals the readiness of the speaker to identify with the basic goals of the Party. It draws a clear boundary line between true and distorted Marxism-Leninism. The ideology of the HSWP also reflects the strong authoritative tendencies of classical Marxism-Leninism. Thus, a 'liberal' like Gy. Aczél goes as far as questioning the wisdom of democratic procedures in an attempt to legitimize the monopoly of the Party in political decision making:

> There are issues — and practically all issues are more or less of this kind — in which it is difficult to reach clear decisions. If people are given a chance to vote on how many flats should be built in the next fifteen years, I think all of them would vote unanimously for the highest number. But if I added that the maximum would imply that our educational establishment would deteriorate, the commercial network would become less satisfactory, transportation more complicated, then the vote would show the opposite extreme: even the optimum number would be voted with difficulty . . . The wise conciliation of interests helps to find the optimum in which the necessary number of flats are built, yet the schools, the commercial network etc. are developed to the satisfaction of the people . . . In socialist societies, decisions have to reflect familiarity with the actual situation.[17]

As legitimation patterns become more realistic, they reveal an increasingly defensive attitude. Party leaders openly state that as long as scarcity conditions prevail, there can be no fully democratic decision-making. The 'fault', then, lies with economic constraints. Politburo member Károly Németh expressed this aspect clearly in his exposé on the 5th five-year plan (1976-1980): 'Net investment can grow by only 25-26 per cent. Therefore, it will be impossible to satisfy many legitimate needs. The selection of goals has to take the availability of material resources into account and this is why we must insist on a *rigid ordering of priorities*' (emphasis added).[18] The leaders seem determined to realize economic priorities in spite of the social problems that may ensue and in spite of the possible limitations for democratic decision procedures. The present has priority over a vague utopian future. Therefore, the Party leaders have no compunctions about a return to heavy-handed methods in critical situations. One of J. Kádár's recent statements illustrates this attitude:

> However faulty the earlier attitude was, according to which socialist construction goes hand in hand with the intensification of class struggle, so would it be incorrect to believe that the permanent softening of the class struggle is the only realistic alternative. That always depends on the domestic and the international power relations.[19]

Also, the determination of the HSWP leadership to remain loyal to the Soviet cause is no mere lip-service. What appears to be a strategy oscillating between Hungarian nationalism and Communist internationalism is a firm commitment to Soviet interests that keeps the Soviets fully informed about domestic policy without challenging control mechanisms.[20] There are deeply ingrained attitudes behind such declarations as

> Our party learns and has learned from every communist party and revolutionary force. For us, the rich theoretical and practical experiences of the CPSU, founded by Lenin, is of especial significance . . . The acceptance of these experiences does not mean their mechanical imitation, and the violation of independence . . . Our Party places great emphasis on the creative application of the universally valid teachings of Marxism-Leninism according to the historical, political, economic and other conditions of our homeland. Thereby the HSWP expresses its dual nature as a patriotic and internationalist party.[21]

Changes in Party Structures and Functions

While questions of ideology and legitimacy undoubtedly are given increasing attention as a result of the Party's commitment to improve its democratic profile, the capacity of the Party to meet the challenge of an increasingly complex situation quickly and effectively appears to be very limited.

The main reasons for the present difficulties must be sought in the structural weakness of the Hungarian economy. It cannot compensate for the rising supply costs incurred by increased exports to capitalist markets, and at the same time create the funds necessary to finance the Party's social objectives which, in turn have been adopted as a result of the failure of the Stalinist model.

The situation of the world economy in the 1970s has forced Hungary to orient her foreign trade and production system increasingly towards the West. As the limits of extensive growth have been reached, the transfer of Western technological know-how becomes more important than ever before: 'Our historical task is the elimination (ledolgozás) of our underdevelopment. Of necessity, in that process the production forces of the developed capitalist countries serve as a model; in the fulfillment of our tasks, one of the most important methods is the transfer of their more highly developed technology.'[22] The present situation is characterized by rapidly growing imports; between 1971 and 1975 consumption of imported industrial goods increased by 58 per cent, whereas that of domestic industrial goods increased by a mere 28 per cent. Planners therefore advocate a decrease in domestic consumption to safeguard a net increase of industrial production over consumption.[23] The situation also necessitated a tightening of the screws in the planning system. The economic reformers in 1968 had envisaged a gradual replacement of obligatory plan figures by contractual relations and indirect state control.[24] However, as a belated consequence of the recognition of social interest groups, the measures adopted under the premise of social strategy in the fields of social security, family support and distributive policies have indeed strained the economy of the country beyond its capacities, while the anticipated positive return effects for the economy did not live up to expectations. Whatever reasons may otherwise be found for the dysfunctions of economy, it remains a fact that the increasing quantitative and qualitative demands for commodities and infrastructure performance resulted in an imbalance, both in foreign management and the domestic economy, within the existing organization and management structures; the elimination of this imbalance exceeded the given power and control capacities of the state. After countless attempts to improve the finance and pricing system, the service sector, and the structure and quality of production, the Party stood up to its responsibility for the economy and changed the previous course of economic policy in 1978; the disposition of the national income was no longer to be defined by consumers' demands, but by the task of balancing the economy.

The main burden of improving economic efficiency and of restructuring measures now considered necessary was passed from public expenditure to the population; state subsidies were cut in every branch of industry, which considerably hit the production plants, but also certain classes of the population (e.g. because the prices for meat products, certain services, restaurants, hotels and recreation facilities have risen markedly).

Nevertheless, raising the standard of living has been retained as an element of economic policy. The population is not to be solely — and extensively — restricted as a consumer but should also be challenged as a producer. The political leadership endeavours to stabilize not only production, but also the spheres of circulation and distribution. Here, however, emphasis has shifted from social policy to legitimation; given the critical economic situation of the country, the distribution of burdens and benefits, which is both justifiable and intelligible, is aimed at encouraging unity of action throughout society.[25]

In trying to reaffirm its position in economic decision-making and in elaborating a programme for the further 'construction of Socialism' in Hungary the Party poses as an active political force in society. In reality, Party politics are to a large degree dictated by the exigencies of an increasingly critical situation. István Huszár, the chairman of the Planning Office, writing in an English-language journal, is quite explicit about the plight of the decision-makers:

> In the years to come the highest priority must be accorded, both by planning and management, to the restoration of the foreign trade equilibrium and to a reduction of the country's hard currency loans. Growth, investment, and the objectives of living standard policy must, for a time, be subordinated to this task . . . A brake on the growth rate is not an objective but a consequence.[26]

As external pressure on the Party is mounting, it tries to improve its strike capacity through structural adaptation. The norms of inner party-life are interpreted to serve primarily the maintenance of party unity; according to Article 2 of the Rules of the HSWP (1975) the Party member is 'obliged to . . . strengthen and defend the Party's ideals and its political, organizational and actional unity, to fight the formation of factions'. The expansion of intra-party democracy was postponed by the laconic announcement in the Guidelines for the XIIth Congress of the HSWP that 'the Rules presently in force serve the Party's activity and development well and correspond to the tasks we are facing'. The Guidelines see the most important elements of Party work in 'the uniform interpretation of decisions, the organization of their implementation and the mobilization of the masses.'[27]

Cadre policy is to provide the social basis for a genuine Marxist-Leninist programme of action, reduce the Party's dependence on non-Party specialists and keep the Party from becoming an outpost for various social interest groups. However, the conflicting tendencies resulting from these partly incompatible goals cannot be harmonized in practice.

Although the Party has been campaigning for increased recruitment among the manual workers since 1971[28] — 'The most important recruitment basis for the Party are the workers in large enterprises' in the wording of the 1979 Guidelines for the XIIth Congress — the results are modest. In 1979, out of a total of 800,000 Party members, around 75 per cent were said to be workers or peasants according to their original occupation.[29] In 1975, the exact figure was 72.2 per cent.[30] Recent figures that relate to the type of jobs actually held have not yet been released. In 1970 and 1975, the percentage of manual workers and collective farmers was 46.8 and of intellectuals 43.6 and 40 per cent, respectively.[31] The weight of the white collar professions within the Party is striking, especially when compared to the occupational composition of Hungarian society (according to the 1979 'Guidelines' 59 per cent workers, 13 per cent collective farmers, 25 per cent intellectuals and employees, 3 per cent entrepreneurs). Disproportionate white collar representation is due to the fact that the strategical social positions that are liable to Party control are held by this group and conversely, that white collar careers are linked to Party membership. On the other hand, many workers cannot satisfy the demands of party-membership; their educational level and political commitment are relatively low. This especially pertains to the one million commuters, of whom eighty per cent are manual workers. Their political activity is particularly low. A 1973 investigation revealed that in Dunaujváros the proportion of party-members amongst the commuters amounted to four per cent, whilst the proportion amongst the town work-force was 13.5 per cent. In addition, it is much more difficult to organize political training and education in an industrial enterprise than in administrative institutions. In the latter, the work-process is economically less rigidly organized, the socio-economic status of the employees is higher and they have more free time.[32] The ideal type of the communist cadre has changed greatly since 1956 — the mere ability to carry through Party orders has been supplemented by the requirement of technical skills; 'party soldiers' have become 'administrative specialists' and 'planners'. However, the Party has gradually begun to realize the pitfalls of this development: 'The number of non-manual workers is rising faster than real social demand and also their distribution between various fields shows disproportions. This negative process must be changed by the rationalization of work, the intensification of social control and the repression of bureaucracy'. This formulation of the 'Guidelines' is counterbalanced by the insight that the role of white collar professions 'will grow with social development and scientific-technical progress'. The odds are, then, that Party representation of non-manual labourers and the intelligentsia will not be strengthened in the long run.

As far as the top leadership positions in the HSWP are concerned, they are held by people who are neither of a stalinist nor of a recent managerial-technocratic vintage. The majority of the Politburo and Secretariat members are of 'old bolshevik' extraction; their average age is 59 and almost all of them joined the Party before or in 1945. This means that a significant part of their political experience stems from illegal work, the period of the regime establishment, and the following phase of class struggle in Hungary. The few newcomers are colourless men, a few are economic specialists with a university education. The 'old bolsheviks' are a significantly smaller group among the Central Committee members (about 20 per cent). In this body, the strongest group is composed of state functionaries, most of them with a background in economic administration (c. 30 per cent).[33]

There is certainly a potential for political change emanating from within the Party. The Party at large is relatively young (average age 44; 44.1 per cent of the newly recruited were younger than 26 years in 1975).[34] One may assume that the value system of the future generation of communist leaders differs significantly from that of the present leadership as a result of the exposure to twenty years of a relaxed domestic and international climate. Symbols such as 'stalinism' or 'capitalism' are relatively meaningless to them because they are not tied to personal experience. Thus, they can afford to view their environment pragmatically and without the basic distrust that is so typical of the 'old bolshevik' personality. However, this potential can unfold only under special conditions; there are still formidable obstacles between individual pragmatism and collective pragmatic action.

The Party in Social Communication

The attempts of the Party to regain initiative and its independence from specific demands has not led to a more uniform pattern of communication between Party and society. Because the formal organizational network (Party and state bodies, social organizations such as the trade unions) limits communication to 'legitimate' inputs on the one hand and formal decisions and declarations on the other, both Party and citizens try to open up new alleys that bypass the existing communication channels. Citizen and social groups try to get direct access to the decision-making centres and leaders want to be aware of social developments that are reflected only partially and in a distorted form in the information obtained through official reports. Thus, a wide gap exists between informal and formal communication systems. The average citizen is politically pathetic and tends to withdraw into the pursuit of material wellbeing. Low political interest and a catastrophic lack of political education is a reliable indicator for this attitude.[35] Citizens advancing specific demands obviously do not place much trust in the official grievance-solving mechanism, but resort to putting pressure on the administration through personal connections, letters of complaint published in the press, or by trying to mobilize support in the mass media.[36] The latter variant was adopted in February 1976, when a regulation on the classification of kindergarten, primary and secondary school pupils had aroused widespread consternation, among both parents and teachers. Yielding to the pressure of public opinion, efficiently flanked by the literary weekly *Elet és irodalom* and Radio Budapest's weekly political magazine '168 Hours', the Ministries of Education and Labour, which issued the decree on classification, were compelled to reword it.[37] The establishment of a blue jeans factory which will produce on a licensed basis is a classic case of unofficial pressure group activity under socialism. Although jeans are still being frowned on as a symbol of Western petty-bourgeois decadence, the planners obviously preferred to meet this strong consumer demand by domestic production facilities rather than spend convertible currency for largescale imports.[38] Growing exports of jeans to other socialist countries are anticipated to counterbalance licence costs. Thus, economic and consumer interests entered a strange coalition against a traditional Party value.

The wage increase for industrial and construction workers decided by the November 1972 and November 1973 Party Plena was an
extraordinary measure that increased the living standard of more
than 1,500,000 workers and employees.[39] Whatever the concrete
Party interests behind this step, they led to the satisfaction of large
non-party groups' demands. The case of commuters is an example
of a tug-of-ware between planners who try to implement centrally-
set industrialization priorities and a large socially-declassed group
that is affected by economic growth policy. As in other East European countries, the high rate of commuting is due to the preference
given to 'productive' investments that in the final analysis has a
detrimental effect on urban infrastructure. The industrial enterprises frequently oppose by all means possible — legal and illegal
— the transfer of their production and administration out of the
towns. The press occasionally reports in great detail on the clash of
interests which this leads to. The poorer sections of the population
cannot compete with the new middle class on the urban property
market or are unable to obtain living space in the cities via the state
redistribution system. Daily commuting and night-lodging are the
inevitable (but of course unwanted) consequence.[40] The two alternatives open to the planners, namely the allocation of more funds
to dispersed smaller centres or increased investments in urban infrastructure in big cities are anathema partly because of the basic industrialization philosophy, partly because they are considered
'destructive' and economically not viable by the planners.[41]
However, the roots of a development can be discerned in Hungary,
which could result in the realization of the first alternative —
locating the production sites closer to the producer and not vice
versa. In recent years, the villages have begun to industrialize and
are experiencing a veritable boom in housing construction.[42] This is
due to the progress in agricultural production that has led to the increased availability of funds for the construction of ancillary industrial facilities. It has happened in spite of the official policy to
curb such development. However, the striking capacity of the commuting group and their families lies with their control of vital parts
of the food production process — the private plots.[43] On account of
their ability to exert pressure on the policy-makers, their interests
have been recognized to a certain degree. The reaction of the
policy-makers   consisted   of   increased   investment   in   the
transportation system. Also official publications have begun to
turn their attention to the problem. In spite of the fact that the

discussion had been opened up by dissidents (Konrád, Szelényi), the official voices recognize clearly the existence of a social conflict and take a mildly critical stance. The most recent contributions were published in the Party's daily *Népszabadság* and in the Party theoretical monthly *Társadalmi Szemle*.[44]

Due to its recognition of the legitimacy of conflicting interests and in spite of its attempts to remain aloof of social infighting, the Party does get involved in interest politics. The most severe danger to the autonomous nature of the Party does not come from the long-term interests of the various social groups that can by and large be calculated and incorporated into social planning, but from the chaotic stream of urgent requests by powerful local or enterprise bosses. Needless to say, their chances of successful intervention are much higher than those of ordinary citizens who have no personal contact within relevant decision-making centres. Because of the danger of informal connections to rational planning, the existence of such networks is discussed openly in the media.[45]

The Party has consistently tried to integrate informal communication into official channels, albeit with limited success. Thus, the 1972 Constitution recognizes the trade union as the interest representative of the workers (Article 2, 4/3); the 1949 Constitution had assigned mainly production tasks to them (Article 56/2). Enterprise democracy, at present still in an embryonic stage, is to receive strong impulses; signalling the sincerity of the leadership, a 1978 Presidential Council decree amended the Labour Code to include an explicit recognition of the participation rights of workers' communities in enterprises. Article 36 of the 1972 Constitution obliges the Council of Ministers to cooperate with the interested social organizations. This constitutional promise has become a routine procedure in legislative practice. The credibility and seriousness of this constitutional regulation was underscored by a number of statutes and ordinances in the late 1960s and early 1970s that brought detailed regulation of the legislative process. Organizations such as the National Council of Trade Unions, the Central Organs of the Cooperative and Youth Organizations were granted the right to propose legislative action, to be consulted on drafts and to decide policies in their spheres of interest. This commitment sets a framework for the processing of future group demands to be processed through existing information channels.

Occasionally, one finds concrete political information in formal documents, too. Article 12 of the 1972 Hungarian Constitution may be cited as an example ('The state recognizes the socially useful economic activity of the small commodity producers. However, property and private initiative must not violate the interests of the community'.). This promise is a direct mapping of social development; it mirrors the growth in the political capacity of private entrepreneurs (*gebines*) since 1949. As of 1977, there were 11,000 private shopkeepers in Hungary who mainly satisfy the consumer interest of a growing middle class.[46]

The systematic bias inherent in every information system that is based on passing reports through hierarchically-structured bureaucracies forces the Party to devise rival systems to tap public opinion. Since communication between central and local Party organizations had degenerated into a system of formal reports, the Party decided to open up direct communication lines between the local organs and their social environment and the decision-making centres. Party activists who have to report back directly to the centre try to tap public opinion in a few selected settings, e.g. industrial enterprises. However, it is very doubtful whether this new approach can overcome the traditional tendency to produce overly optimistic reports.

A more viable alternative is the opening up of information channels through the ministerial system. In the process of policy formulation (e.g. drafting of a decree) the possible reaction of selected groups (mostly the enterprise workers) is tested in informal talks.[47] The establishment of such a procedure is most probably a reaction to a more active public opinion and has most likely been motivated by a fear of 'infection from the Polish disease' (i.e. the events in 1970 and 1976). Together with sociological research data, this channel seems to yield the most reliable political information for the Party decision-makers.

THE STATE

Changes in the Theory of the State

Official theory has traditionally regarded state organization as one of the main fields of socialist democracy. The changes in state practice ushered in by Kádár's reform policies and the institution of a new economic model have prompted an expansion of the traditional Marxist-Leninist doctrine but have left its essential positions untouched. The main theoretical changes reflected by the amendment of the Constitution of the Hungarian People's Republic in April 1972 involved the transition from the Dictatorship of the Proletariat to the higher stage of Socialism, the incorporation of Alliance Policy into the state doctrine (Article 2, Section 3) and a stress on citizens' participation. Commenting on the 1972 Constitutional amendment, a legal scholar states that,

> The widening of socialist democratism is manifest . . . in a development of the political system to the effect that the firmness of socialist state power, the safety of the legal order of the socialist state, are emphasized as before, while at the same time prominence is given to forms which open up possibilities for each citizen of the state to take part sharing actively the power in the realization of the great social objectives, in the complete building of socialism. This expresses at the same time, at the level of political relations, the reciprocity which exists between the many-sided development, the unfolding of the capabilities of the citizens' personality and the tasks faced by the community . . . The fundamental objective in the present stage of our work to build socialism is the complete building up of a socialist society . . . Although a new constitution was not adopted in a given historical situation, the amendments to the Constitution were serving adequately the requirement of a creative enrichment of the Constitution.[48]

In spite of utopian overtones in theoretical works, the theme of the withering away of the state is played down. Only a few authors venture to identify trends that might eventually lead towards the socialization of the state. Some hopes were placed on the economic reform started in 1968, which, however, has not prompted the state to withdraw from economic activity although it allegedly produced de-bureaucratizing effects: 'The limitation of superfluous and exaggerated (state) intervention reduces bureaucracy, because it strengthens . . . social mobilization in lieu of the rigid instruments of state control'.[49] But the 'withering away' is moved into a distant future:

> This process can only start when the internal political contradictions are reduced, when these contradictions can be resolved through the general political mobilization of society. As long as force . . . is needed to handle contradictions, will there be statehood and public power that are characteristic for class societies.[50]

While the Constitution paints an idyllic picture of flawless socialist democracy, relevant Party documents are more outspoken about the possibilities of expanding democratic participation:

The Party invariably considers the development of socialist democracy and the participation of the masses a basic task. The democratic fora have an important mission in the exploration of the various interests in society and for the harmonization of these, for the realization of the basic interest of the whole society. *The stepping up of civic discipline and the joint realization of rights and duties are inevitable conditions for the development of socialist democracy*[51] (emphasis added).

The realities of political decision-making begin to overshadow the brisk optimism of political theory.

Changes in State Structure and Functions

The reform of the economic system in 1968, which granted the production units greater autonomy in management, has had important implications for the overall political climate. In replacing administrative directives by economic mechanisms the reform emphasized the importance of legal and political stability for successful economic activity. Legal and constitutional reform in Hungary enjoyed the backing of powerful economic interests and their eventual success will determine the fate of the economic reform itself. The modification of the Constitution contributed to a redirection of public attention toward the system of state and legislation. It promoted every Hungarian, irrespective of his social origin and political orientation, to a 'citizen' and thus contributed to the gradual relaxation and the elimination of anxieties that suggested a return to heavy-handed methods. The constitution granted Parliament additional functions, e.g. the discussion and adoption of the government programme. The sincerity of parliamentary reform has been underlined by the fact that influential interest groups use the — albeit limited — policy-making capacity of the National Council (Országgyülés) to compete for a higher share of the state budget. Thus, the National Assembly is increasingly becoming a spokesman for agricultural interests; although the representation of industry is numerically larger in this body (29.9 per cent vs. 17.3 per cent), the percentage of deputies with an agricultural background has grown by 6 per cent since 1971.[52] Moreover, the spokesmen for collective farms command a majority in many of the regionally-organized deputy groups and can therefore overrule industrial interests within the group, especially as the conflicts of interest are much more intense among the representatives of industrial enterprises.

However, the process of democratization is contradictory. For one thing, central control was never abandoned completely, but every act of decentralization (e.g. more enterprise independence, greater autonomy for the local councils) was counterbalanced by recentralization in another field (e.g. the extension of the competencies of the Central Planning Office, the State Planning Committee and the Ministry of Finances), thus achieving the dialectical principle of 'democratic centralism'. Furthermore, the administrative structure of the Hungarian economy promotes strong centralizational tendencies. The fierce competition for funds leads to the formation of monopolies, a tendency that is welcomed by the administration because it is easier to bargain with a smaller number of clients. Therefore, responsibilities shift upwards; relevant alternatives to established policies are unlikely to be developed or even discussed at lower echelons. A situation has arisen, in which decisions are made two or three levels above the one affected by a problem, while the central control capacity wanes, due to input and withinput overload.[53] Enterprise democracy, hailed as one of the most salient features in the Hungarian system, has had to remain mainly on paper. Under the given unfavourable conditions, it has remained an empty slogan that provokes little response among the potential addressees. Hungarian observers explain this failure mainly in terms of the influence of economic decision-making in the enterprises, which leaves no room for the workers to voice their direct concerns and interests.[54] They are left frustrated and without any feeling of political efficacy. In a field-study on the effectivness of enterprise democracy, a large part of the respondents stated: 'A production conference takes place very rarely. What matters is what happens every day'.[55] Another study found that only 20 per cent of the trade union functionaries in the sample could give a correct answer when asked to name the competencies of trade union enterprise bodies.[56]

There seems to be a somewhat greater potential for democratization at the level of local politics. The economic reform of 1968 had presented a new challenge to the control capacities of the municipal councils. Throughout all local and regional levels, the councils were to tackle tasks of economic organization which could no longer be dealt with by conventional administrative methods. As a result, the No. I Act of 1971 provided a new foundation for the election and operation of the councils. The act served a three-fold purpose:

a) The position of the councils in fulfilling local administrative tasks and providing for the population was to be strengthened.

b) The population was to be involved more actively in the planning, implementation and control of local operations. These activities were to be furnished with an adequate forum, in line with the development of socialist democracy.

c) The responsibility and independence of the councils was to be increased; yet the efficiency of central administrative control was to increase simultaneously.[57]

Accordingly the position of the councils in the political system has been given a new definition. They are no longer considered part of the state's power structure, and neither are they classified as a mass organization. They are now part of the state representative structure and apparatus: 'The councils are organs of the people's representation, self-administration, and administration, which realize the people's power by operating on the basis of democratic centralism'.

The character of the councils as representative bodies of the people first took shape in the alteration of the election regulations and the local structures. Since 1973, elections to the local and the national parliaments have been held separately. In this way, the difference between the local and national issues and problems may be more easily expressed; accordingly, differing interests may be voiced more explicitly. The new institutional character of the council representative system gives a more pronounced status to local interests. The territorial councils are primarily ascribed administrative functions, and are elected by municipal councils. Members of these councils are delegated to the regional councils to represent the municipal interests at a higher level. Legislation has separated the powers of the two levels. Consequently, the hierarchic structure of the councils was abolished. The municipal councils are to fulfil both administrative functions and tasks of self-administration. Their members are elected every 5 years, and are nominated by public assemblies. The proportion of re-elected council members is increasing slightly, amounting to approximately 80 per cent. The social composition of the bodies shows a relatively balanced distribution among age groups and professions: 10 per cent are under 30 years of age, 30 per cent are over 50 years; the proportion of workers amounts to 20 per cent, while graduates account for 16 per cent. The female proportion is strongest on the municipal level, yet even here it amounts to a mere 25 per cent.[58]

The council members participate in decisions concerning the level of the municipalities they represent, and they put forward the needs and motions expressed by their voters. In general, these decisions are discussed in the four annual meetings of the municipal councils, which are usually held in public. Here, the operative regulations of the elected body are worked out, and motions and decrees are passed. The permanent and ad hoc commissions, however, are also of great importance. On a regional level, they conceive operational schemas for the councils, and development programmes for the district; they also coordinate production between sectors and branches of the economy. On a local level, their main responsibility is to control provisions and to organize social activities for the population.

The assembly of municipal councillors appoints their head (the mayor), his deputies, and the executive (council) committee. One of the most important regulations of the new legislation states that the mayor now presides over the whole municipality, and not only over the executive committee. By emphasizing the responsibility of this body to the council, the law has set a counterbalance to its previous tendency toward making itself independent from the general representative body. On the other hand, the dual responsibility of the executive committees has been retained; they are also subordinate to their superior executive committees, and, in the last resort, to the Council of Ministers. It is along this line that the central administrative regulations are implemented and sectoral objectives are pursued. On the other hand, they cooperate, as organs of the council, in preparing and implementing local decisions. Their new task is to balance the general interests of society with (specific) local interests. The most important institution for the consideration of interests is the communal planning system. Investments in the field of the communal infra-structure and services, in terms of both natural and pecuniary indicators, are projected in the medium-term regional plans. In deciding on the allocation of resources, the regional executive organs are to take into consideration the need and initiative of the municipalities. On the other hand, there is coordination of the regional development plans with the projections and indicators of the national plan. At present, the communes dispose of over 30 per cent of the state budget.[59] In the 5th five-year plan (1976-80), total investments were to amount to 161.5 milliard Forints, an increase of 67 per cent over the preceding period.[60] Most of this was to be made available to the communes for project-linked investments, particularly housing-construction.

The town of Szeged, for example, could dispose of only three per cent of resources itself according to the 1976-80 budgetary plan. Plan proposals of central authorities can in most cases only be endorsed. The town-councils have real decision-making competency only within narrow parameters, i.e. on minor matters.

The commune budget is determined at the regional level. This level also creams off the major part of the state allocation. Between two-thirds and three-quarters of the communes' income derives from the national budget. Yet the municipalities mostly receive nothing. Only 8-10 per cent of funds falls to the municipalities, in which half the population lives.

The financial basis of local autonomy at the lowest communal level is limited to the utilization of its own means. These derive, in essence, from two sources:[61]

— Payments by the inhabitants and local businesses amount to an average of 9.2 per cent of communal incomes. Their proportion in comparison to the years 1971-75 has not altered.

— 'Transferred means' (contributions) are voluntary donations by industrial enterprises and agricultural cooperatives for the construction of apartments, kindergartens, cultural establishments. At 5.8 per cent, their contribution is very modest; yet decrees have already appeared with the aim of reducing them still further.

Thus municipalities which are weak — both in terms of their location and economically — have in general little prospect of revenue and projects within the planning-system. They can, however, take initiatives to secure money for investment from special funds in the state budget. These paths for interest articulation are not yet institutionalized, and hence not documented. Yet the municipalities must use their own initiative for a share of the regional investment-plan, since the planning authorities have to undertake the distribution of funds without any rational system of criteria. There is no list of priorities for the various — yet necessary — improvements to the infra-structure and for the requirements of the municipality, and indeed there cannot meaningfully be one. In the competition between the municipalities for the very limited funds available, the planning authorities can only make use of the general principles issued for reaching decisions, and these principles are directed primarily at concentration. Despite this, it would be improper to conclude that in a hierarchical regulatory system decisions are clearly made by the centre. Goals which appear to be centrally-determined can be the result of interest-integration by lower levels of the organization.[62]

CONCLUSIONS

During the second half of the 1970s, a number of structural problems have become apparent that pose a serious threat to Hungary's 'quiet' social and economic reform; her traditionally non-competitive economy, hit hard by rising world market prices, is unable to satisfy the expectations of a society that, encouraged by the Party itself, wants to recover what it missed during the lean years of Stalinism. The Party has gradually lost the initiative in the reform process and tried to reaffirm its position as a unified and active decision-making force only after long hesitation. The precarious unity of the Party may break apart, as soon as new developmental alternatives appear; moreover, against the background of a chaotic all-out competition for higher budgetary subsidies the implementability of the Party line has become highly questionable.

The Party thus becomes entangled in partly self-created, partly inherited problems that absorb its long-range decision-making capacities. Centralization of Party and state decision-making as an antidote must in the long run lead to a deterioration of the relations between administrators and administered society. The present situation certainly does not encourage the transformation of authoritative decisions into voluntary social action. The authority transfer to the masses, the essential feature of the 'withering away of the state', seems to be excluded by the attitudes of both partners in the bargain; authoritative leadership and passive welfare mentality enter a strong coalition. Thus, Hungary's problem is not the abolition of the state but the preservation of the achievements and the prevention of the withering away of the reform.

NOTES

1. For further details, cf. Charles Gati, 'Hungary: The Dynamics of Revolutionary Transformation', in Charles Gati (ed.), *The Politics of Modernization in Eastern Europe: Testing the Soviet Model* (New York: Praeger, 1975), 51.

2. Ibid., 82.

3. William F. Robinson, *The Pattern of Reform in Hungary: A Political,*

Economic and Cultural Analysis (New York: Praeger, 1973), 5.

4. The importance of creating a social basis for communist power is underlined in András Zsilák, 'The Changes in the Social Structure of Hungary and the Main Question Concerning the Alliance Policy', in Henrik Vass (ed.), *Studies on the History of the Hungarian Working-Class Movement (1867-1966)* (Budapest: Akadémiai Kiadó, 1975), 326.

5. Cf. Iván Szelényi, 'Regional Management and Social Class: The Case of Eastern Europe', *AIAS Informationen*, No. 1/2 (1977), 31.

6. Zsilák, op. cit., 329.

7. Peter A. Toma and Iván Völgyes, *Politics in Hungary* (San Francisco: W.H. Freeman, 1977), 13; *A Szocializmus Útján* (Budapest: Akadémiai, 1970), 325.

8. János Kádár, *Vorwärts auf dem Wege des Sozialismus* (Berlin-Ost: Dietz Verlag, 1967), 348. István Katona, 'Pártunk fö Iranyvonalainak Húszéves Alapelvei', *Társadalmi Szemle (TSz)*, Volume XXXII No. 6 (1977), 13.

9. Katona, op. cit., 14; Kádár, op. cit., 77.

10. *A MSzMP XI Kongresszusa* (Budapest: Kossuth, 1975), 71.

11. János Kádár, 'A szocializmus épitésének néhány magyarországi tapasztalata', *TSz*, Volume XXXII (1977), No. 2, 5.

12. Ibid., 5.

13. Imre Pozsgay, 'Socialist Society and Humanism', *New Hungarian Quarterly (NHQ)*, Volume XIX No. 70 (1978), 23.

14. Valéria Benke, 'A marxista-leninista propaganda és a társadalmi valóság', *TSz*, Volume XXXIV No. 5 (1979), 7.

15. Pozsgay, op. cit., 25.

16. István Katona, op. cit., 13.

17. György Aczél, 'Workdays and Prospects', *NHQ*, Volume XIX No. 71 (1978), 31.

18. Károly Németh, 'Otödik ötéves tervünk — nepgazdaság töretlen fejlödésének programmja', *TSz*, Volume XXX No. 1 (1976), 6.

19. Kádár, 'A szocializmus', 8ff.

20. Toma and Völgyes, *Politics*, 90.

21. Kádár, 'A szocializmus', 4.

22. Robert Hoch, 'Fogyasztáspolitikánk elméleti alapjaihoz', *TSz*, Volume XXXII No. 9 (1977), 14.

23. *Ungarn* 1978 (Budapest: Pannonia Verlag, 1979), 84.

24. Cf. 25 *Kérdés es válasz gazdaság-politikai kérdésekröl. Interjú Nyers Rezsö elvtárssal* (Budapest: Kossuth, 1969), 17.

25. András Tábori, 'Eletszinvonalról, hatékonyságról' and Lajos Héthy, 'A gazdasági munka partirányitása és az érdekegyeztetés', *TSz*, Volume XXXIV No. 2 (1979).

26. István Huszár, 'The Economic Equilibrium and the Foreign Trade Balance', *NHQ*, Volume XX No. 73 (1979), 18.

27. 'A MSzMP Központi Bizottságágnak irányelvei a párt XII kongresszusára', *Népszabadság*, 9 December 1979.

28. Toma and Völgyes, *Politics*, 22.

29. 'A MSzMP Központi Bizottsagának irányelvei', loc. cit.

30. *A MszMp XI Kongresszusa*, op. cit., 7.

31. Ibid., 7.

32. Antal Böhm and László Pál, 'A bejáró munkások társadalmipolitikai magatartása', *TSz*, Volume XXXIV No. 10 (1979).

33. Calculated from data in *A MSzMP XI Kongresszusa*, loc. cit.

34. *A MSzMP Kongresszusa,* op. cit., 7

35. Cf. Toma and Völgyes, *Politics,* 142.

36. This was admitted to the authors during an interview with a member of the parliamentary bureaucracy. The original statement was: 'One *Ludas Matyi* (a satirical magazine) is better than three Presidential Councils'.

37. RAD Background Report/36 (Hungary, 10 February 1976).

38. *Pest Megei Hirlap,* 6 August 1976.

39. Toma and Völgyes, *Politics,* 35.

40. Iván Szelényi, 'Regional Management and Social Class: The Case of Eastern Europe II', *AIAS Information,* 1977, No. 3/4, 121 ff; Roland J. Fuchs and George J. Demko, 'Commuting in the USSR and Eastern Europe. Causes, Characteristics and Consequences', *East European Quarterly,* Volume XI No. 4 (1977), 463 ff.

41. Szelényi, op. cit., 130.

42. Data in Konrád and Szelényi, 'Social Conflicts of Underorganizations: The Hungarian Case', in Mark G. Field (ed.), *Social Consequences of Modernization in Communist Societies* (London and Baltimore: Johns Hopkins University Press, 1976), 162ff.

43. Szelényi, op. cit., 129.

44. Mód Aladárné, 'Bejáró életmód-cél és valóság', *TSz,* Volume XXXIII, No. 6 (1978), 67 ff; *Népszabadság,* 10 May 1979.

45. Cf. e.g. Huszár, op. cit., 17.

46. *Magyar Nemzet,* 26 April 1977.

47. Akos Balassa, 'A vállalati kozéptávu tervezés eredményei es tanulságai', *TSz,* Volume XXXII No. 2 (1977).

48. György Antalffy, 'Recent Traits in the Development of State and Law in the Light of the Amendment of the Constitution of the Hungarian People's Republic', *Hungarian Law Review,* No. 1 (1975), 7.

49. Peter Schmidt, 'A bürokratizums forrásai az államigazgatásban', *TSz,* Volume XXXIV No. 2 (1979), 66.

50. Ibid., 68.

51. 'A MSzMP Központi Bizottságagnak irányelvei', loc. cit.

52. Toma and Völgyes, *Politics,* 61.

53. Mihály Bihari, 'A döntési mechanizmus szervezeti, hatalmi és érdekkörnyezete', *TSz,* Volume XXXIV No. 3 (1979), 111.

54. József Balogh, 'A Vállalatgazdasági és politikai funktióinak kapscolata', *TSz,* Volume XXXII No. 12 (1977), 69.

55. Ibid., 69.

56. Miklós Vass, 'Ismerik-e a dolgozók a demokratikus jogokat', *TSz,* Volume XXXIII No. 2 (1978), 78.

57. Gizella Sóvári, *A Tanácsok Gazdálkodása* (Budapest: Kossuth, 1974), 20.

58. Ibid., 16.

Age structure of the Hungarian population:

below 15 years	—	20.5%
15-39 years	—	37.0%
40-59 years	—	24.3%
over 60 years	—	18.2%

Women: 51.4%
University graduates: 5.1%

Source: *Magyar Statisztikai Zsebkönyv* (Budapest: Közgazdasági és Fogi, 1979); *Ungarn 78,* op. cit.

59. 'A tanácstörvény a gyakorlatban. Kerekasztal-beszélgetés a szerkesztoségben', *TSz*, Volume XXIII No. 8/9 (1978), 81.

60. Ferenc Biró, 'A tanácsi tervezö munka fontosabb tapasztalatai', *TSz*, Volume XXXII No. 7/8 (1977), 52.

61. Ibid., and Gábor Vági, 'Versengés a tervezésért. Feltételezésk a helyi-teruleti érdekek érvényestésének társaldalmi mechanizmusairól', *Valóság*, No. 3 (1979).

62. Gábor Vági, op. cit., 57-58.

8 Indochina — Militarization of the State

Dennis Duncanson
University of Kent at Canterbury, UK

INTRODUCTION

Relations between the Communist Party and the state, or states, in Indochina have undergone no definite break between the historical phases of revolution and of government: except for its first fifteen formative years, the Indochinese Communist Party (ICP) has been continuously a revolutionary party and a party-in-power at the same time. As a result, public administration has been subject all the time to the imperatives of allocating resources — and of cutting a figure in the wider world — in ways that facilitated the next extension of the Party's political dominion.

Notwithstanding a vociferous parade of nationalism from time to time in quest of temporary allies, the ICP, although among the earliest advocates of what today we call 'Eurocommunism', has never been a national Party but has always worked towards the establishment of a mini-USSR in Indochina — a plurality of 'autonomous' national States with one Marxist-Leninist Party and Politburo paramount over all. The leaders' ambition is not the only reason for balancing plurality of states with unity of Politburo. Decolonized Indochina does not fit easily into the nation-state system of the post-1945 age: in addition to numerous hill tribes straddling all the frontiers of the region, including that with China, there have been six modern states in the Indochinese plains, each of which can advance historical precedents for retaining its independence: two in Vietnam (disunited until 1804), one in Cambodia, and three in Laos, united for the first time by France in 1941-46. The Vietnamese Emperor (of 'Dai Nam') claimed at various times to be suzerain over all the others, and the French colonial administration, superseding that suzerainty, aimed, whilst respecting the native monarchies in their traditional fields of government, to create a single super-state for the Union Indochinoise in new departments entrusted with modernization and development; at the moment of colonial emancipation, Paris still envisaged the region remaining a federation in which this framework would be preserved by the three individually sovereign Etats Associés de l'Indochine. During the first Indochina war (1946-54), the Vietnamese communists demanded the right of succession to French suzerainty by virtue of their having taken up arms in 1946 in the name of independence; at their 2nd Party Congress in 1951, they spoke of Lao and Khmer branches of 'the Party' that did not exist and at the Geneva Conference in 1954 made a bid for seats for two representatives of 'resistance governments' which they claimed they had themselves constituted 'somewhere' in Laos and Cambodia in opposition to the constitutional monarchies France had gradually devolved power to.

After the outbreak of the Cambodian-Vietnamese war in 1978, Hanoi spokesmen declared that they had put aside for good their fifty-year old plans for an Indochina Federation; yet history shows that Vietnam is difficult to hold together in a single state unless its perennial rebels are prevented from intriguing with the rulers of Cambodia and Laos, so that Hanoi's declared intentions, if genuine, would have been imprudent. However, the military occupation of Laos and Cambodia by the People's Army of Vietnam, the replacement of Pol Pot by one of his subordinates (Heng Samrin) amenable to the Hanoi Politburo, the signing of a tripartite network of 'special-relationship' treaties, the routing of the external trade of Laos and Cambodia (such as it is) through Vietnam, the establishment of administrative links between provinces on either side of the frontiers, and the resettlement of Vietnamese peasants in districts of Laos ceded under one of the treaties, as well as in districts of Cambodia abandoned by their frightened inhabitants, now refugees, all point to revival of imperial and colonial policy in the Marxist-Leninist constitutional guise exemplified by Party-state relations in the USSR. At one time, there were Western analysts who argued, from the cultural divide between a Vietnam historically part of the Chinese world and a Laos and Cambodia drawing their civilization from India, that political fusion was out of the question. Yet, reinforced by modern communications, Marxism-Leninism stands a good chance of triumphing over differences in traditional political culture and taking the political suzerainty ('hegemony') of imperial and colonial times into a tighter association of three states, whose autonomy is temporary if not literally 'withering', under one Politburo.

In domestic administration, the Indochinese communists have had before them all the time both the Russian and the Chinese models for Party-state relations, the latter of which is rooted in Leninism anyway. In the 1930s, the Party leadership was directed by the Comintern, and the August Revolution closely imitated the October Revolution; but, since those days, Maoist 'people's war' has been the chief instrument of revolution, whereas Stalinist examples have guided methods of government. The Cambodian communists, however, till overthrown by the Vietnamese invasion, followed the Maoist example both in their fighting and in their dictatorship, which amounted to a *reductio ad crudelissimum* of the Great Proletarian Cultural Revolution. It is no quest for an ideal form of government that has motivated recent policies in Indochina: 'progressive socialist revolution' has taken precedence, especially in Vietnam, over recovery from the effects of civil war, notwithstanding the decline in production which the Politburo expected would result from it.[1]

THE PARTY

Indochinese Parties and Fronts

The ICP was founded by Ho-chi-Minh in 1930 as a section of the Comintern, of which he was an employee; he remained a *sovyetnik* (adviser) to it, not a member of it, on through the dissolution of the Comintern, until he took over the Secretary-Generalship in 1956. Until shortly before that date, the Party had no headquarters or lists of members, so that different spokesmen gave inconsistent figures for their number; Moscow had no compunction about dispatching new secretaries from time to time with instructions to inaugurate changes of policy by whoever the leaders on the spot might be, irrespective of the existence or otherwise of a mass membership. During its first quarter century of history, it is hard to determine at times what the Party consisted of, and in 1945 it was declared dissolved, even though the same stream of directives to cadres continued to emanate from it.[2] 'The Party' — referred to in Vietnam from 1945 to 1951 and in Cambodia from 1975 to 1977 as 'the Organization' — has usually been the named source of authority when the communists were the government; but in contexts of revolutionary activity, its place has been taken by Fronts, the other constituents of which have in the main been individuals the Party designated to speak as representatives of sectional, sectarian or interest groups, including at times 'the Catholic community'.[3] For long periods, only the Fronts have featured in publicity — a Democratic Union in the 1930s, the Vietnamese Revolutionary League (*Viet Minh*) in the 1940s, the United Popular Front of Vietnam (*Lien Viet,* which included Laotians as well as Chinese or Vietnamese 'representatives' of Cambodia) in the 1950s, and the Fatherland Front (North Vietnam) and National Liberation Front (South Vietnam) in the 1960s. Longest-lived of the Fronts was the Lao Patriotic Front (*Neo Lao Hak-xat* alias *Pathet Lao*), started in 1945 by Vietnamese dressed as Lao[4] and used as a cover for successive campaigns on Laotian soil by the Vietnamese People's Army; it set a precedent for the Vietnamese conquest of Cambodia at New Year 1979 in the name of a Cambodian Patriotic Front. Each of the Fronts purported to entail CP power-sharing, but, after its demise, has been acknowledged to have been the Party alone in disguise; both the Party and its Fronts were notional rather than 'objective' political entities and evidently consisted, in the revolutionary phase — in North Vietnam till 1954, in the rest of Indochina till 1975 — of a small number of activist cadres without organized rank-and-file.

Similar insubstantiality marks the record of the two non-Marxist parties which in Vietnam are supposed to round off the National Liberation Front (NLF) and the Fatherland Front, the second of which was said to have absorbed the first by 'democratic-centralist' decision in 1978: the Democratic Party and the Socialist Party. Both were started by leaders of the ICP (in 1944 and 1946 respectively), the former 'to help the bourgeoisie participate in the struggle for . . . the policies of the working class and the Workers' Party', the latter 'to unite intellectuals in close association and tight unity with the Workers' Party'.[5] The chief founder of the Democratic Party, Hoang-minh-Giam, has, according to his official biography, long been Deputy Secretary-General of the Socialist Party.[6] These arrangements reflect the theory of class parties; only proletarians ought to be members of the Communist Party, whereas middle and intellectual classes should have their own parties. Thus, within the NLF, the Chairman, Huynh-tan-Phat, being a middle-aged builder (sometimes 'architect'), was said to be a member of the Democratic Party, while the first Secretary-General, Nguyen-van-Hieu, being younger and a lawyer, was said to be Secretary-General of the Socialist Party. In fact, not above half a dozen names ever seem to have been mentioned in print as members of either party, North or South. The only activities of the two parties reported in the newspapers have been the passing of resolutions in support of CP initiatives — resolutions at the 3rd Party Congress approving the new campaign of people's war in South Vietnam, the 1960 Constitution and 1978 draft constitution, some of the state plans for closer social control, and the 'bourgeois' Democratic Party endorsing the ICP's land reform designed 'to crush the bourgeoisie'.[7] In between, for years on end, they seem to have been forgotten altogether.

A third category of subordinate Front comprises three post-1960 People's (Revolutionary) Parties (PRPs) in South Vietnam, Cambodia and Laos. There was no suggestion that communists in South Vietnam were members of any party but the ICP until the 'founding' of the NLF; but after 1960, because the intention was that the Front should appear to be conducting its revolution independently of the government in Hanoi, the ICP could not play the indispensable role of 'vanguard' in it; and so the PRP was said to have been 'founded' in 1962 expressly for the purpose. As long as the war continued, no distinction was drawn between the cadres of the PRP and those of the NLF, or between either and the commanders of guerrilla units, whose rank-and-file were the only 'masses' associated with the PRP. After the fall of Saigon, no bones were made about it — the PRP had had no existence separate from the ICP in Hanoi: Comrade Pham Hung, member of the Hanoi Politburo, revealed himself as both Secretary-General of the PRP and Secretary of the Hanoi party's Centre Office for South Vietnam in charge of the political direction of the fighting from 1960 to 1975.[8] Thenceforward, the identity of the two parties was taken for

granted — 'two States in Vietnam but only one Party' was the common phrase — and the former 'Chairman' of the putative PRP was
appointed a member of the Hanoi Politburo, thus joining his
Secretary-General.

The People's (literally 'proletarian') Parties of Laos (*Phak
Pasason*) and of Cambodia (*Phak Pracheachon*) have misleadingly
appeared to act more independently of Hanoi because instructed,
in pursuance of New-Democracy (or National-Front) coalition, to
put up candidates for elections and accept ministerial office in the
two Royal governments while these were still in being. In Laos, the
'parliamentary road' was followed under the terms of the two
Geneva Agreements of 1954 and 1962, and communist candidates
for the National Assembly as well as ministers who took portfolios
in the Royal Government did so in the name of the Patriotic Front.
In Cambodia, the People's Party acted openly, in direct bargaining
with Prince Sihanouk who, with his very emphatic protestations of
cold-war neutralism, was deemed specially manoeuvrable into the
ICP orbit by coalition methods, his whole government being ex-
ploitable itself as a kind of front. Again, neither 'national CP' had
a mass membership, headquarters, constitution, party cards or
subscriptions: the function of both was diplomatic, as part of the
front apparatus rather than of the command structure between the
ICP and either guerrillas or masses — that being provided for by
Vietnamese communists and People's Army officers. The
Pasason/Pracheachon were working not merely with a view to
establishing communist rule in their two countries but, in a shorter
term, with a view to securing the two Royal governments' tolera-
tion of the Ho-chi-Minh Trail in Laos and, in Cambodia, of People's Army bases bordering Cochinchina — as well as transport in
Cambodian lorries of Russian and Chinese munitions required by
the Party in South Vietnam. When Sihanouk was deposed in 1970
and the Vietnamese communists had to fight for their positions in
Cambodia, 'People's Party' was dropped again, and they adopted
the designation National United Front to indicate the Cambodian
guerrillas they trained, equipped and fought alongside until the fall
of Phnom Penh in 1975.[9]

Theory of the Party

Not until after taking power, when the need for 'national fronts' of 'temporary allies' was at an end, did the communists in any of the Indochina countries declare themselves for what they were. The ICP named itself the 'Vietnam Workers' Party' in 1951 and the 'Vietnam Communist Party' in 1976, whilst the Khmer People's Party similarly became a Communist Party in 1977; the Lao Party, one step behind, 'emerged' from the Patriotic Front as the Lao PRP (not yet CP) in 1976. The change in each case was a stage on the road from the national democratic revolution through proletarian dictatorship and socialism to communism. The Vietnamese held a 4th Party Congress at the end of 1976 by way of *rite de passage* — of special interest because it really did take place, as did the 3rd in 1960, at which the chief Party historian told participants that congresses the Party claimed it had held in the past had not necessarily met at all but, 'in accordance with Marxist-Leninist principles', *counted* as having been held.[10] We always knew that the 1st (1935), if it did take place, had only seven comrades present, and that the credibility of the 2nd (1951), 'somewhere in the jungle', was no greater; it was the communiqués for the latter, distributed to the outside world by the New China News Agency, which adopted the first Party statute and laid down the framework of the intended communist state constitution for post-colonial Indochina.

Today, in Vietnam, the Party has developed into a mass party with a million and a half members who become so, as in other communist parties in power, by invitation, probation and training. The suspect 2nd, the 3rd and the recent 4th Congress have all been marked by purges of 'temporary allies' useful in the previous phase of the struggle and by the inauguration of a new campaign of 'Party-building' with individuals more promising in the next phase. The present statute goes back to the 3rd Congress and organizes the membership, on principles of democratic centralism, into workplace, collective, and territorial branches at village, district, and province echelons; officials are elected collegiately at each echelon. At the top is a Central Committee of a hundred (more than doubled at the 4th Congress) which meets in the customary annual or more frequent serially-numbered 'plenums' to ratify political decisons of major import. But the brain of the Party is the Politburo, augmented at the 4th Congress from eleven to fourteen members (plus three alternates). First brought together in 1945, at the time the Party was 'dissolved', the oligarchy has remained almost unaltered, except for deaths, for thirty years, and it is from it that all authority is derived. That authority is transmitted both through the hierarchy of branches and down the chain of command of the Army. Relations between Party and Army are formally like those in the USSR — that is, the Army is controlled by political commissars who share responsibility with field officers. Not only the commissars, but all officers and NCOs are Party members; the commissars probably constitute a KGB element and talk to the Politburo direct, whereas Party branches in the Army limit themselves to troop indoctrination. Under conditions of revolution, Party, Fronts and guerrillas have been all the same men; under conditions of government too, the Army — conventional units, not guerrillas — has sometimes overridden state organs and exercised direct authority in the name of the Party: conduct of the land reform in North Vietnam in 1955-56 was one example, discharge of police duties in Hanoi from time to time another, the management of camps for 'remoulding through labour' (in foreign publicity, 're-education') and the conduct of political courts with unlimited powers of punishment a third and fourth.

As in South Vietnam, so in Laos and Cambodia, during the revolutionary wars the Army line of communications provided the Party's channel for control over the mobilizable masses, and its officers — the majority Vietnamese — were the 'cadres'. Relations between the nominal leaders of the Lao PRP and the Hanoi Politburo are obscure: in 1977, on the eve of the signing of the three State treaties with the SRV, Radio Vientiane named five ministers as 'members of the PRP Politburo', one of them being Prince Souphanouvong; when the Royal Government was negotiating under international pressure the terms for the last coalition preceding the communists' takeover of Laos, Souphanouvong, spokesman for 'the Patriotic Forces', had refused to divulge to his brother, Prime Minister Prince Souvanna Phouma, the identity of the political body he was instructed by and was committing for the future, the inference being that it was the Politburo in Hanoi.[11] The prevarication continued until the election which set up the People's Democratic Republic of Laos: voting was then compulsory, the candidates, all communist-sponsored, kept out of sight, and they used code names on the ballot papers, only unmasking after the event.[12] Given the dependence of its State and Army on Hanoi, the putative Laotian Politburo cannot be expected to enjoy — or even to desire — greater freedom of action than do many East European Politburos.

The Comintern, when Ho-chi-Minh was first active, had been
unable to subvert young Cambodians in France, and little headway
was made by the Vietnamese communists with Cambodian
recruiting until after the Cambodian war began in 1970 and they
could send 'armed propagandists' into the villages: the handful of
members of the 1951 Pracheachon were Chams, Malays, Chinese,
Vietnamese or even tribesmen brought in from Laos by the People's Army,[13] and when the latter tried to seize Phnom Penh after
the fall of Sihanouk in 1970, they could muster fewer than a hundred Cambodians for Front purposes.[14] Pol Pot's strength was
built up for him by the People's Army after 1970 and, apart from
Vietnamese troops, consisted exclusively of guerrilla forces these
had trained and armed, so that there is perhaps a grain of truth in
his assertion, once in power, that the 'Phak Komunis Kampuchea'
dated, not from the founding of the Pracheachon, but from his
assumption of the Secretary-Generalship within it in 1960.[15] Like
him, the half dozen other members of his faction were 'ideological
communists' from post-graduate courses in the University of Paris
in the 1950s (three of them hold the *doctorat d'université*) who had
their own ambitions, not disciplined recruits of the international
movement in the Comintern tradition. When Vietnamese combat
formations left Cambodia to man the final offensive against
Saigon, leaving behind only artillery and other technical services,
Pol Pot and his handful of close associates were left with a
monopoly of control over their country and, with help from the
Chinese People's Republic (CPR) in foreign exchange and munitions, were able to adopt an attitude of hostility towards their
former patrons, who they no doubt assumed would not dare accept the challenge.[16] The Organization or Party comprised only the
fighting force of untrained, illiterate adolescents.[17]

THE STATE

Theory of the State — Cambodia and Laos

The State is quickly disposed of in the context of Cambodia: there
was none under Pol Pot, and at the time of writing Vietnamese
plans for administration are not foreseeable. The Party, in 1975,

stood in the usual need of a 'repressive apparatus of proletarian dictatorship' with which to overawe opposition, but made use of its untrained adolescents to set about the task in the most direct way possible — by slaughter of the entire civil service and professional class and of anybody who answered back (two and a half million, or one in three of the population, according to Radio Hanoi on the eve of Vietnamese intervention) and by evacuation of the towns, abolition of all institutions (schools, pagodas and rural hospitals) as well as of money and private property; the whole achievement of modernization under colonial and post-colonial rule was taken apart, families were split up, and the survivors divided the seasons of the year between hand tillage of the ricefields and the digging of a huge network of new irrigation canals. A State constitution was published on 6 January 1976 over Radio Phnom Penh — there no longer being printing presses at work in the country — and issued as a book, perhaps from dictation, by Cambodians in Paris. It made no mention of Marxism-Leninism and was vague about administrative structure (president and vice-presidents, elected People's Assembly, and 'administrators to execute laws and lines laid down'); it concentrated on rationalizing the social transformations of collectivized living, which implied 'collective mastery of the means of production' (a term made much of by the Vietnamese too); rural authority was exercised by 'people's organs', while 'state power' was entrusted to 'the Revolutionary Army'. One of the Yugoslav Party delegations invited to Phnom Penh inquired into the central government and found that what purported to be ministries were all but empty offices; the three or four individuals to be found in any of them spent their time growing vegetables in the park and generally undergoing ceaseless 'remoulding through labour'.[18] The true explanation of this unique, but recognizably Marxist-Leninist, system, lacking both party and state, probably has nothing to do with ideas but lies in the opportunities and constraints of the moment; when jointly conspiring to put the ex-Parisian *cénacle* of Khieu Samphan and Pol Pot nominally in power, Peking seems to have expected Khmer public servants to follow Sihanouk blindly into the Chinese fold and to be available to go on running the administration, Hanoi to have expected to be able to put in its own cadres — whereas in fact other hands frustrated both programmes.

Comparable radicalism has not attended the establishment of the Lao Democratic People's Republic (LDPR). The northeastern provinces of Laos have been under Vietnamese Army occupation for a quarter of a century now; the inhabitants are mostly tribal minorities, and while the northern districts are widely believed to have been administered by Chinese political agents and Liberation Army from about 1958 to 1975 — possibly until eviction of Chinese 'technical assistants' in March 1979 — the others were mobilized ad hoc to service the supply needs of the Vietnamese forces.[19] Although there was ostensibly a communist capital at Sam Neua, it did not pretend to be a *State* capital and was reputed to be cramped into limestone caves. Only since the takeover of the ethnically-Lao plains provinces has a formal State apparatus been alluded to — ministries and a People's Assembly at the centre — scheduled to be removed ultimately away from the bamboo curtain and nearer to Hanoi in the tribal lands, whither the deposed king has been carried off. Village affairs are evidently managed by a cadre (unspecialized as to Party, Front or Army command) presiding over an executive people's (or sometimes, 'revolutionary' or 'administrative') committee; but there is no evidence as to actual practice.

So long as the capital remains at Vientiane, the main function of the ministries will probably continue to be the reception of foreign aid and portrayal abroad of an independent Lao State; in this respect, Souphanouvong and Kaysone Phomvihan are communist heirs to the Royal Laotian seat in the UN, as Khieu Samphan and Pol Pot were to the Republican Cambodian seat at a time when, ironically, communist Vietnam had to negotiate for an entirely new 'national seat'. The ascertainable local duties of the state administration in the LDPR, such as it is, are the conversion of what remains of the 're-education' camps housing former Lao bureaucracy and bourgeoisie into state farms in the upland country, the break-up and resettlement of slash-and-burn minorities, and attempts to collectivize the hundreds of thousands of Lao smallholdings in the plains.

Theory of the State — Vietnam

In contrast to the unsophistication of the smaller Indochina States, the Socialist Republic of Vietnam, (SRV), like the Democratic Republic (DRV) that preceded it, is thoroughly orthodox by Stalinist standards. Voluminous explanations of lines for Party relations with the State and the masses have been published in Hanoi since 1954, the most important among them attributed to Le

Duan, successor to Ho-chi-Minh as Secretary-General of the Party though not as Chairman of the State; the latter office is currently filled by an obscure sailor, Ton-duc-Thang, veteran of the French mutiny in the Black Sea. That 'the party cannot slacken its leadership over government organs, but neither can it charge itself with government work' has, over the years, been a continual refrain; the judiciary is no more than a department of the government, charged like it with ensuring that the Party line is adhered to by the masses,[20] the law itself providing 'guides not to be followed too slavishly'.[21] In practice, the State is a scapegoat, not only legitimating but also taking the blame for unpopular lines.

The DRV approved its first constitution in November 1946 — one that was bourgeois-democratic in the image of the regime it tried to convey and, in order that the Party should not have to hold a general election, never went into effect;[22] 'a gang of traitors' (that is, non-Marxist temporary allies) 'having taken part in the drafting, it lacked a progressive character', the masses were told.[23] In 1958, four years after the takeover of North Vietnam, the Party judged the time come 'to strengthen dictatorship, enlarge and centralize democracy, and fortify the machinery of the State under the leadership of the Party'.[24] The resulting 'socialist' constitution went into effect in 1960. Under it, supreme power was vested in the people, but through a hierarchy of councils, organized by democratic centralism 'under the leadership of the local Party Committee' at all levels and culminating in a National Assembly, all of whose powers were exercised by a Standing Committee (as under Stalin); the Assembly was the sole interpreter of the laws (not the courts). Allocation of powers between Chairman of the Republic,[25] Council of Ministers, ministers and lower councils was left to be guessed by the reader; as late as 1967, administrative responsibilities and procedures had not been worked out for the territorial, as distinct from the departmental, administration.[26]

To voice opposition to either democratic centralism or unification of South Vietnam with North was a treasonable offence. The right of national capitalists to own private means of production was safeguarded 'temporarily' as a Leninist New Economic Policy measure. It was an offence to exercise democratic freedoms against the interest of the State, since, Ho-chi-Minh explained, 'under a socialist regime, rights of individuals dissolve into those of the collectivity'.[27] Labour discipline became a constitutional duty, as did military service, without distinction of sex. No limits were set on the powers of authorities at lower levels of the administration, since they must act solely as executives of Party lines. Public order was entrusted to rural collectives or urban 'neighbourhood blocks'; both had control by democratic centralism of all social services and provided a means for families to watch over one another under a revival of the imperial system of China, Japan and Vietnam known as *pao chia/bao giap*.[28] Similarly, rural collectives and urban blocks alike enforced the *jus receptum* of corvée.

At every echelon, People's Councils were to be elected by councils below them from among candidates chosen by the council above, but had the power to dismiss any of the councils which had elected them. Procedure for elections for the National Assembly in 1960 allocated one in seven of the seats to ethnic minorities, the remainder to ten-member constituencies at the rate of one to 50,000 rural inhabitants, one to between 10,000 and 30,000 urban inhabitants, on Russian and Chinese principles; candidates had to have the approval of the Fatherland Front acting under the supervision of the Central Committee of the Communist Party, and voting was either at workplaces or by small districts of 500 to 2500 voters, the counting of ballots being carried out on the spot by 'the cells' — presumably of the Party.[30] At the 1964 election, the Fatherland Front selected candidates from the Communist Party and the Socialist and Democratic Parties on a class basis, exclusively from among persons who had 'fought' for unification in the civil war and were known to be loyal to Socialism; it then 'told the people which ones it was their duty to vote for'. Balloting was by striking out one in four or five names on each list, and, in addition to the 336 thus elected, 89 extra candidates were returned 'unopposed', having been designated by the Fatherland Front to carry on from the previous Assembly as spokesmen *in partibus infidelium* for the South.[31] Meetings of the 1964 Assembly grew rarer and shorter (none after 1968), until, in 1971, another election was held; this time, to support the fiction of a separate Communist government in South Vietnam,[32] membership was confined to the putative representatives of the North elected in 1964, who were now declared re-elected in a body, with 54 new names. Over the years, however, voting by this system for People's Councils as well had become discredited, and the Front was constrained to explain to the electors that 'even in a democracy, there has to be leadership, and candidates must have the unanimous approval of the people before they stand' — a unanimity of which the Front (i.e. Party) was best judge.[33]

This deliberate imitation of the USSR in the state structure of the pre-1975 DRV was paralleled in many details of practical administration, especially in public finance and accounting (what resources are profit, what investment, what tax, etc.) The development of state forms, even if we include the pre-1954 period, when ministries and departments of the DRV 'in the jungle' had no more substance than the Provisional Revolutionary Government of the Republic of South Vietnam was to have from 1969 to 1975, took place *pari passu* with the adoption of Stalinist models for the structure of the new Chinese People's Republic; consequently, both when they relied on Soviet advisers directly and when they relied on Chinese ones (with an occasional nod, as in the Party statute, to 'Marxism-Leninism co-ordinated with Mao Tsê-tung's revolutionary ideas'), the Vietnamese communists adopted the same procedures. Imitation of common Russian and Chinese methods for establishing social control was reflected in the brutal land reform and in assimilation of minorities by socialist transformation; organization of the armed forces, militia and police also followed common Russian and Chinese lines, as did the neglect of civil and commercial law (mostly rendered superfluous by abolition of private property) and assertion by the courts of 'class justice' in criminal law — the Vietnamese procuratorates going so far as to compete with other government departments for challenge cups in State 'emulation' campaigns.[34]

In the event, the management of a specialized bureaucracy — for all the sophistication of the Vietnamese by comparison with the Laotians and Cambodians — overtaxed their capacities, as it did those of the Chinese: in both countries in the same year, 1960, central statistics ceased to be published (had probably never been collected), Russian advisers became disillusioned, and lists of names of ministers, vice-ministers and directors of departments were shown to be little more than honorifics. Threads of influence on the Vietnamese in this period are all the harder to unravel because the truth was that Khrushchev, for all Mao Tsê-tung's condemnation of him for 'bureaucratism', had embarked on a decentralization of control whose purpose was very like Mao's own; but the Vietnamese Party's need at this time, derived from the civil war, was to move society and economy away from a guerrilla mentality, and it set in train a gradual alienation from Chinese ways in favour of deepening sympathy with the Russians. The Politburo's remedies for what was quite simply 'underdevelopment' were therefore not pressed to the extremes of the Great Leap Forward or the Cultural Revolution, but a resemblance to Chinese ideas is traceable in decentralization of social services to the collectives and in the entrusting of authority, not only for defence of the regime and maintenance of law and order, but for political supervision of State activities at a distance from the capital, to the Army; only the rationalization was different in Vietnam — permanent warfare instead of permanent revolution (tacitly, external aggression instead of internal class struggle). No less similar than the Party's remedies for the problems was the masses' passive resistance to the collectivized way of life pressed on them for reasons of social control at whatever cost to productivity;[35] disappointed in hopes that socialist transformation was going to generate the New Man, the Party had to acquiesce in private plots as a lesser evil than disintegration of collectives.[36]

Party and State in the Socialist Republic of Vietnam

Less has been given away in the Party press about public administration since the absorption of the South in 1975 than in the heyday of Stalinism from 1955 to 1965; for example, nothing was said about the compilation of an electoral register or procedure for nominating candidates for the general election in April 1976, which preceded the act of union on 1 July, and therefore the institution of any body with powers to pass an electoral law. A new Council of Ministers (with thirty nine members) was appointed, although only six of them hailed from the South; many names of junior officials have come to light in the South in connection with tasks such as rationing food and supplies, control of the education system and the medical services, and other needs arising from the political change, but there is no clue how they may relate to the new pan-Vietnamese ministries far away in Hanoi. Deurbanization and the drafting of undesirables ('unemployed') to 'new economic areas' (= 'virgin lands'), as reported many times in *Liberated Saigon,* has not been a duty of the State but of the Party itself acting directly and employing the Komsomols to do the work of preparing rough housing and rounding up and accompanying the families designated by Party branches. When all private commerce was declared unlawful in Saigon-Cholon in March 1978 and all existing stocks of goods had to be declared to the authorities (the action which set off the exodus of Chinese), again it was the Komsomols who went around making the inventories and putting seals on warehouses[37] — in derogation, one might have thought, from Le Duan's clear distinction between spheres of Party and of State authority. Ministries may have been relegated to the industrial sector and to a technical, largely planning and advisory, role in other sectors, while contact with the masses is maintained, especially in the rural areas, by the security forces — People's Army, militia, Komsomols or police. It is likely that there is still uncertainty, informality and arbitrariness in relations between departments, and much overlapping between rivals for control — likely not least because of the frequent admissions of corruption among both military and civilian cadres.[38]

A new constitution for united Vietnam has been under discussion in Party branches and at workplaces. Under its general principles, 'the Party leads, the people exercise collective ownership, and the state manages'; it is not only the means of production that are owned collectively, but the individual's labour as well, in order that it can be managed in the interests of the whole nation by the state, which in so doing translates the Party's will into law.[39] Collective ownership is in fact identical with state ownership under Party leadership.[40] The state is democratic, but democracy is emphatically collective and exercised for the people vicariously by the Party; the people's wishes are known by inference from what the Party judges to be 'political requirements'.[41] Though disappointing in its economic results, socialist transformation through strict adherence to Party lines even in the family circle, as well as through collectivization of the means of production, has to be pressed on with in the interests of social control.[42] The Party contrives to move with an appearance of meticulous legality; for example, union of South Vietnam with North was hurried in 1976, in spite of its known unpopularity[43] and of undertakings in the Paris Agreement to proceed 'gradually' (now declared 'irrelevant');[44] only after unification did mobilization of Southern manpower for the army (against their wish) commence,[45] in anticipation of armed struggle against the Cambodian communists.

The long programme of deurbanization the Party has in mind affects not only the newly-conquered Southerners, but some four million from the whole country (one in ten of the population). The new latifundia are being organized, not as collective but as state farms.[46] In fact, the state farm is considered the ideal pattern for agriculture in the future, largely in order to make the best use of manpower: the existing hamlet and village settlement will be liable to reorganization throughout Vietnam and dwellings brought together on infertile land, releasing the maximum of fertile land for tillage.[47] Old communities will be broken up, families recombined according to their capacity for work in new ones planned to facilitate the mustering of labour by whole administrative districts at a time; this project for regimentation and proletarianization of the peasantry is all to be entrusted to the army to carry out, not excluding contingent civil administrative reforms.[48]

CONCLUSIONS

It therefore appears that the People's Army has become the principal executive for the Party's authority throughout the Socialist Republic as much as for the exercise of power over the Laotians and Cambodians, and that the Stalinist bureaucracy which characterized the preceding Democratic Republic has suffered extensive atrophy. What has happened can be accounted for in a variety of ways, all of which contain elements of truth; none of them corresponds to the 'withering away of the state' forecast by Engels — the withering of the *proletarian* state as a consequence of socialist transformation. Under the DRV, the Party acknowledged the failure of socialist transformation to change mass conduct and perfect the New Socialist Man, capable only of spontaneous communist behaviour. In part, the inappropriateness of Engels' prediction arises from his ignorance of the future complexity of public administration — of the necessity for regulation of new kinds of social action resulting from human technical inventiveness reaching far beyond the 'means of production' that cramped his vision. The decline of the state in Indochina — after a period of steady growth under colonial rule and after colonial emancipation in response to technical, developmental, needs — has been functional: state bureaucracy, legal restraints on rulers, individual justice, and rigid rules for accountability in public finance all constricted the freedom of action of the Politburo, however subservient the bureaucrats might be. In Cambodia, the Party, having abolished the 'bourgeois' state and the Buddhist church by killing the bureaucrats and bonzes, had no cadres capable of manning a 'proletarian' state: it abandoned every responsibility of modern government and contented itself with holding the masses down by forced labour and through fear of juvenile gun-toters. In Laos, because the Royal government had only been administering a small if populous area of the country and offered no fight at the end, the transition to a proletarian state could be relatively gentler; however, 'the Laotians lack the level of culture and capacity for management that are necessary' even to make a Stalinist state work,[49] and there are few signs of public administration outside the two capital cities beyond action by the army — by a disciplined army with formal command structure. In Vietnam, public accounts evidently are kept, a few statistics are published again, laws are promulgated, and courts are convened from time to time, if only for political campaigns as in China. But in the remoter rural areas, it is the army which alone represents authority.

As was said at the beginning, the ICP has conducted revolution and government through much of its history simultaneously, using the latter primarily to mobilize resources for the former; the army was the Politburo's principal, if not sole, agent in the former aspect, so that strong reasons (reasons of Party, not 'national', interest) would be required for relinquishing it after victory. Political risks are incurred by demobilization even in conditions of peace; but the Party's social control was at all times uncertain in parts of North Vietnam to the same degree as today in the South. Conversely, the possession of a strong army, expanded after 1964, retrained and equipped after 1968 for the conquest of South Vietnam, and kept under arms for social control, was a tempting instrument for extending the Party's domain into Laos and Cambodia even if the Politburo had not already nourished ambitions in those lands. Opposition from greater force would seem to be the only deterrent against the ICP's keeping its divisions under arms and continuing along the same lines west of the frontiers of Indochina as it has east. One can imagine circumstances that would persuade the Party in the future to revive its state apparatus again — for example, if the army ceased to be the chief repository of skilled manpower in the country. But for the time being, the state throughout Indochina can be expected to continue its decline, superseded by the army, for reasons and by a progression far beyond the ken of Engels or even Lenin.

NOTES

1. Prime Minister Pham-van-Dong reported in *Nhan Dan* (The People), Hanoi, 1 September 1977.

2. 'By "Party of the masses" Lenin did not mean a party with a large number of members' — a Mongolian Party official quoted from a Russian source by X. Eudin and R. North, *Soviet Russia and the East 1920-1927* (Stanford: Stanford University Press, 1957), 207.

3. In 1946, the Vietnamese bishops reached a tacit concordat with Ho whereby the Church was left unmolested as administrator of rural parishes on condition that they sought Vatican recognition of the revolutionary regime — Piero Gheddo, *The Cross and the Bo Tree* (New York: 1970), 26 and 142.

4. Disclosure by Tran-van-Dinh, in charge of the manoeuvre, after his defection from the ICP — N. S. Adams and A. W. McCoy, *Laos: War & Revolution* (New York: Harper & Row, 1970), 424-425.

5. *Doc Lap* (Independence), Hanoi, 3 December 1960; *Nhan Dan,* 28 July 1961.

6. *To Quoc* (Fatherland), Hanoi, 1 June 1960.

7. *Vietnam Information,* Rangoon, 10 July 1953.

8. Radio Hanoi, 14 May 1975, taken with Radio Saigon, 7 June 1975.

9. Though concealed at the time, the total Vietnamese command over the campaign became a matter of boast after victory — e.g. Comrade Hoang Tung of the VCP's Central Committee interviewed in *Far Eastern Economic Review,* 21 April 1978.

10. Comrade Tran-huy-Lieu (ed.), *Nghien-cuu Lich-su* (Historical Review), Hanoi, No. 15, 1961.

11. Mangkra Souvanna Phouma, *Agonie du Laos* (Paris, 1976), 58. The Prime Minister conveyed his uncertainty to me personally during an interview in August 1973.

12. Mangkra Souvanna Phouma, 68-69.

13. Allegation of Sihanouk, *Agence Khmère de Presse,* 1 February 1968 and 11 June 1969.

14. Or so it is claimed by Hoang Tung, loc. cit.

15. After murdering his pan-Indochina-minded predecessor, according to Hanoi — charges and counter-charges over Radios Hanoi and Phnom Penh, February-March 1978.

16. It was the Cambodians who started the skirmishing, according to themselves — Radio Phnom Penh, 10 May 1978.

17. So described by Radio Phnom Penh, ibid.

18. *Tanjug,* Belgrade, 21 March 1978.

19. Sisana Sisane (Laotian Minister of Information) to *Far Eastern Economic Review,* 6 April 1979.

20. Directive No. 1033 of 23 September 1959 quoted by V. Kolesnikov, 'Supreme People's Court in the DRV', *Bulletin of the Supreme Court of the Soviet Union,* No. 3, 1961 (transl. Joint Publications Research Service, Washington, No. 4940).

21. Chief Justice Hoang-quoc-Viet (untrained in law) in *Nhan Dan,* 8 November 1961.

22. Stated at the half-day's proceedings of the National (Constituent) Assembly that approved it: *Le Monde,* Paris, 15 November 1946.

23. Liberation Radio some time in 1951, quoted in US Dept. of Defense, *US-Vietnam Relations 1945-67* (Pentagon Papers), Washington, 1971, Vol. i.B. footnote 56.

24. Prime Minister Pham-van-Dong, *Nhan Dan,* 18 April 1958.

25. In Vietnamese, as in Chinese, there are separate words in modern usage for 'chairman' (*chu tich/chu hsi*) and 'president' (*tong thong/tsung t'ung*); communists use the former for their head of state, non-communists the latter, e.g. Mao Tsê-tung compared with Chiang Kai-shek, Ho-chi-Minh compared with Ngo-dinh-Diem.

26. Criticism in *Nhan Dan,* 3 July 1967.

27. Ho-chi-Minh, *Ećrits,* Hanoi 1971, 229.

28. *Hanoi Moi* (New Hanoi), 31 July 1973.

29. Ibid., 22 August 1973.

30. *Nhan Dan,* 15 January 1960, 13 March 1961, 20 April 1961.

31. Ibid., 28 June 1964.

32. Ibid., 13 February 1971. That the 'Provisional Revolutionary Government of the Republic of South Vietnam' represented by its peripatetic 'Foreign Minister' Mme Nguyen-thi-Binh, never was a concrete political entity has been admitted by Comrade Nguyen-khac-Vien of the Central Committee, chief editor of foreign propaganda — television interview reported in *Le Figaro,* Paris, 14 April 1977.

33. *Quan-doi Nhan-dan* (People's Army), Hanoi, 16 April 1967; *Nhan Dan,* 7 April 1967.

34. The latter detail a recent disclosure — *Nhan Dan,* 22 May 1978.

35. Admission of Pham-van-Dong, *Nhan Dan,* 1 September 1977.

36. For the danger in China, see disclosures about Chekiang in *New China News Agency,* Peking, 22 December 1976; for that in Vietnam, see *Nhan Dan,* 13 April 1959 and 16 June 1962.

37. *Tin Sang* (Morning News), Saigon, 4 and 12 April 1978; *Thanh Nien* (Youth), Hanoi, June 1978.

38. Corruption has been a running complaint in the Party press since about 1964; two typical recent allegations concern 'universal thieving among transport workers' (*Giao-thong Van-thai* — Transport and Shipping, Hanoi, 20 June 1978) and bribery over issue of travel permits (*Hanoi Moi,* 5 April 1978), which attained its extreme form in the treatment of 'boat people' (*Far Eastern Economic Review,* 15 June 1979).

39. *Tap-chi Cong-san,* July 1978.

40. 4th Congress resolution in *Nhan Dan,* 15 February 1977.

41. *Tap-chi Cong-san,* April 1978; *Luat Hoc* (Law Studies), Hanoi, January-March 1978.

42. *Nhan Dan,* 14 January 1977; *Tap-chi Giang-vien* (The Lecturer), Hanoi, July-August 1978.

43. 'We would be lucky if even one in three Southerners wanted it' — Prime Minister Pham-van-Dong in *Nhan Dan,* 29 November 1975.

44. Radio Hanoi, 4 December 1975.

45. 'Either military service is by conscription and therefore as in the bad pre-socialist days,' they argued, 'or it is voluntary, and I can opt out' — *Tap-chi Quan-doi Nhan-dan* (People's Army Review), Hanoi, April 1978.

46. *Nhan Dan,* 14 January 1977.

47. *Nghien-cuu Kinh-te* (Economic Research), Hanoi, June 1976.

48. *Quan-doi Nhan-dan,* 12 January 1978. For the significance of the district in the political culture of the Chinese world, see Duncanson, *Government and Revolution in Vietnam* (London: Oxford University Press, 1968), 235.

49. Lao Party chief, Kaysone Phomvihan, Radio Vientiane, 6 March 1978.

9 The USSR: The Revolution Reversed?

Ronald J. Hill
Trinity College, Dublin, Eire

Timothy Dunmore
University of Essex, UK

Karen Dawisha
University of Southampton, UK

INTRODUCTION

The general direction of Soviet political life in the 1960s and 1970s appears particularly difficult to identify. Many Western observers have noted a cautious, conservative trend;[1] in the literature the concepts of 'immobilism', 'decay', 'degeneration' and 'petrification' have repeatedly been given an airing.[2] At the same time, however, Western scholars have also identified (and generally welcomed) tendencies towards 'pluralism' in one form or another, as the rigidities of Stalinist totalitarianism have given way to greater flexibility and openness in internal political life;[3] in this connection one commentator has referred to 'the change to change' in Soviet and communist politics.[4] A number of writers have drawn our attention to the possibility of 'interest group influence' in the policy-making process,[5] while the evidence of an aggressive policy towards the so-called dissidents has been widely publicized in the West and has challenged the proponents of a 'reformist' model of Soviet politics.[6]

The apparent conflict in these various perceptions is perhaps as revealing of the state of Western sovietology as it is of Soviet reality. The change in the manner of writing about Soviet politics reflects both the change in generations of scholars in the West concerned to understand the Soviet system,[7] and also the far greater access to reliable information about Soviet political life. Not only have the preoccupations of Western scholars undergone a significant change of emphasis (in part, at least, a reflection of changes in political science), but our greater knowledge of the Soviet scene has also revealed significant areas of ignorance that were of relatively small concern to the specialists of a generation ago. One thing is clear, however: Soviet society is itself complex, complicated, full of paradoxes and contradictions, which can no longer be summed up in a neat formula or model, and which are reflected in the differing interpretations and constructions placed on them by Western observers. In this paper we wish to review briefly certain developments in the Soviet political system, particularly those that affect party-state relations, and examine some of the implications of the elements of continuity and change in Soviet politics, as the society grows through the phase of 'developed socialism'.

The concept of 'developed' or 'mature' socialism (the two terms are used interchangeably), which has been introduced and incorporated into Soviet political rhetoric and social science vocabulary since the late 1960s, can be seen as the most important theoretical pronouncement since Khrushchev's notion of the 'all-people's state' or 'state of the whole people'.[8] The reasons for the new concept are several. First of all, its association with the ascendancy of Leonid Brezhnev is clearly intended to guarantee him a secure place in the history books as the leader under whose guidance the USSR moved to a fresh stage on the way towards Communism: Lenin introduced the dictatorship of the proletariat; Stalin induced the building of socialism; and Khrushchev's attempt at introducing a further phase — cumbersomely named 'the unfolding building of communism' — has given way under Brezhnev to the much more positive-sounding era of developed socialism. Secondly, at a stage where other socialist countries were clearly seen to be approaching the USSR in terms of economic development and their general 'socialist' orientation, the argument that 'developed socialism' is the 'pinnacle of contemporary social progress',[9] 'civilization's highest achievement in the contemporary epoch',[10] and a 'necessary stage' through which all societies must go en route to communism,[11] helps to place the Soviet Union firmly back in the leading position in the world socialist league. Thirdly, and more significantly from the point of view of the present paper, the assertion that a qualitatively new stage in societal development has been reached opens up the way for a re-examination of the various elements in the economic, social and political systems, and permits changes in emphasis and structural modifications that will bring consistency to the relationship between the economic base and the social and political superstructure. This point was emphasized by Leonid Brezhnev when introducing the 1977 USSR Constitution: 'Why was it necessary to create a new Constitution?,' he asked rhetorically, and he gave the following answer:

> Because, comrades, in four decades in our country and in the whole of our socie-ty profound changes have taken place.
>
> When the 1936 Constitution was adopted, in essence only the creation of the bases of socialism had been accomplished. The collective farm system, still young, was still not firmly established. The technical level of the economy was still far from the level of the most developed industrial countries. In various spheres of life, the remnants of pre-revolutionary times continued to be felt.
>
> But now in the Soviet Union a developed, mature socialist society has been built. *Major fundamental changes have touched all sides of social life.*[12]

Furthermore, Brezhnev stressed the need for further significant developments in legislation to bring the political system into line with developments in the base of society, and for fresh emphasis on the performance of the various elements in the political system.[13]

Soviet academic writers have underlined the point. V. Guliev and A. Shchiglik, for example, wrote in 1975 that 'the developed socialist society . . . is called upon to develop further and to perfect the democratic institutions and norms of socio-political life'.[14] The new Constitution was immediately identified as 'serving as the basis for further developing Soviet legislation and improving the whole of law-making activity',[15] while another writer, in a party journal, referred to it as 'a powerful means of further developing and deepening socialist democracy'.[16]

The concept of developed socialism has been further elaborated by Soviet scholars, taking up the call to examine its nature. Since the early 1970s the social science publishing houses in the USSR have been putting out large numbers of monographs, symposia and collective works, in which the characteristics of the present Soviet society are explored, and the need for particular developments argued. One of the points raised concerns the need to perfect the political system and develop democracy,[17] and a favoured argu-ment in support of this relates to the increasing sophistication of the population, in terms of improving levels of general education and the acquisition of political information and experience, all of which is said to fit them to play a more active part in the country's political life. Thus, G.N. Manov has identified 'a raising in the consciousness and political culture of Soviet citizens, a development in their public activity. Their interest is growing in participation in governing public affairs and in the effective use of democratic institutions'.[18]

However, the key element in the concept of developed socialism, as this has been expounded in the official press, by leading ideologists and by scholars, is the fresh assertion of the relationship between different sets of political institutions, in particular the central position of the party in the political system. The most symbolic expression of this appears in the 1977 Constitution, article 6, which sums up the picture that has been developed in the literature:

> The leading and guiding force of Soviet society and the nucleus of its political system, of all state organizations and public organizations, is the Communist Party of the Soviet Union. The CPSU exists for the people and serves the people. The Communist Party, armed with Marxism-Leninism, determines the general perspectives of the development of society and the course of home and foreign policy of the USSR, directs the great constructive work of the Soviet people, and imparts a planned, systematic and theoretically substantiated character to their struggle for the victory of communism.
>
> All party organizations shall function within the framework of the Constitution of the USSR.[19]

In that article we find the basic elements in the Soviet political system:[20] it refers to the ideology, the party as the institutional linchpin of the system, the state organizations and the public organizations; it indicates the methods of party rule (providing the nucleus in non-party institutions); it broadly depicts the party's general role (setting out the basic policy guidelines for the society); and it repeats the Leninist dictum that the party operates constitutionally.

'Developed socialism', then, serves certain political purposes, internally and in the international arena (where it has been joined of late by the concept of 'real' or 'existing' socialism in justification of the Soviet system before the eyes of the world).[21] It has been elaborated in such a way as to justify a reassertion of the communist party's dominant role in Soviet society. However, in so far as it is a novel concept — certainly not envisaged by the founding fathers of Marxism-Leninism — it is in need of theoretical and empirical elaboration by philosophers and social scientists. As such, it serves as a vehicle for a fresh scrutiny of the nature of Soviet society and its political system, and also perhaps a means of introducing reforms into that system. Indeed, the past decade or more has witnessed reformist developments and other forms of change in the institutions of both the party and the Soviet state.

THE PARTY

One of the central elements in the model of a developed socialist society is the assertion of the centrality of the communist party's 'leading and guiding' role: we saw this above expressed with reference to the political system, but the view extends beyond that to the whole of society. Indeed, according to the chapter heading of a recent book on the subject, 'Increasing the leading role of the communist party (is) the objective requirement for the development of Soviet society'.[22] Another collective work, which appeared in English translation, asserts that

> The activity of the Communist Party of the Soviet Union is indissolubly linked with the life, work and vital interests and strivings of the people. The unity of the party and the people becomes stronger in the course of building communism, acting as the decisive factor in the development of socialist democracy. Building a new society demands broader and stronger links between the party and the people and a thorough analysis and consideration of their practical experience.[23]

Indeed, the party's leading role is seen as a 'general principle' in a society that is supposedly building communism, and to deny this (as the reformist leaders under Dubček in Czechoslovakia were said to have done) amounts to a denial of the need for political leadership in general, and leads to the chaos and spontaneity that is so feared by Soviet commentators.[24]

Hence, as society itself continues to change and develop, so the party's role too is to be expanded. Moreover, it has increasingly been recognized and argued that the party must itself change if it is to play its enhanced role effectively: in particular, there is a need for the scientific study of the party and its performance, and a need for greater intra-party democracy, involving recruitment policies, the disposition of personnel, improved information channels, and structural modifications.[25] Attempts to introduce some of these have already been made.

Changes in the Party's Structures and Functions

The general structure of the party, and the distribution of power within it, remain as they have always been: it is a centralized institution, in which the Politburo and the central Secretariat remain the locus of real power. In the 1970s there have been relatively few changes at that level; but the role of the 200,000 or so 'apparatchiki' (officials) and the sixteen million-odd 'non-cadre' members, and the structures within which they operate, have been the subject of comment and some modification.

a. *The Leading Bodies of the CPSU*

Stability and regularity have been the keynotes of Brezhnev's leadership, in contrast to both Khrushchev's blustering and incompetent wilfulness and Stalin's crude and bullying enforced conformity. This stability has manifested itself above all in the upper echelons of the party, where the Politburo, central Secretariat and Central Committee have experienced remarkably few changes, compared with the number of dismissals and promotions under Khrushchev and with the rate of governmental changes in non-Communist political systems. Between Brezhnev's assumption of the party leadership, in 1964, and the year 1979, only seven individuals had been forced out of the Politburo; in 1976, no fewer than 89 per cent of the 1971 Central Committee were re-elected. As Robert Blackwell notes, 'Cadres stability . . . has been higher at each of the three party congresses since Khrushchev's removal than it was in either 1956 or 1961. Leadership continuity, moreover, has steadily increased throughout the Brezhnev period . . .'.[26] The structure of the central apparatus (essentially the Secretariat) has not been fundamentally altered since Khrushchev's day, and we know little more about the operations of the central bodies than previously: between the 24th and 25th congresses (1971 and 1976) the Politburo met 215 times and the Secretariat 205 times (i.e., approximately weekly),[27] while the Central Committee meets twice a year and appears to deal almost exclusively with economics and foreign policy; (since 1965 it has declined to publish the stenographic records which Khrushchev introduced).

It seems clear that these bodies (and particularly the Central Committee and Politburo) are now carefully balanced so as to serve as forums for the articulation of certain regional and functional interests. Thus, the Politburo contains the first secretaries of the Ukrainian, Belorussian, Kazakhstan, Georgian, Moscow and Leningrad party organizations, thereby providing for the representation of the interests of some of the larger, economically most powerful, or ethnically most sensitive parts of the country; and the representation in the 1970s of ministers of defence, culture, industry, foreign affairs, the secret police and formerly also agriculture, plus the most significant institutional hierarchies (party Secretariat, Council of Ministers, Supreme Soviet Presidium) ensures wide functional representation, so that the Politburo more closely resembles the *government* in a cabinet system. The composition of the Central Committee even more clearly reflects its role as a forum for the representation of a broad range of special interests, including in particular the interests of regional party organizations and most branches of the governmental administration. [28]

At the same time, despite the obvious functional aspects of the membership of these bodies, one possible interpretation of the changes that have taken place is that they favour Brezhnev. Shelest, Shelepin and possibly Mazurov opposed his policy of détente with the West, and were duly ousted from the Politburo; Shelepin had long been a political rival before his removal in 1975; Polyanskii and Voronov were made to take the blame for failures in agriculture, a field that Brezhnev, like Khrushchev before him, seems to have made his own; Podgornyi may have opposed some parts of the new Constitution (possibly even the bold article referring to the party's position: he was head of state, after all). And some of the replacements are clearly 'Brezhnev men': Chernenko is the most obvious example, but Shcherbitskii and Kunaev too have been identified as protégés, while Aliev and Kuznetsov are known to be strong supporters. [29] Moreover, Brezhnev's re-assumption in 1977 of the post of president, while retaining his party post, clearly strengthened his hand, ousting Podgornyi in the process, and possibly violating the unwritten rule that an individual may not hold top party and state posts simultaneously (although that 'rule' most obviously applies to the party general secretaryship and the post of chairman of the Council of Ministers, or premier, a position that has been held by Kosygin since October 1964).

Yet there is a strong current of opinion which plays down the Brezhnev 'personality cult'. Jerry Hough, in particular, has argued that Brezhnev seeks the approval of his colleagues in policy decision-making, and may in any case be more interested in foreign than domestic affairs. [30] Hough quotes one of Brezhnev's close colleagues, Georgian first secretary Eduard Shevardnadze, thus: '. . . one of Leonid Il'ich (Brezhnev)'s best qualities is that he does not clothe himself in the mantle of a superman, that he does not try to do everyone's thinking and working'. [31] One might at least comment that someone of Brezhnev's advancing years and ailing health must be presumed still to command a fair measure of genuine support from his colleagues, who otherwise would have taken steps to remove him from office, on the same grounds as Khrushchev was removed in October 1964: advancing age and failing health. One possible reason why Brezhnev has allowed them a relatively free rein is that he has simply not been fit enough to do otherwise. But whatever the reason, it seems as though some form of collective leadership has survived.

The stability has also brought its problems, specifically the general ageing of the ruling group, and possibly associated with it a lack of energy and industry, not to mention the likely frustration that is building up among second-rank leaders who might have aspired to top positions. Even the most probable eventual successors — the younger men currently in the Politburo: Romanov, Grishin, Demichev — are themselves already or approaching sixty, and for them the problem of dealing with rivals of their own age, likewise moulded in the political experience of the post-war, post-Stalin Soviet Union, and patiently waiting in the provinces, is likely to present an acute political problem in the early 1980s.

b. *The Apparatchiki*

One problem that has arisen in the past decade is that of identifying an appropriate role for the relatively non-specialized workers in the party apparat. An interview with a former official of the central Secretariat painted a very uncomplimentary picture of the 900 staff workers in the Central Committee apparatus, concerned with the privileges of office and using their influence to settle scores. [32] Hough's portrayal of the obkom (provincial committee) first secretary (and probably the first secretaries of the communist parties in the union republics, except for the RSFSR) as essentially a political broker, who can cut through red tape and other blockages, seems to be reasonable. [33] However, the position of other full-time party officials is by no means so clear. The state apparatus has recruited and trained its own staff of loyal and well-qualified managers and administrators, closer to the practical problems of running the country than the party officials are, and more experienced in doing so; therefore, the party official as someone distinguished by his expertise — which was no doubt common in the past — is already outdated, and party apparatchiki seem more willing to 'leave it to the experts'.[34] Their own role becomes one essentially of checking on or verifying the performance of the state bureaucracy,[35] which may cause resentment among the state managerial and administrative officers.

A further important function of the party apparatus is in the ideological field, where a new policy of improving agitation and propaganda was adopted in the spring of 1979, to counteract years of formalized and ineffectual political education measures that have been a continual source of adverse comment in recent years.[36] However, although the 'intensified ideological struggle' in the international arena may be used to justify this effort, one might slightly cynically speculate that its main value is in creating a 'useful' role for the staff of the party apparatus itself.

c. *Lower Party Bodies*

The most noticeable changes in the party have taken place at the level of the primary organization (PPO), reflecting both the growing size of the party and of some PPOs and also changes in the administration of the economy since 1973. They also reflect the increased responsibilities placed on the lower levels under Brezhnev for supervising the work of state institutions.

With the continued growth of the party, the average PPO now has more than forty members; in industry they may be much larger — over 10,000 members in some of the production associations founded in Soviet industry since 1973. Obviously there is a danger that the member will feel out of touch with the leadership in his organization, and much debate and experimentation has been undertaken in order to find suitable structural forms for avoiding that problem.[37] In particular, the workshop party organizations and party groups have been established and vitalized, in some cases being given their own committees, and sometimes divided into small groups of ten or so members, in which it is hoped that the ordinary communist will find a team of colleagues with whom he can identify. At the level of the very large PPO, enlarged committees have been tried, consisting of 45-55 members, often with about fifty per cent shop-floor representation.[38] Even so, it is not yet clear that these new structures will have the desired effect in preventing a sense of alienation among rank-and-file members, who are still not granted real opportunities for displaying initiative and acting outside certain limited, approved channels. Hence the calls in the work of scholars for far more effective information flows downwards, and for the right of the ordinary membership to criticize their local officers to be respected in practice.[39]

A further matter raised in the wake of the industrial restructuring concerns relations between primary organizations and district committees (raikoms), and their respective roles in checking on the functioning of management. Different industrial units within the same production association may be situated in different districts, or even different towns, so the relationship among the various parts of the PPO, and the question of which higher committee they are subordinated to, affects the success of the party at local level in fulfilling its self-appointed role. Nor is it certain whether that role is properly restricted to economic questions, or allowed to extend more widely to general questions in the life of the district. The vested interests of existing PPO secretaries and raikom officers also play their part in the argument — or, at least, in its resolution — and parallels with Khrushchev's bifurcation of the party into industrial and agricultural sections come to mind as one follows the Soviet debates.[40] The question of the most appropriate structural arrangement has not so far been resolved. An attempt to provide co-ordination by creating still a further body, the Council of Secretaries, linking the PPO secretaries of the various branches of an industrial association, has not met with overwhelming success: these councils meet infrequently and have no executive authority, so there is no distinct function that they can perform. Clearly, this search for appropriate local structures will continue into the 1980s.

Changes in the Party's Composition

In the sphere of party membership, the Brezhnev period has been characterized by the 're-proletarianization' of the party, as a deliberate policy by the leadership to encourage 'guided' participation and activism among the mass membership; it is also a means of improving 'feedback' from the masses to the leadership and of reinforcing the regime's legitimacy,[41] as well as bringing under party discipline important sectors of the working class. Some 57.6 per cent of new admissions to the party over the period 1971-75 were workers, who also accounted for 58.6 per cent of the 1976 intake, and constituted 42.0 per cent of the total party membership at January 1977: Leonid Brezhnev expressed himself 'profoundly satisfied' with these figures at the last party congress.[42]

There is some doubt, however, about how these statistics should be interpreted.[43] They do not appear to be compatible with figures for the numbers of party members with higher education, and so may reflect the social origin of members, rather than their current occupation. But what is also clear is that even those recruited from among the working class tend increasingly to come from the technologically advanced industries such as chemicals and petrochemicals, electronics, automobiles, radio technology, instrument-making and so forth[44] — far removed from the traditional 'working class', and much closer to the technical intelligentsia in training and work. 'Employees and others' (i.e., non-manual workers) still provided 44.4 per cent of the party membership in 1977 (compared with 45.9 per cent in 1967), while the proportion of collective farmers fell from 16.0 per cent to 13.6 per cent in the decade to January 1977.[45] The purge of the party's ranks, in the form of an 'exchange of party cards' that was undertaken between the twenty-fourth and twenty-fifth congresses, gave the party authorities a modest amount of room to manoeuvre in bringing about the desired social balance of the CPSU's ranks. However, this is a very complex question, with many different aspirations pulling in different directions: the party wishes to be a vanguard, a party of the whole people (implying broad representation of the major nationalities and other social groups), a party of the working class, a party consisting of the politically most-aware citizens, and also a party of government. So complex is the task of adjusting recruitment policies to satisfy these several aims that the problem is likely to trouble the leadership in the future.[46]

To sum up, the CPSU seems to have become confronted with a serious crisis of identity. On the one hand, it fervently proclaims its own indispensability to the society in building communism; yet, on the other hand, it seems unable to solve the problems associated with performing its role — or even identifying what that role is at local level. It is an organization of nearly 17 million members, with a permanent staff of almost a quarter of a million: a 'vanguard' of nearly ten per cent of the adult population. It consists moreover of a relatively well educated and sophisticated body of men and women: they may well feel a growing sense of frustration at the leadership's inability or unwillingness to introduce reforms that would permit them to play the active part in the life of the country that exhortatory propaganda encourages them to do. The long-standing problem of the relationship between the party and the state becomes even more acute for party workers, as the state bureaucracy expands, its officers and officials develop special managerial skills, the task of running the society becomes more complex, and the representative institutions too are revitalized. In the next section, we shall examine some of these developments in the state structure.

THE STATE

The Soviet political leadership has shown itself more willing to modify the structures of the state apparatus over the years than it has to alter the institutions of the party. Khrushchev's abolition of the ministries in 1957, replacing them with the economic councils, subsequently abolished and replaced by a re-born system of ministries, is one example of major structural changes in the sphere of state administration; the abolition of the raion (district) as an administrative unit, to be replaced by agricultural administrations, is another of Khrushchev's reforms undone by his successors.[47] Khrushchev, indeed, was particularly anxious to demonstrate that the state was indeed withering away, as a means of showing that progress towards communism was being made under his personal tutelage. Scholarly comment in the early 1960s even suggested the complete abolition of village soviets, with the transfer of their functions to the collective and state farms.[48] Much of Khrushchev's tinkering was reversed by his successors, although some changes have remained, such as the transfer of certain welfare functions to the trade unions.

Under Brezhnev a more stable institutional structure has been established, and such unsophisticated attempts to induce the withering-away of state have been abandoned. In fact the trend has been in quite the opposite direction, following the elaboration of the concept of developed socialism. It is recognized and asserted that the transition to communism is still to be a lengthy process, indeed longer than was foreseen, and that developed socialism is 'a stage during which society has to resolve plenty of complex problems, to eliminate deficiencies that still exist in the field of economic management, science and culture, and in the behaviour of citizens'; the incalculable impact of the technological revolution also needs to be taken into account.[49] Hence, the 'withering away' cannot be forced.[50] These fundamental changes in society, it is argued, require a general enhancement in society's political superstructure, in order to control the direction of development.[51] For, as the 1961 Party Programme noted (and its basic principles, if not specific details, are still formally accepted and asserted by Soviet writers), 'Unlike all previous socio-economic formations, communist society does not develop spontaneously, but as the result of the conscious and purposeful efforts of the masses, led by the Marxist-Leninist party'.[52]

Improving the Administration

It is clear, then, that the state administration, rather than being hastily induced to run down its operations, is to remain in being for a considerable time, and needs to be developed, in order to cope with the increasingly complex problems that face society. The transformation of the economy in the era of the 'scientific and technological revolution', the growing complexity of the tasks of forecasting and planning economic and social development, and the rising levels of education and public involvement of the masses are some of the reasons given for the need for a more sophisticated administrative system than hitherto.[53] And that does not simply mean more government, more administration, or even further structural modifications, but rather a different approach to state administration, and *more competent* government, by better trained and more highly qualified public servants.[54] This is a question that has been accorded much attention by Soviet scholars in recent years, and politicians too have taken up the theme. The cybernetics and decision-making approaches have been applied, with emphasis on the need for more and sounder information, and for the recruitment of a type of official who (in Brezhnev's words) within himself organically combines party commitment with profound competence, discipline with initiative and a creative approach to affairs. Alongside that, at every level, the leader is also obliged to take into account socio-political and educational aspects, to be sensitive to people, to their needs and requirements, to serve as an example in work and in his everyday life.[55]

These sentiments have been taken up and expanded by others, who call for the establishment of a new 'administrative culture' or 'state service ethic';[56] others have called for a statute on servants in the state service[57] and for competitive appointment to such positions.[58] In other words, the trend for the immediate future, as revealed in current thinking, is towards a greater professionalization of the state administration.

Furthermore, a range of legal reforms were introduced in the early 1970s, in order to enhance the effectiveness of state administration, particularly at the local level. One problem that had been long recognized was the completely uncoordinated development of industry, housing and other measures, under the sponsorship of various ministerial apparatuses, each of which operated on the basis of its own criteria of efficiency and effectiveness. As the chairman of the Moscow provincial soviet executive committee (oblispolkom) noted in 1968, frequently a new factory is cited in a town by a particular industrial ministry, without adequate provision for housing and all the other services required, since these come within the purview of other ministries or authorities;[59] local government had no powers to control this. Similarly, the effective functioning of local administration was hampered by their lack of material support, in terms of both finance and facilities, in the form of adequate premises and office equipment, and even auxiliary staff.[60]

Reforms set in motion during 1971 were intended to improve the existing position in these respects. The party Central Committee issued a statement on 14 March that year, which was followed by a statement from the USSR Council of Ministers, charging the governments in the union republics with 'providing during 1971-75 the executive committees of district and town soviets with well-appointed quarters, and also means of transport, articles of office machinery, equipment, furniture and stocks'.[61] In the absence of such basics, it is easily appreciated how little the local administrators could do against powerful ministries. A further measure introduced at the same time gave the local authorities certain powers to coordinate the activities of various industrial enterprises on their territory, and transferred some enterprises to the direct control of local government. In addition, it was enacted that the local budget should benefit by the diversion to local control of part of the profits of such enterprises and part of the turnover tax on goods produced over and above the planned production. In principle, the local authorities would thus have a material interest in encouraging these local enterprises to produce as much as possible.

Important as these measures are in terms of redistributing a degree of power from the centre to the localities, two further factors, however, need to be borne in mind in evaluating them. First, the Soviet administrative system remains governed by the principles of 'democratic centralism' and 'dual subordination', which place the executive and administrative organs at one level under the authority not only of the soviets (representative institutions) to which they are attached, but also to administrative bodies and soviets further up in the hierarchy, and the ministries still have paramountcy (along with the planning authorities) in running the economy. Second, and related to the last point, the performance of the economy depends too much on factors that are outside the control of local administration for the latter to have complete influence over it: the allocation of resources — financial or material — depends on the planning system, which is coordinated through Gosplan, the state planning commission. A local authority finds it difficult even to ensure that street lights operate, since it depends on an allocation of lamp bulbs, as a local administrator ruefully noted in the provincial press.[62] There is no sign of a desire to alter these basic ground-rules that govern the state administration.

Yet over the longer term the recruitment of a new generation of competent and sophisticated officials, loyal, versed in modern administrative techniques, and experienced in running a diversified modern society, may encourage the central authorities to have confidence that genuine decentralization of power might be attempted without the risk of harming the nature of the system. However, this very development also threatens to create a distinct class of administrators, a 'technocracy' that rules over the masses. Although Soviet commentators point out that this is not so,[63] there is no sign that administration is being so simplified that (as Lenin put it in one of his more utopian moments)[64] 'every literate person' can perform the tasks involved in it. Moreover, the current response to the potential problem is *not* to make everyone an administrator but to strengthen democratic control over the apparatchiks, by putting them in their rightful place, subordinate to the representative institutions. In this connection the revitalization of the soviets (renamed Soviets of People's Deputies) occupies a central position.

Revitalizing the Soviets

The strike committees (as they were essentially) that so attracted Lenin in the revolutions of 1905 and 1917 changed their nature when they became formalized as the institutional basis of the new revolutionary state to which they gave their name. During the thirty-five years of Stalin's domination, they enjoyed no significant development,[65] and their political role became largely ornamental. Research by Soviet scholars since the early 1960s has devastatingly revealed how inadequately they were able to perform their constitutional representative role. The lack of choice given to the voters over who shall represent them, and other weaknesses in the electoral system; the unrepresentative composition of the deputies; the infrequency and brevity of meetings, which prevented popular control over current issues, and also hindered the deputies in gaining and using political experience; the rapid turnover among deputies, which had a similar effect; the domination of the sessions by local administrators; the triviality of the topics debated: these and other basic weaknesses have been thoroughly explored in research,[66] and it is no longer possible to ignore them.

Indeed, within four years of Stalin's death, the CPSU Central Committee issued a statement entitled 'On improving the activity of the soviets and strengthening their links with the masses' (22 January 1957), and set in motion a policy that has continued until today, aimed at breathing fresh life into these institutions and identifying an appropriate role for them in modern Soviet society. Since the late 1960s, new normative legislation has been introduced, redefining the legal powers and responsibilities of the various soviets in the hierarchy, and a particular item of legislation (which is accorded great significance by Soviet writers on the subject) is the Statute on the Deputies' Status (1972), intended to give the deputies greater authority vis-à-vis the administrative bureaucracy. Moreover, just as there has been a move towards the recruitment and training of more sophisticated administrators, so in the sphere of the representative institutions proper there has also been a tendency to stress the need for greater erudition, experience of life, indeed professional competence[67] on the part of those whose duties, as it is continually stressed, consist in representing the interests of their constituents.[68] And if little change has been made in the conduct of the sessions,[69] the deputy's role as a kind of Ombudsman, intervening with the authorities on behalf of his electors, seems to have expanded considerably.

These developments reflect, in our view, a significant development in Soviet social and philosophical analysis that has taken place since the death of Stalin: namely, a reassessment of the nature of *interests* in society. The groundwork was laid in 1955 by G.M. Gak, who identified various types of interests that may arise in a socialist society, including individual interests.[70] In subsequent writings, Soviet scholars have explored the question further, and distinguished a whole range of interests — societal, group, and individual — that exist, and that may not always be compatible with one another: the word 'collision' has been used in this context.[71] Hence it is argued that 'the socialist state must in its activity take into account both the general and the specific interests of classes and social groups in society, and resolve the possible non-antagonistic contradictions among them, reconcile them, directing them into the common stream'.[72] An important means of feeding these interests into the system is intended to be the deputies.

Other methods of discovering what the Soviet public wants include the formal study of public opinion, and the encouragement of citizens to engage in direct communication with representatives of the administration and political system. As to the first of these, R.A. Safarov, the Soviet Union's most enthusiastic student of public opinion, has repeatedly called for the establishment of an Institute of Public Opinion,[73] and others have urged that the referendum should be adopted as an important element in the Soviet system of government.[74] As far as direct communications are concerned, the party and government press in the 1970s has carried many items urging officials of both party and state to be more attentive to letters from the public, since 'Behind the letter there is a person'.[75] The central authorities have on more than one occasion turned their attention to this question, criticizing the state of affairs in particular parts of the country, and, as a means of encouragement, assuring citizens that the proposals contained in such letters are taken into account in decision-making.[76]

Caution is needed, however, in interpreting these developments.

They do no doubt reflect a different perception from the Stalinist one of the importance of interests and opinion and their significance for the political system. There may even be an inference to be drawn that the CPSU no longer asserts its infallibility in identifying at all times and in all circumstances what is in the interests of people — apart from the broad basic common interest of building communism. Yet the fact that the point needs to be repeated and stressed so frequently in the press and in official statements bears witness to the lack of enthusiasm with which the personnel in the apparatus are responding to the change of emphasis. So while these tendencies in Soviet thought may indicate the firm aspirations of some articulate sections of the intelligentsia and the political leadership, the development of a political system based on the notion that government devises policies on the basis of the articulated and aggregated demands of the population is by no means to be taken for granted. The concept of a 'pluralist' system, which some Western scholars claim to see emerging in the Soviet Union, has been rejected explicitly and with contempt by some Soviet writers,[77] for whom it is too close to bourgeois government or to anarchy. Instead, Soviet policy seems to be to extend the scope for individual participation in political processes, through carefully 'guided' recognized channels: letters to the press and to politicians, elections, working in the soviets as deputies or volunteer activists, participating in the various 'social' or 'public' organizations. In these ways, it is hoped, and through bolstering up political culture-formation by means of continuous political education,[78] people will acquire the political skills and experience that will be needed under 'communist self-administration'.

It may be argued, however, that Soviet society has an even more basic need: to establish a political system that is based on law, after centuries in which the law operated to the benefit of a ruling circle — tiny and remote from the mass of the population — and after a generation in this century when 'infringements of socialist legality' (the standard post-Stalin euphemism for the evils of Stalinism) were the rule rather than the exception. More than one Soviet writer has drawn attention to the lack of respect for the law and ignorance of its provisions on the part of those who are ostensibly charged with administering it.[79] Many areas of existence were totally unregulated by law, leaving much scope for malpractice on the part of officials whose sole overriding objectives were to ensure maximum output and to maintain political conformity. Writers today stress that 'Reinforcing legality is closely linked with the further development of socialist democracy. Genuine legality exists only in a society operating on a democratic basis'.[80] It is interesting and significant in this regard that the final draft of article 6 of the 1977 Constitution differed from the original version in its inclusion of the sentence, 'All party organizations shall function within the framework of the Constitution of the USSR':[81] the fulfillment of this 'promise' to all citizens (and perhaps reminder or warning to party officials around the country) is a basic element in the development of legality in the Soviet system.

CONCLUSIONS

The Soviet political system at the threshold of the 1980s ought also to be on the threshold of profound political change, occasioned by the transformation of society's economic and social base into a complex, diverse, well-differentiated and increasingly sophisticated society, in which the methods of rule that may have been adequate forty or fifty years ago have become plainly inadequate. At least two trends in Soviet society can be identified. One is towards consumerism, passivity, political indifference, selfishness and philistinism,[82] which backs up evidence of the well-known social and economic problems of alcoholism, delinquency, divorce, absenteeism, labour turnover and so forth. These are the problems of an advanced urban industrial society, which were not foreseen by the generation of leaders who embarked upon building 'socialism in one country' in the 1920s. The other trend is towards greater sophistication and discrimination, a reflection of a long tradition of education as a means of social mobility, coupled with growing wealth and increased leisure, all of which ostensibly equip people to play a far more positive participatory role in political life than they have done to date.[83] This second trend is also seen in the presence of a body of scholars — philosophers and social scientists — who are able to analyze the processes that are taking place in Soviet society, and have shown themselves not backward in identifying problems and putting forward proposals for change.[84] What is lacking, it seems, is a willingness on the part of the political leadership to introduce the wide-sweeping reforms that may be necessary.

Nevertheless, there are signs in their speeches and their policies that the leaders, or some of them, have recognized the problems for a number of years past. They have taken some steps to bring the political fabric up to a level where it can match the needs of the economy and society, by inducing changes of various kinds, in both the party and the state apparatuses, in structures and in personnel. The promulgation of the concept of 'developed socialism' has been valuable in giving a justification for such reforms, and the notion of participation has been central to the theme.

However, the nature of that participation is in some doubt. Although it has been argued, particularly by Hough,[85] that there has been a significant advance in the scope for popular involvement in running the society, we saw above that nothing like free, spontaneous political action is either possible or contemplated. Certain groups, it is true, are being admitted to the ranks of the party (the most important political institution in the country); others, in significant numbers, are drafted into the soviets to serve as deputies for a two-and-a-half-year term of office; and the masses are encouraged to join the 'public organizations' — trade unions, Komsomol, special interest societies — sponsored by the regime. Whether these forms of 'participation' are significant as political acts is open to debate; so far, it appears to be largely participation in the application of policy rather than in policy-formulation. It may be best to think of this 'guided' participation as part of the process of political culture-formation: it involves people in the work of institutions that may possibly in the future be given enhanced political roles, as a means of giving the experience and skills that will be needed when (if?) 'communist self-administration' is attained. After all, whether one takes as a base the year 1917 (when the Bolsheviks were faced with an illiterate peasant population with no experience of participation in politics) or the year 1953 (when, on the death of Stalin, the leaders were still faced with a population that had been forcibly denied the opportunity to develop participatory political skills and attitudes), Soviet society under the leadership of Khrushchev and his successors has had a long way to catch up. A political culture cannot be changed overnight, and few political leaderships would run the risk of inducing their system's collapse by establishing political institutions and conventions that could not be expected to operate effectively. That is particularly the case when, as we have seen, the ideology eschews and mistrusts spontaneity — a point at which the ideology is in tune with the political culture.[86] These considerations are in addition to the vested interests of a regime in power that must have played a great part in motivating the Soviet leadership.

So in the 1970s the Soviet leaders have been cautious, not to say conservative, in their approach to political reform. Certainly we have seen nothing that matches Khrushchev's grand reformist gestures — which may perhaps be no bad thing. Caution has been the watchword: an attempt to introduce change gently, without upsetting basic political relationships, and without antagonizing strategically placed groups whose loyalty needs to be maintained — specifically party workers, the loyal intelligentsia, and the technologically advanced ranks of the working class; it does not, of course, include overt dissidents.

In 1979 the leadership that took over from Khrushchev — basically still intact — is obviously reaching the end of its career, and the 1980s are bound to witness a change of generations.The new leadership, when it becomes established, will have to tackle certain problems more forthrightly, and it may be necessary to adopt greater boldness in encouraging political development, so that the political system will be able to cope with the increasing demands placed upon it as 'developed socialism' continues to mature.

The state, it seems, cannot wither away. The tasks that require authoritative, large-scale resolution are likely to grow, rather than diminish, and only an increasingly competent — technically and politically — administrative profession will be able to perform this decision-making role. As that happens, there will be a greater need for some 'watchdog' institutions, to keep a democratic eye on the administrators: so the soviets, the representative side of the state apparatus, are also likely to continue their developmental path. That leaves the party, whose role of 'leader' or 'guide' seems more nebulous and more unnecessary as the population develops a loyal participant political culture, and begins to operate institutions without requiring guiding instructions from the CPSU. That, indeed, is the party's policy for political development towards communism, so is it already sounding its own death-knell? For a variety of reasons it will not happen: but perhaps the *party* should begin to 'wither away'.

NOTES

1. See, for example, Alec Nove, *Stalinism and After* (London: Allen & Unwin, 1975), 159; Archie Brown and Michael Kaser (eds), *The Soviet Union Since the Fall of Khrushchev*, 2nd edition (London: Macmillan, 1978), 245, 249; Jerry F. Hough, 'The Brezhnev Era: The Man and the System', *Problems of Communism (PoC)*, Vol. 25 No. 2 (1976), 8-9.

2. Zbigniew K. Brzezinski, 'The Soviet Political System: Transformation or Degeneration?' *PoC*, Vol. 15 No. 1 (1966), 1-15; Robert Conquest, 'Immobilism and Decay', *PoC*, Vol. 15 No. 5 (1966), 35-37; Jerry F. Hough, 'The Soviet System: Petrification or Pluralism?', *PoC*, Vol. 21 No. 2 (1972), 25-45.

3. Hough, 'The Soviet System'; Stephen White, 'Communist Systems and the "Iron Law of Pluralism"', *British Journal of Political Science*, Vol. 8 (1978), 101-117; Darrell P. Hammer, *USSR: The Politics of Oligarchy* (Hinsdale, Ill.: Dryden Press, 1974), 223-256.

4. William Taubman, 'The Change to Change in Communist Systems: Modernization, Postmodernization, and Soviet Politics', in Henry W. Morton and Rudolf L. Tökés (eds.), *Soviet Politics and Society in the 1970s* (New York: The Free Press, 1974), 369-394.

5. For example, Joel J. Schwartz and William R. Keech, 'Group Influence and the Policy Process in the Soviet Union', *American Political Science Review (APSR)*, Vol. 62 (1968), 840-851; Philip D. Stewart, 'Soviet Interest Groups and the Policy Process: The Repeal of Production Education', *World Politics*, Vol. 22 (1969), 29-50; and especially the work of Gordon Skilling, particularly *Interest Groups in Soviet Politics* (ed., with Franklyn Griffiths) (Princeton, NJ: Princeton University Press, 1971).

6. On dissidence, see especially Rudolf L. Tökés (ed.), *Dissent in the USSR: Politics, Ideology, and People* (Baltimore and London: Johns Hopkins University Press, 1975); on the Soviet treatment of dissidents, see Sidney Bloch and Peter Reddaway, *Russia's Political Hospitals* (London: Gollancz, 1977); see also Frederick C. Barghoorn, *Détente and the Democratic Movement in the USSR* (New York: The Free Press, 1976).

7. Peter H. Solomon, Jr, *Soviet Criminologists and Criminal Policy* (London: Macmillan, 1978), 1-4; also Stephen White, 'Political Science as Ideology: The Study of Soviet Politics', in B. Chapman and A.M. Potter (eds.), *W.J.M.M. Political Questions: Essays in Honour of W.J.M. MacKenzie* (Manchester: Manchester University Press, 1975), 252-268.

8. See Alfred B. Evans, Jr, 'Developed Socialism in Soviet Ideology', *Soviet Studies (Sov. Studs)*, Vol. 29 (1977), 409-428.

9. L.A. Grigoryan, *XXV S"ezd KPSS i Aktual'nye Problemy Sotsialisticheskoi Demokratii v SSSR* (Moscow: Znanie, 1977), 36.

10. P. Fedoseev, 'Nauka i Ideologiya', *Partiinaya Zhizn'*, No. 22 (1979), 20.

11. For one of many statements to that effect see G. Glezerman and M. Iovchuk, 'Sovetskii Obraz Zhizni i Formirovanie Novogo Cheloveka', *Kommunist*, No. 4 (1978), 119.

12. L.I. Brezhnev, 'O Proekte Konstitutsii Soyuza Sovetskikh Sotsialisticheskikh Respublik' (Speech to CPSU Central Committee Plenum, 24 May 1977), reprinted

in *Sovety Deputatov Trudyashchikhsya* (*SDT*), No. 7 (1977), 32-39; the quoted passage appears on p. 32 (original emphasis).

13. Ibid., 37-38.

14. V.Ye. Guliev and A.I. Shchiglik, 'Partiya i Gosudarstvo v Sisteme Sovetskoi Sotsialisticheskoi Demokratii', *Sovetskoe Gosudarstvo i Pravo* (*SGiP*), No. 4 (1975), 10.

15. M.A. Shafir, 'Etapy Razvitiya', *SDT*, No. 10 (1977), 15.

16. A. Krukhmalev, 'Konstitutsiya SSSR i Dal'neishee Razvitie Sotsialisticheskogo Demokratizma', *Partiinaya Zhizn'*, No. 19 (1978), 19.

17. See, for example, Yu.Ye. Volkov et al. (eds.), *Razvitoi Sotsializm* (Moscow: Politizdat, 1978), Chap. 10.

18. In Yu.A. Tikhomirov (ed.), *Demokratiya Razvitogo Sotsialisticheskogo Obshchestva* (Moscow: Nauka, 1975), 276.

19. *Constitution (Fundamental Law) of the Union of Soviet Socialist Republics* (Moscow: Novosti, 1977), Article 6.

20. 'Political system' is a concept that has now come to be accepted in Soviet writings (including, as we have just seen, the Constitution) in place of the separate reference to the state and party organs as though there were no connections between them.

21. See, for example, B.N. Ponomarev, *Existing Socialism and its International Significance* (Moscow: Progress Publishers, 1979). Recent comment sees 'existing socialism' as one of the three 'basic currents in the present revolutionary process' and 'the most dynamic and leading force of historical progress': see Fedoseev, op. cit., 20.

22. A.F. Yudenkov et al. (eds.), *Rukovodyashchaya Rol' KPSS v Usloviyakh Razvitogo Sotsializma* (Moscow: Mysl', 1979), Chap. 1.

23. D.A. Kerimov (ed.), *Soviet Democracy in the Period of Developed Socialism* (Moscow: Progress Publishers, 1979), 38.

24. On party leadership as a general principle, see G. Kh. Shakhnazarov, *Sotsialisticheskaya Demokratiya (Nekotorye Voprosy Teorii)* (Moscow: Politizdat, 1972), 76-77. The notion that communism will not be attained spontaneously is enshrined in the 1961 CPSU Programme: 'Programma KPSS', reprinted in *KPSS v Rezolyutsiyakh i Resheniyakh S''ezdov, Konferentsii i Plenumov TsK,* Vol. 8 (Moscow: Politizdat, 1972), 301; see also below.

25. For a fuller argument, see Ronald J. Hill, *Soviet Politics, Political Science and Reform* (London: Martin Robertson, 1980), Chaps. 6 and 7.

26. Robert E. Blackwell, Jr, 'Cadres Policy in the Brezhnev Era', *PoC*, Vol. 28 No. 2 (1979), 31; Blackwell fully explores the question of the stability of cadres policy under Brezhnev, and the implications.

27. Figures given by Brezhnev at the 25th CPSU Congress (1976): see *XXV S''ezd Kommunisticheskoi Partii Sovetskogo Soyuza: Stenograficheskii Otchët* (Moscow: Politizdat, 1976), Vol. 1, 91-92.

28. See Michael P. Gehlen and Michael McBride, 'The Soviet Central Committee: An Elite Analysis', *APSR,* Vol. 62 (1968), 1232-1241; Robert H. Donaldson, 'The 1971 Soviet Central Committee: An Assessment of the New Elite', *World Politics,* Vol. 24 (1972), 382-409; Robert V. Daniels, 'Office Holding and Elite Status: The Central Committee of the CPSU', in Paul Cocks et al. (eds.), *The Dynamics of Soviet Politics* (Cambridge, Mass.: Harvard University Press, 1976), Chap. 5.

29. Blackwell, op. cit., 37, Note 20.

30. Hough, 'The Brezhnev Era'.

31. The quotation is from *XXV S"ezd KPSS,* Vol. 1, 186.

32. A. Pravdin and Mervyn Matthews, 'Inside the CPSU Central Committee', *Survey,* Vol. 20 (1974), 94-104.

33. Jerry F. Hough, *The Soviet Prefects* (Cambridge, Mass.: Harvard University Press, 1969).

34. See A.G. Tannenbaum, 'Soviet Party Apparatchiki Attitudes Towards Change', *Comparative Political Studies,* Vol. 9 No. 1, (1976), 93-106.

35. This point was made by Brezhnev at the 25th CPSU Congress: see *XXV S"ezd KPSS,* Vol. 1, 94-95.

36. See Stephen White, 'Political Socialization in the USSR: A Study in Failure?', *Studies in Comparative Communism,* Vol. 10 No. 3, (1977), 328-342. The new policy was announced by the CPSU Central Committee in a statement publicized in *Pravda,* 6 May 1979, 1-2, and backed up editorially in *Pravda,* 7 May 1979, 1.

37. For a fuller account, see Timothy Dunmore, 'Local Party Organs in Industrial Administration: The Case of the Ob"edinenie Reforms', *Sov. Studs,* Vol. 32 No. 2, (1980), 195-217.

38. See, for example, *Leningradskie Khozraschëtnye Ob"edineniya* (Leningrad: Lenizdat, 1975), 27.

39. On the need for freer information flows see, for example, V.A. Kadeikin et al. (eds.), *Voprosy Vnutripartiinoi Zhizni i Rukovodyashchei Deyatel'nosti KPSS na Sovremennom Etape* (Moscow: Mysl', 1974), 158; *XXIV S"ezd Kommunisticheskoi Partii Sovetskogo Soyuza: Stenograficheskii Otchët* (Moscow: Politizdat, 1971), Vol. 1, 119-120. On the need for criticism see Kadeikin et al., op. cit., 14-15, 96-98; Tikhomirov, op.cit., 102-103.

40. On Khrushchev's 'bifurcation' reform (which lasted from November 1962 until November 1964, being hastily unscrambled by his successors) see John A. Armstrong, 'Party Bifurcation and Elite Interests', *Sov. Studs,* Vol. 17 (1966), 417-430.

41. See Jerry F. Hough, 'Political Participation in the Soviet Union', *Sov. Studs,* Vol. 28 (1976), 3-20, and T.H. Rigby, 'The Soviet Communist Party Under Brezhnev', *Sov. Studs,* Vol. 28 (1976), 317-337.

42. *XXV S"ezd KPSS,* Vol. 1, 88.

43. See, for example, Rigby, 'The Soviet Communist Party Under Brezhnev', 330-332; A.L. Unger, 'The Soviet Communist Party Under Brezhnev: A Comment', *Sov. Studs,* Vol. 29 (1977), 306-316; and Rigby, 'A Rejoinder', *Sov. Studs,* Vol. 29 (1977), 452-453.

44. Kadeikin et al., *Voprosy Vnutripartiinoi Zhizni,* 168.

45. Figures from 'KPSS v Tsifrakh', *Partiinaya Zhizn',* No. 21 (1977), 28.

46. See Hill, *Soviet Politics, Political Science and Reform,* 129-131; and, for a fuller account, Darrell P. Hammer, 'The Dilemma of Party Growth', *PoC,* Vol. 20 No 4 (1971), 16-21.

47. On these and other points see Jerry Hough, 'Reforms in Government and Administration', in Alexander Dallin and Thomas D. Larson (eds.), *Soviet Politics Since Khrushchev* (Englewood Cliffs, NJ: Prentice-Hall, 1968), 23-40.

48. L.M. Karapetyan and V.I. Razin, *Sovety Obshchenarodnogo Gosudarstva* (Moscow: Politizdat, 1964), 159.

49. B.N. Topornin, *Sovetskaya Politicheskaya Sistema* (Moscow: Politizdat, 1975), 7.

50. Ts.A. Stepanyan and A.S. Frish (eds.), *Razvitoi Sotsializm i Aktual'nye Problemy Nauchnogo Kommunizma* (Moscow: Nauka, 1979), 174.

51. Ibid., Chap. 11.

52. 'Programma KPSS', op. cit., 301.

53. See, for example, Stepanyan and Frish, op. cit., 169; *Apparat Upravleniya Sotsialisticheskogo Gosudarstva,* 2 (Moscow: Yurudicheskaya Literatura, 1977), 28-29. Another source refers to the presence of 'aggressive imperialist forces' as a further factor that demands the strengthening of the Soviet state: see Volkov et al., op. cit., 292.

54. Volkov et al., op. cit., 294.

55. *XXV S"ezd KPSS,* Vol. 1, 95-96.

56. A.Ye. Lunev et al. (eds.), *Nauchnye Osnovy Gosudarstvennogo Upravleniya v SSSR* (Moscow: Nauka, 1968), Chap. 10; Yu.M. Kozlov, *Kul'tura Upravleniya i Pravo* (Moscow: Znanie, 1978); *Apparat Upravleniya,* 235-238.

57. Tikhomirov, op. cit., 217.

58. Ibid., 131, 218; Shakhnazarov, op. cit., 157.

59. N.T. Kozlov, 'Povyshenie Roli Mestnykh Sovetov na Sovremennom Etape', *SGiP,* No. 9 (1968), 5-6. For a Western study of this and related problems see William Taubman, *Governing Soviet Cities* (New York: Praeger, 1973).

60. For example, in 1965 it was reported that the State Planning Commission in Kazakhstan employed 24 shorthand-typists, yet not one of them knew shorthand: see M.I. Piskotin and Yu.A. Tikhomirov, 'Sovershenstvovanie Organizatsii i Metodov Deyatel'nosti Apparata Gosudarstvennogo Upravleniya', *SGiP,* No. 9 (1965), 5.

61. The texts of these statements were reprinted in *SDT,* No. 4 (1971), 11-15, 30-31.

62. V. Nebylitsa, 'Litso Raionnogo Tsentra', *Sovetskaya Moldaviya,* 12 November 1971, 2.

63. See, for example, Shakhnazarov, op. cit., 122; Tikhomirov, op. cit., 112.

64. V.I. Lenin, *The State and Revolution* (various editions), Chap. 3, Section 2.

65. Theodore H. Friedgut, 'Citizens and Soviets: Can Ivan Ivanovich Fight City Hall?', *Comparative Politics,* Vol. 10 (1978), 464.

66. For documentation on these points see Hill, op. cit., Chaps 2-4.

67. See, for example, N. Arutyunyan, 'Deputat i ego Delo', *Izvestiya,* 4 March 1969, 1.

68. See, for example, A.A. Bezuglov, *Soviet Deputy (Legal Status)* (Moscow: Progress Publishers, 1973), 21.

69. The 1972 Statute on the Deputies' Status required the deputies to be fully provided with documentation in advance of the sessions, to allow them to come properly prepared for a businesslike debate; however, the avalanche of materials which has followed, in some parts of the country at any rate, led two experienced deputies to suggest in 1977 that sessions should be held less often, since the preparation for sessions, in mastering the paperwork alone, was proving too burdensome and time-consuming — partly because much of it concerned trivial matters that ought to be resolved administratively: see T. Slepneva and V. Mineeva, 'A Ne Luchshe Li Raz v Kvartal?', *SDT,* No. 9 (1977), 22-23. Clearly, the problems of the adequate functioning of the soviets are far from solved.

70. G.M. Gak, 'Obshchestvennye i Lichnye Interesy i ikh Sochetanie pri Sotsializme', *Voprosy Filosofii,* No. 4 (1955), 17-28.

71. Yu.S. Zav'yalov, 'Vyrazhenie Interesov v Sotsialisticheskom Prave', *SGiP,* No. 6 (1970), 104; B. M. Lazarev, 'Sotsial'nye Interesy i Kompetentsiya Organov Upravleniya', *SGiP,* No. 10 (1971), 86.

72. I.P. Il'inskii et al. (eds.), *Sotsialisticheskoe Gosudarstvo: Sushchnost', Funktsii i Formy* (Moscow: Mysl', 1976), 16; the phraseology here is taken from Brezhnev's speech to the 24th CPSU Congress, in *XXIV S"ezd KPSS,* Vol. 1, 97. The metaphor bears a striking resemblance to Western views of interest articulation and aggregation.

73. See, for example, R.A. Safarov, *Obshchestvennoe Mnenie i Gosudarstvennoe Upravlenie* (Moscow: Yuridicheskaya Literatura, 1975), 92, Note 1; R.A. Safarov, 'Obshchestvennoe Mnenie v Usloviyakh Razvitogo Sotsializma', *Kommunist,* No. 12 (1977), 40.

74. See, in particular, V.F. Kotok, *Referendum v Sisteme Sotsialisticheskoi Demokratii* (Moscow: Nauka, 1964). The 1977 Constitution incorporates this device in Article 5, although it remains to be seen how significant it will prove to be in the functioning of the political system.

75. See, for example, *Pravda,* 5 June 1975, 1; *Sovetskaya Moldaviya,* 18 March 1975, 1; the point is also stressed by Safarov in his article 'Vyyavlenie Obshchestvennogo Mneniya v Gosudarstvenno-pravovoi Praktike', *SGiP,* No. 10 (1967), 51-52, and also by the Central Committee, in *Kommunist,* No. 8 (1976), 3-5.

76. The most explicit statement to this effect was made by Brezhnev at the 25th Congress: see *XXV S"ezd KPSS,* Vol. 1, 92. Other examples of statements by the central authorities on this question are to be found in *KPSS v Rezolyutsiyakh,* Vol. 9 (1972), 369-373 and Vol. 12 (1978), 269-272, and elsewhere.

77. See, for example, M.N. Marchenko, *Politicheskaya Sistema Sovetskogo Obshchestva i eë Burzhuaznye Fal'sifikatory* (Moscow: Izdatel'stvo Moskovskogo Universiteta, 1973), 100.

78. For a recent assessment of the effectiveness of the Soviet government's efforts at political enlightenment see White, 'Political Socialization in the USSR', and his lengthier treatment, *Political Culture and Soviet Politics* (London: Macmillan, 1979).

79. See, for example, Shakhnazarov, op. cit., 80-82; Tikhomirov, op. cit., 121-122. Brezhnev too has spoken of a need for 'strengthening the legal basis of state and public life': see *XXV S"ezd KPSS,* Vol. 1, 106.

80. A.S. Pigolkin and I.N. Rozhko, *Sovetskoe Zakonodatel'stvo i ego Rol' v Kommunisticheskom Stroitel'stve* (Moscow: Znanie, 1976), 51.

81. This phrase, according to Moshe Lewin, was a party promise 'made in 1919, never repeated, and never fulfilled': see his *Political Undercurrents in Soviet Economic Debates* (London: Pluto Press, 1975), 243.

82. See Tikhomirov, op. cit., 277-278; Yu.A. Tikhomirov (ed.), *Sovetskoe Gosudarstvo v Usloviyakh Razvitogo Sotsialisticheskogo Obshchestva* (Moscow: Nauka, 1978), 58; the author in both cases is G.N. Manov.

83. See, for example, Tikhomirov, *Demokratiya Razvitogo Sotsialisticheskogo Obshchestva,* 86.

84. This point is argued at length in Hill, op. cit.

85. Hough, 'Political Participation in the Soviet Union'.

86. Archie Brown emphasizes the 'fear of chaos' as an important element in the Soviet political culture: see his *Soviet Politics and Political Science* (London: Macmillan, 1974), 93.

10 Yugoslavia: Toward Self-Management?

Ralph Pervan
University of Western Australia

INTRODUCTION

In the communist world and indeed the world as a whole, Yugoslavia has an importance far beyond what one would expect of a country of its size and economic strength. This is due to various interrelated factors most of which derive from Yugoslavia's position, precariously poised between East and West. These factors include the remarkable resistance movement of World War II, the successful defiance by its leaders of Stalin, its leading role in the nonaligned movement and its bold socio-political model known as self-management.

Yugoslav spokesmen claim this model as a major step towards Marx's 'association of free producers', that is, towards a system in which all have a real opportunity to participate as equals in the decisions affecting them in both the workplace and community.

As a substitute for directives from the state apparatus, emphasis is given to workers' control within particular economic and communal collectives and to 'self-management agreements' and 'social compacts', which establish mutual rights and responsibilities and which are worked out in negotiations between these separate collectives. Similarly, 'delegation' rather than 'representation' is stressed as a means of reaching such agreements and compacts (as well as determining any laws which may still be necessary) with the aim of ensuring that power remains in the hands of the working people. In short, it is urged that not only has there been a substantial reduction in the role of the state but that, largely through the delegate system, the state has been transformed from something above the working class to the instrument of that class.

And what is the role of the Communist Party, or rather, as it is known, the League of Communists of Yugoslavia (LCY)? It is insisted that the dramatic transformation in the role of the state has not been achieved by enlarging the role of the communist organization; on the contrary, the role of the League has been reduced primarily to one of guidance, so paralleling these other changes.[1]

The self-management model emphasizes the determination of the rights and responsibilities of individuals and groups through discussion leading towards consensus; it therefore assumes a considerable sense of community and responsibility. However, it is difficult to imagine a country which has more obstacles than Yugoslavia to the development of such attributes.

The chief obstacle is the enormous diversity of its peoples, a diversity born of both its history and geography.[2] For centuries the region was a battleground between rival religions (most notably Catholic, Orthodox and Islam) and between rival empires. From the beginning of the sixteenth century only the city state of Dubrovnik (at least until 1805) and the tiny, mountainous and barren Montenegro maintained a precarious independence. It was not until 1878 with the decay of the Turkish Empire that Serbia formally won its independence and it was only with the collapse of the Austro-Hungarian Empire in World War I that the last major empire was pushed from the region. The different circumstances and historical experiences of the various groups led to the development of profoundly different and often mutually suspicious and habitually hostile societies. At one extreme, for example, the traditional values stressed 'honour', while at the other, values of hard work and thrift were developed. According to one Yugoslav sociologist, the range and diversity might best be appreciated by imagining a country containing both a Switzerland and a Syria[3] — one is tempted to add 'and just about everything in between'. The experience of generations of foreign control and exploitation, often implemented by soldiers and officials of another south Slav ethnic group, bred a suspicion of outsiders as well as a feeling that government was the enemy to be fought, fooled, bribed or evaded. Conversely, clan, district and, to a lesser extent, ethnic 'connections' became of central importance. These connections, rather than regulations and laws, were the primary means by which one sought to survive and prosper.

It was not until after World War I that the peoples of present-day Yugoslavia were even brought within the same boundary. From the beginning there was bitter dispute especially between the Serbs and the Croats — the Serbs, dominant within the central governmental structures, favoured a greater concentration of power; conversely, the Croatians sought its dispersal. Another dimension to the conflict within Yugoslavia was seen in the activity of the Communist Party.

These conflicts, some of which grew out of and were stimulated by the desperate economic situation, led to the discarding of the parliamentary system in 1929 and the assumption by the monarch of virtually complete powers. At the same time the name of the state was changed from the Kingdom of the Serbs, Croats and Slovenes to Yugoslavia, and the various south Slav ethnic groups were proclaimed as 'tribes' of the one Yugoslav nation. However, the ethnic problem was not one that could simply be defined away. And despite the harsh measures directed against the Communist Party and the decimation of its ranks, the party survived to provide the framework on which was built first a guerilla movement and then an army during World War II. The assumption of power by the communists at the end of this war was in large part due to their leadership of this major resistance movement; this sharply distinguished them from the other regimes of Eastern Europe.

During the war almost eleven per cent of the population lost their lives, more than half of them at the hands of their 'fellow Yugoslavs' and this often not in battle but in cold-blooded slaughter[4] — such was the intensity of the political, ethnic and religious hatreds which divided these peoples. The new leaders of Yugoslavia insisted, however, that, despite these events, a new relationship based on the 'brotherhood and unity' of the various ethnic groups had been forged in the Partisan struggle.

The new government quickly set about consolidating its control and embarking on new policies. The first included the removal, often local and spontaneous, of both past and potential rivals.[5] The second meant nothing less than endeavouring to build a modern industrialized society almost overnight through a political and economic system closely modelled on that of the Soviet Union in which the state controlled and regulated almost every aspect of life.

There was only one significant exception. No doubt recognizing the danger of alienating that group which had formed the basis of the Partisan movement and which now formed the backbone of the army, police and party, the Yugoslav leaders refrained from the collectivization of agriculture.

All their plans, however, were thrown into confusion by the break in 1948 with Stalin and the consequent expulsion of the 'Tito clique' from the communist fraternity. For some time there had been differences and even tensions between the Yugoslav and Soviet leaders. In particular, the ambitions and pride of the Yugoslav leaders meant that they did not easily accept that they should totally subordinate themselves to Stalin's grand design or stand idly by as the Soviet leadership sought to have its agents infiltrate the major organs of society.[6] The Yugoslav leadership vehemently insisted that this latter action was unnecessary and that it impugned their loyalty to Stalin and the Soviet Union. However, it would be surprising if wounded pride were the only reason for their protestations; Tito at least, with his long experience of Stalin's methods, could not have been unaware of the threat this penetration posed. Nevertheless, while the Yugoslav leaders were prepared to resist on such points, they were devastated when they found themselves suddenly thrown out of the parental home. Their initial reaction was to proclaim their fervent loyalty to Stalin and to urge that the dispute derived merely from misunderstandings. To prove both their loyalty and their ideological integrity they even embarked on a vigorous programme of agricultural collectivization and generally strengthened central controls.[7] But to no avail — the breach remained.

To justify the continuation of this breach the Yugoslav leaders then began to criticize the Stalinist system — the model which until very recently they had faithfully followed — and proclaimed a dramatically new model, that of self-management. This model entailed nothing less than the dismantling of those centralized structures. A new and important era in the history of world communism had begun.

THE PARTY

In 1920 the Communist Party of Yugoslavia had some 65,000

members and significant electoral support. Shortly afterwards, however, the party began a precipitous decline down to a mere 500 members. Most significant in this decline was its persecution by the government which included the banning of the party, but also of relevance was the factionalism which rent it from within.[8]

The deteriorating domestic and international situation in the late 1930s provided both the opportunity and desire for the new party leadership (headed by Josip Broz) to expand the party's ranks, and by July 1941 membership had grown to 12,000.[9] This membership became the nucleus around which the overwhelmingly peasant-based resistance struggle of World War II was organized.

As a means of maintaining and extending control, the party leadership drew an increasing number of these new recruits into the party — by the end of the war the party had grown to just under 150,000. These recruits often appeared to accept the party not so much because of its economic and social policy, but rather because it was the most vigorous opponent of the occupiers and their domestic allies. This new influx, together with the decimation of the ranks of the pre-war Communists (only 3,000 of the 12,000 survived the war) meant that the party became overwhelmingly a party of the resistance movement, overwhelmingly a party of peasants.[10]

In the immediate post-war period, the party, together with the security forces, was the leadership's principal weapon of control. Many communists found themselves placed at this time in positions which were often beyond their experience, qualifications or even abilities; they received these posts in part because the number of positions was expanding rapidly as the Yugoslav leadership sought to bring about dramatic change, in part because they were adjudged the more reliable in what was still seen as an uncertain political situation and in part because of the time-honoured tradition that to the victor belong the spoils. Concerning this last point it is noteworthy that, in marked contrast to the ascetism which was preached and often observed during the war itself, most of these new office-holders were quick to claim the privileges they deemed appropriate to individuals in such exalted posts. The old, much admired model of the 'gospodin', the gentleman who never deigned to soil his hands, quickly reappeared as the model for the functionaries of the new regime.

Inevitably, as the months passed, as the problems of transforming the economy and society became more apparent and

as officials at various levels became increasingly attached to their
new life style, revolutionary fervour began to wane. Nonetheless
the sudden announcement in 1948 of the split with Stalin came as a
stunning blow. For those with the greater commitment to Marxist
ideology the dilemma was clearly a serious one. A minority
wavered (or threatened to waver) toward the Soviet position and
found themselves quickly purged from the party and in many
cases imprisoned. The overwhelming majority however swung
behind Tito, the crucial factor appearing to be opposition to
foreign domination.

To strengthen its position in this crisis the leadership made
vigorous efforts to boost party membership; hence, despite the expulsion of those members who showed less than complete support
of the new party line, membership increased by over 60 per cent in
the years 1948-52.[11] As had been the case during the war, one
suspects that the major motivation for many of these new
members, leaving aside personal ambitions, was not so much doctrinal conviction as support for those resisting the external threat.
These points concerning the nature of the party membership must
be borne in mind when considering later debates concerning the
party's role.

As noted, the rift evoked vehement protestations that the breach
stemmed from misunderstandings. As time passed, with only a
worsening of the dispute and with the Yugoslav leadership retaining its control both within the party and the country, it was no
longer sufficient or necessary to maintain that the Soviet leaders had
made an unfortunate error; rather, it was necessary to explain how
they could persist in this error. Consequently, the Yugoslav leaders
began to assert that the Soviet Union under Stalin's domination
had distorted the basic tenets of Marxism and had built a system
characterized by the growing, rather than declining, power of the
state apparatus, and had developed a bureaucracy which stood
above the masses in an exploitative relationship. Similarly, the relationship between the Soviet state and the other socialist states was
described as being essentially a relationship of exploitation rather
than mutual benefit.[12]

Thus, as they sought to explain and justify the past, the Yugoslav
leaders were forced onto a new path. And, with the passage of
time, what began as reluctant and nervous steps away from the
Stalinist pattern developed into an eloquent elaboration of an alternative model, 'self-management'. It was observed that the term

'management' customarily meant that one man, or group of men, dominated other men; the new system of 'self-management' negated this contradiction as man became both worker and manager. (Incidentally, it is worth noting that recent explanations by Yugoslav spokesmen of the abandonment of the Soviet model play down the rupture with Stalin, presenting it more as a catalyst than a cause.)[13]

The self-management system was presented as crucial to the construction of a truly socialist society; it was asserted that socialism could not be built or imposed from above but rather had to grow from below, from the people themselves, that the state apparatus must be permitted to 'wither' away, and that it was no longer appropriate to have the party as a directing and controlling force.[14] This must be borne in mind when considering comments of Yugoslav spokesmen regarding the necessity of recognizing the right of each country to determine according to its own particular circumstances its own path towards socialism; it is difficult to avoid the impression that they often seek to imply that one path is smoother and more direct than some they are too diplomatic to name.

To symbolize the changed role of the party from that of direction to guidance, its name was changed from the Communist Party to the League of Communists (1952). Inevitably there was confusion. At one extreme were those who believed that a drastic reduction in the role of the League was imperative, most notably one of Tito's closest associates, Milovan Djilas. However, his colleagues were not prepared to accept his views for a variety of reasons — fear that the level of socialist consciousness within the League and society was too low, that their own positions and privileges might be jeopardized and even that if the League withdrew too precipitously the secret police and army might fill the resultant gap. They dismissed Djilas as a 'pseudo-liberal', who sought to reduce the league to a discussion club with no responsibility to struggle against anti-socialist tendencies and for socialism.[15]

At the other extreme, a significant number were described as behaving as though the eloquent principles of self-management were mere slogans in a propaganda war.

The principal exponent of this tendency was alleged to be Aleksandar Ranković, also a close associate of Tito; indeed, prior to his fall from favour in 1966 he was seen as Tito's right hand man and probable successor. He was charged with having used his position as organizational secretary of the League and his influence over the secret police to establish an apparatus through which reforms and self-management itself were gravely undermined; by means of massive domestic spying and the spreading of false information he had been able to slant discussions within even top party circles and politically to destroy large numbers of officials and then to replace them with his own supporters — in Tito's words, there was a 'considerable resemblance' between Ranković's methods and Stalin's. Even his immediate colleagues were subjected to telephone taps and listening devices. Indeed Ranković may have lost the crucial support of Tito because of the latter's discovery that such devices were apparently being used against himself.[16]

The situation within the League was far more complex than the bald presentation of these two positions suggests; both positions continued to exist within the party and often within the same individual. Which one appeared to predominate at a certain time often depended on particular circumstances, both foreign and domestic, and on a variety of factors, some 'principled', some pragmatic and some personal (the importance of some of these factors is elaborated below).

Ranković's removal provided the opportunity for those leaders at the republican level who had chafed under his domination to strengthen their own positions. It is important to note that it was not merely the so-called liberals in Slovenia and Croatia who spoke out against the Ranković system, but also the so-called conservatives from the other republics.

Their efforts to strengthen their positions were seen in two broad areas. First, only some 10 per cent of the delegates to the subsequent republican party congresses had previously attended such a congress and only some 31 per cent of the republican central committees retained their positions.[17] Those brushed aside tended to be older members of the League, often of the Partisan group, who were suspected of being sympathetic to the Ranković 'firm hand' centralist policies. Second, the League appeared to change into a confederation of separate republican organizations rather than a single body. For example, in contrast to previous practice, members of the central organs of the LCY were elected by the various republican congresses rather than coopted from above, and these central organs were reconstituted on the basis of strict parity of representatives for each republic and 'appropriate' representation for each autonomous province.[18]

Increasingly, the republican leaders of the League seemed concerned with maintaining their republican base and, increasingly, decisions of the central organs of the League appeared to be the result of negotiations between representatives of separate republican organizations. Arising out of this were the changes in the federal constitution (sketched in the following section) which weakened the power of the central state organs and strengthened those of the several republics. In turn there was the gradual clogging up of the central organs of both the state and League machinery. The new system in effect provided structures in which consensus between the views of the separate parts was to be reached; however, forces had been unleashed and stimulated which made the reaching of consensus increasingly difficult.

Inevitably, the League became far less effective in carrying out its role. The guidance of the League continued to be described as crucial because the socialist consciousness of many was such that they often saw only their immediate interests. It was the task, for example, of communists within a collective to explain how the 'real' interests of the collective could be harmonized with the interests of individuals, other collectives and with the interests of the socialist community as a whole without a detailed and inevitably clumsy central plan. Take the policy of a factory collective concerning scholarships for university students and concerning the employment of graduates; it was the task of communists to point out that the long-term interest of the collective lay, first, in providing scholarships to ensure the availability of appropriately qualified experts, and second, in employing these experts when they had completed their studies. This would improve the factory's productivity and at the same time the interests of the entire socialist community would be advanced by policies which led to the education and employment of experts who were actually needed. As for the students, they could expect the assistance of a particular collective and, at the end of their studies, worthwhile employment.[19] This at least was the theory.

With the gradual relaxation of central controls within the League following Ranković's removal, League policy became increasingly vague. This may have been inevitable, given the wide range of attitudes and interests of the members; in addition there were no simple solutions to the worsening problems of high inflation, unemployment and uneven regional development. Further, it was apparent that there were some who felt these problems were best left for the market to resolve. This reflected, according to a subsequent judgement of the League leadership, the fact that the League had become more a party of the middle and upper levels of society (bureaucrats, managers and the like),[20] because for the ambitious, League membership remained useful, indeed almost indispensable. Many were described as using the influence which came from League membership to obstruct League policies not to their advantage. Thus they might resist the employment of young experts in their collective, fearing the effect on their own careers, or they might urge pricing policies for their collective simply on the basis of what the market would stand.[21]

The effect of the changed structures and climate in the post-Ranković era became most visible and significant in Croatia. In addition to providing greater scope to 'liberal technocrats', the leaders emphasized what they termed the injustices still suffered by their republic, despite the reforms, and the manner in which the implementation of some of the reforms (especially regarding banks) had been to Croatia's disadvantage. This greatly strengthened their position within the republican League organization because it aroused a responsive chord with many in that organization and the community. However, this heightened support in turn became pressure to expand their demands. For example, the leadership in Croatia now began to urge that Croatia should keep the foreign currency it 'earned' through its enormous number of foreign tourists. As has been cogently argued,[22] this would have destroyed a unified Yugoslav market and led to bewildering counter claims. For example, would Croatia be required to pay foreign currency for the food it purchased from other republics for its tourists?

The expression of increasingly strident nationalist views, mass demonstrations, a student strike and so on led to increasing tensions particularly between Serbs and Croats within Croatia and increasing concern even from liberals in other republics that the Croatian leadership might have gone too far. According to Tito there was even the threat of civil war. Eventually the situation was defused, at least for the time being, through a major purge in Croatia in late 1971.[23]

Not long afterwards the purge was extended to the other republics, most notably Serbia. Here the post-Ranković leadership had tended towards a more liberal position, in no small part because Serbia, for reasons elaborated in the succeeding section, had found itself doing much better under the economic reforms than had been expected. As was also the case particularly in Croatia and Slovenia, the leaders had allowed substantial scope to the market and thus to 'liberal technocrats'. These leaders were described by some, including most notably Tito himself, as having failed to deal adequately with developments which stemmed from the unchecked operation of market forces, developments which included the stimulation of Serbian nationalism. Justified or not, the clear inference was that these leaders sympathized with and supported these developments and therefore had to be removed. Significantly, so firm was the resistance of the Serbian League that Tito was obliged to use all his prestige and authority to force the resignation of the key figures.[24]

Subsequently, the balance within the top ranks of the League in all regions was shifted toward more conservative and often older cadres and the organization's unity and role was strengthened in several major areas. The dominance of the central leadership was reasserted; the League, as demonstrated by substantial personnel changes in the media, publishing, universities and the like, resumed a major role in appointments; it sought a more direct role in socio-political organizations; and it urged greater worker and youth representation at lower and middle levels of the League so as to dilute the influence of 'liberal technocrats' and enhance the possibility of its policies being implemented. In short, according to the distinguished Yugoslav political scientist Dušan Bilandžić, the slogan that the League should not interfere was suppressed and the view that it was responsible for developments in society was renewed.[25]

THE STATE

Several major obstacles impede the ready understanding of the changing role of the state apparatus in Yugoslavia: the major debates were rarely conducted directly and openly, the principal declarations may in fact mask a very different underlying trend and there is an enormous mass of relevant material — since World War II there have been no less than four different constitutions (the latest of which runs to 406 articles over some 160 pages) as well as several major constitutional amendments. However, one thing is clear in all of these changes — at least until relatively recently, there has been a strong trend towards a diminution of the powers of the central government and state bureaucracies in general.

In the immediate post-war period, economic enterprises functioned merely as branches of government. As noted earlier, it was not until after the rupture with Stalin that changes occurred and most of them were more significant in theory than in practice.[26] For example, legislation in 1950 gave workers the formal right to manage their enterprises, but, since state organs continued to decide production, income and investment, the essentials of the administrative state were preserved.[27]

Nevertheless, a new set of principles had been invoked and it would not be easy to turn back. For example, those who favoured further change, for whatever reason, tended to base their case on self-management, thus forcing their opponents into the untenable position of appearing to be against it.

Efforts to meet the expectations aroused by this new rhetoric, as well as to deal with the burgeoning economic problems, prompted further changes which were proclaimed as enhancing the independence of individual enterprises. The avowed goal was to stimulate greater productivity by providing greater incentives and reducing 'irrational' political controls and at the same time to make self-management more of a reality. But again the changes were much less significant than heralded and the consequences not always what was predicted or expected.

For example, efforts towards the expansion of the role of local authorities often led neither to the more efficient use of resources nor to the expansion of self-management. Factories in various communities would be opened frequently on the basis of overly optimistic or even deliberately misleading presentations and often the approval for such proposals came for political and personal reasons rather than economic. Once established, local pressure coupled with these political and personal links ensured the factory's continued survival through regular financial support from government funds.[28]

On the one hand, the leadership proclaimed the necessity of reducing the drain of these so-called 'political factories' and of expanding self-management rights and responsibilities. On the other hand (and here the influence of Ranković was of paramount importance), subsidies continued to be provided for these enterprises, and controls, albeit of a different sort, continued to be exercised. The significant consequences therefore were not so much the expansion of self-management as the stimulation of localism and the expansion of Ranković's authority.

Even at the formal level the change in the position of enterprises was far less than it at first sight appeared. The division within the League leadership meant that a particular proposal providing for substantial change might be agreed to only after it had been qualified virtually out of existence. For example, beginning in 1952, enterprises were relieved of detailed regulation by state organs so that they could independently determine such matters as the type and quantity of production. However, in practice, incentive to change was limited because any increase in revenue would not be their own and any significant loss was usually covered by government subsidy; the apparently decentralized decision making process occurred within a centralized system of collection and disbursement of funds. The reforms of 1958 had similar justification and similar effect.[29]

In 1961 there were further changes which reduced the role of the state — but almost immediately economic difficulties prompted government intervention, which appeared to herald the imminent return to central controls. A vigorous debate ensued.[30] The frequently veiled statements make it difficult to determine the principal positions, but there appeared to be two major camps. Some opposed the reduction of central controls, urging that the economic achievements since the war demonstrated the value of such methods while the current economic difficulties demonstrated their need. In their opinion the market at least unless carefully regulated was an imperfect and dangerous tool. Others however urged that there were basic weaknesses in the methods adopted to date or at least that they were now outmoded. They claimed that political controls led to serious distortion and waste, that long term economic strength required integration into the world economy and that this could not occur while potentially strong industries were drained or neglected while others with minimal prospects continued to be subsidized. As for the current economic difficulties, they only confirmed the need to place the economy on a more realistic footing.

Members of the more conservative group expressed concern that the greater reliance on the market and the consequent encouragement of 'consumerism' would lead to the weakening of socialist values. Others, however, insisted that the present restraints prevented working people from realizing their self-management rights and from enjoying the benefits of their own endeavour. Further, the strength and legitimacy of the system depended to no small degree on its capacity to meet the aspirations of the populace for better living standards; these could only be satisfied by further changes.

Many among the more conservative group appeared concerned that greater emphasis on the market would seriously retard growth in the less developed regions by the destruction of their infant industries in open competition and by the reduction of state investment funds. Continued support for these regions was urged as a demonstration of socialist solidarity. They pointed to the bitterness deriving from the gulf between the richer and poorer regions, a bitterness fuelled by the conviction that the wealth of the more developed regions was to no small extent due to the artificially low prices they paid for raw materials from the less developed regions and the artificially high prices for finished products which they obtained within a protected Yugoslav market. By contrast, members of the more liberal group suggested that effective development of these regions could only flow from rational economic policies and certainly not from policies which bled efficient collectives so as to prop up waste and inefficiency.

As the latter points show, the division was not a simple philosophical one but one overlain with regional and ethnic considerations. To a remarkable degree the divisions within Yugoslavia reflected the cleavage in international politics between 'developed' and 'developing'; it was no coincidence that most of those described as liberals came from the more developed republics of Slovenia and Croatia, nor was it coincidence that most of those described as conservatives tended to come from the less developed regions. However, the battle lines were neither clear nor permanent. Coalitions formed and re-formed as the economic climate changed, as concessions were made or as new possibilities or dangers were seen.

At first in 1962/63 the conservatives seemed to have the upper hand but economic difficulties weakened their confidence and support. The leaders of some of the less developed regions moved closer to the liberal position, in part because of their view that the present system kept them too much under the control of Belgrade and in part by the promise of a special fund to assist the less developed regions.[31]

This led to decisions which described the market as the decisive factor in economic regulation, which made banks rather than state organs the primary source of investment funds and which brought prices closer to world prices. The role of the central state apparatus was thus substantially reduced; however it still retained responsibility for broad monetary and fiscal policy.[32]

Almost immediately there were economic difficulties.[33] Some urged this was due to external factors, others that the reforms had gone too far while others seemed to believe that the reforms had been sabotaged, largely by forces led by Ranković. As noted earlier, his removal gave the various republican leaders the opportunity to root out his actual or potential supporters and to consolidate their own positions; with that came a substantial shift of power within the LCY from the centre to the various republican organizations. In turn there was a dramatic change of the formal structure and rules of the League and of the state apparatus. In part this reflected what the republican leaders managed to win and in part it reflected the desire at the centre to placate the grievances felt within the separate republics and which had grown out of the previous system. Thus the 'sovereignty' of the republics on most subjects was officially conceded and the powers of the federation were limited to what were in general terms described as foreign affairs, defence and steps necessary to preserve a single Yugoslav-wide market and ethnic equality. It was also insisted that there should be equitable representation for all within the federal organs. Thus a collective presidency was established consisting of equal representation from each republic and 'appropriate representation' from the two autonomous provinces. The changes in economic policy which were now implemented substantially boosted production. However, significant problems also resulted, in particular, inflation, unemployment and economic disparities all increased rapidly. In turn this exacerbated or revived the resentments of various groups which had, under the reformed structures of both party and state, greater opportunity for expression.[34]

Most bitterness was expressed in Croatia both within the League and by leaders of outside groups (students and the major Croatian cultural organization) which flourished in the freer atmosphere. They insisted that they were robbed of their rightful share of foreign exchange earnings and complained of the growing might of the central banks based in Belgrade; central government funding had been largely ended but the effect of the reforms was to replace it with funding by banks concentrated in the Serbian capital. These banks became increasingly significant in economic policy-making.

At a more general level fears were expressed concerning broad societal developments now that the role of the state had been greatly diminished and the League as a whole and its members were proving unable and/or unwilling to provide significant guidance. The emphasis in the economy was also entirely on increasing income at both the personal and the collective level. Thus, banks, export/import agencies and those with a near or actual monopoly in a particular product were described as charging virtually what the market would bear and consequently income differentials between collectives soared. Within particular collectives the emphasis was not so much on the development of self-management as on profit, and managers often sought and received a virtual free hand.

Inevitably there were strong resentments at the manner in which some were able to boost their incomes. Particular resentment was directed at banks which were seen as making enormous profits on the money earned by others. However, others retorted that allowing banks to determine investment policies independently of government interference was the best means of encouraging general economic growth.[35] The emphasis on profit, income and consumerism together with the encouragement of small scale private business heightened concern regarding the future of socialism; in the words of the frequently-heard quip, Yugoslavia was demonstrating the possibility of the peaceful transition from socialism to capitalism.

Confusion, uncertainty and resentments were rife, all of which help explain the points made earlier concerning how the decision-making process at the federal level was virtually stalemated, how different interests came to be expressed, how nationalism was described as having become a major problem and how ultimately Tito decided on a purge of leaders, especially in Croatia and Serbia.

In the aftermath of these expulsions and demotions, greater attention was given to the so-called 'workers amendments' to the Constitution made in 1971; hitherto, they had virtually been ignored because of the focus on the amendments relating to the federation. The amendments had the avowed aim of providing workers with a real opportunity to control their own affairs; for example, large enterprises were to be broken down into smaller, self-contained entities called Basic Organizations of Associated Labour. The decisions of particular collectives regarding the allocation of funds for personal incomes, social services and investment, regarding prices and the like were to be decided according to criteria set by 'self-management agreements' and 'social compacts', which were voluntarily entered into by the various organizations. Further, public services were to be provided not by state organs but by 'self-managing communities of interest'. These bodies would bring together delegates from collectives which provided a particular service and delegates from those collectives which benefitted from that service. The assembled delegates would decide, for example, what the education system was to furnish within the commune and decide the support to be provided by the various work organizations.[36]

As noted earlier, of fundamental significance was the insistence that all these agreements and compacts (as well as any laws, which might still be necessary) were made by 'delegates'; bourgeois representative democracy was specifically rejected as being outmoded and undemocratic. According to the theory of the delegate system, a topic was discussed and a position reached at each level; delegates were then obliged to present this position at the next level and then, after the matter was decided among the assembled delegates, to report back to their collectives.[37]

It seems that a major aim of implementing this reform was to provide some means of restraining 'liberal technocrats' without dramatically increasing the role of state organs. Each collective would be obliged to observe limits set in negotiations with delegates from other collectives; adequate worker representation in these delegations was also emphasized, such delegates being seen as more responsive to guidance by the League; further, because of their direct and real links with other groups, workers would be less easily manipulated by liberal technocrats within their own collectives and more readily kept under League control. The need to justify their policies in negotiation with other collectives, particularly since many of the delegates were at the same time members of a League in which discipline had been significantly tightened, was seen as an effective means of ensuring that the separate collectives were more successfully restrained than in the past.

The avowed aim remained to keep the role of the state to a minimum; however, that minimum was now seen as substantially greater than had been the case in the near past. Thus the most recent Constitution emphasizes the broad right and responsibility of the state to act as a guardian of socialism — for example, to intervene, 'if serious harm has been caused to social interests'.[38] In explaining this reversal of what was a consistent trend it was urged that previously the major threat to self-management came from bureaucratic forces, hence reducing the power of the state was the progressive course. However, this reduction of state power opened the way for liberal technocrats who then became the principal danger so in this situation the withering of the state was the reactionary course;[39] and, of course, the development of the delegate system was described as transforming the contemporary state into the instrument of the working people.

CONCLUSIONS

Of all the countries of the communist bloc, Yugoslavia stands out as the one which has made the most radical change in its basic political system. Almost overnight the party which had seemed more Stalinist than Stalin's own became the bitterest critic of the centralized Soviet model and almost overnight a dramatically new model emphasizing participation, not only as the right of all working people but also as essential to the construction of socialism, was proclaimed. According to the party's principal theoretician, Edvard Kardelj, 'No state, no system and no political party can bring a man happiness'. Rather, the opportunity must be provided for individuals and groups to voice their own interests and to determine their rights and obligations in discussion and negotiation within particular collectives and between collectives.[40] In this system the role of the state is substantially reduced and the nature of the state fundamentally transformed to ensure it does not stand above the working people. Similarly the League is described as having been altered from something above society (in the manner of the traditional single-party) to an organization which is an integral part of society, guiding and inspiring, but also learning and adapting according to circumstances which include the views of the working people themselves.[41]

Clearly this is a most ambitious model — it requires substantial basic agreement and a degree of interest and participation far above that of our own. It is especially ambitious when one has regard for the traditions and cultures as well as the circumstances of contemporary Yugoslavia. Those being asked to decide complex economic and social policy often have limited knowledge of urban, industrial society, most of them being scarcely one step removed from a traditional, insular peasant background. (In 1948, two thirds of the active population were engaged in agriculture and in 1953 four fifths had not even completed primary school.) One suspects that most of those who have flocked to the cities since the war (reducing those engaged in agriculture to 31 per cent of the total by 1977) are preoccupied with coping with the massive dislocation in their personal lives.[42] In addition there are the bitter ethnic rivalries (compounded by the growing assertiveness among the Moslem minorities, which constitute at least 16 per cent of the total population), low and uneven economic development coupled with high and growing expectations, a low level of socialist consciousness and commitment in the community and the League itself, a strong commitment to private interests and personal connections and the seriousness and complexity of many of the current economic problems.

Prior to 1966 the most overt consequences of such factors appeared to be held in check by the controls largely organized by Tito's close associate, Aleksandar Ranković. Indeed it might be claimed that despite profound formal changes many aspects of the 'bureaucratic' system were preserved.[43] Ranković's deposal opened the way for significant changes, providing substantially greater opportunity for the expression of particular demands. However this greater freedom only revealed how deep and irreconcilable many of the cleavages were.

Since the early 1970s the leadership, while vigorously proclaiming the further evolution of self-management, has clearly sought to tighten controls so as to eliminate what it termed these nationalist and liberal-technocratic excesses. The methods include increasing the representation of youth and workers within all sociopolitical bodies, strengthening the role of the state and tightening discipline within and enhancing the role of the League. In this vein it is important to note that Kardelj, in the same work in which he lauded the rights of individuals and groups to pursue their own interests and spoke of the need for the League to revise its policies 'when the prevailing social consciousness is still not ready to accept them', insisted on the continued need for 'special repressive measures' against the forces of 'bourgeois and technocratic-bureaucratic counter-revolution'.[44] In simple terms, this means that 'anti-socialist' ideas and developments cannot be permitted. The critical question is who determines what is, or is not, 'anti-socialist'? Here there can be no doubt that the leadership of the League insists that it alone has the final say.

The leadership has significant problems. The effort to restrain 'liberal-technocrats' and enhance the influence of the League leadership through an expanded role for youth and workers in delegations and in the League may have but limited success. It is clear that workers are still greatly underrepresented in delegations and further that they appear overwhelmed by the volume and complexity of materials they are expected to master outside their normal working hours. As for increased worker and youth representation within the League it is clear that this is frequently secured through 'campaign methods'. By implication, the members chosen in this way are unlikely to have the qualities or desire to play the role avowedly expected of them. Second, these new inexperienced members make up an enormous proportion of the League membership; of the membership in late 1977 some 40 per cent had joined in the previous four years. Just over 30 per cent of the new members were 'workers' bringing the percentage of workers in the total League to just under 30 per cent.[45] It may be that the leadership will be obliged to endeavour to devise policies at the top and then endeavour to force their implementation. The dilution of the existing membership with youth and workers who can be expected to be more amenable to League 'guidance' may, at least, make the latter a little easier by reducing the prospect of open resistance.

However, as the outline of the current problems suggests, it will not be easy in the post-Tito era to decide policies for the entire country despite, indeed partly because of, the elaborate structures providing for balanced representation of the various regions and ethnic groups and the system of annual rotation in League and state positions. These methods, designed to allay suspicions and fears (although presented primarily as a means of preventing the re-emergence of 'bureaucratism') only demonstrate how strong such feelings are. Further, there is the problem of tightening controls without jeopardizing vital Western economic support, without arousing substantial domestic opposition and without making a mockery of what is fundamental to the regime's claim to legitimacy, the system of self-management. It would be a mistake however to overlook the support for the recent, tighter policies; many citizens appeared concerned at the trends of the recent past, not necessarily because of a strong commitment to the system, but often because of a fear that any substantial change is likely to be for the worse.

NOTES

N.B. Where possible reference has been made to English language materials. Two admirable books which proved especially helpful for the present chapter were Dennison Rusinow, *The Yugoslav Experiment 1948-1974* (London: Hurst, 1977) and Dušan Bilandžić, *Historija SFRJ* (Zagreb: Školska Knjiga, 1978). I also had the benefit of valuable comments from Dr John Besemeres.

1. See 'Basic Principles' of the *Constitution of the Socialist Federal Republic of Yugoslavia* (hereinafter cited as *Constitution*) (New York: Merrick, 1976) and Edvard Kardelj, *Democracy and Socialism*, translated by Margot and Bosko Milosavljević (London: Summerfield, 1978), passim.

2. Useful historical background is contained in Fred Singleton, *Twentieth-Century Yugoslavia* (London: Macmillan, 1976); Wayne S. Vucinich (ed.), *Contemporary Yugoslavia: Twenty Years of the Yugoslav Experiment* (Berkeley and Los Angeles: University of California Press, 1969); and George W. Hoffman and Fred Warner Neal, *Yugoslavia and the New Communism* (New York: Twentieth Century Fund, 1962).

3. E. Pusić, 'The Yugoslav System of Self-Management', *Encyclopaedia Moderna*, Volume IX, Nos. 32-35 (1976), 114.

4. Singleton, op. cit., 86.

5. Rusinow, op. cit., 14-15.

6. Ibid., 24.

7. Singleton, op. cit., 120.

8. Pero Morača and others, *Istorija Saveza Komunista Jugoslavije* (Belgrade: Rad, 1976), 19-23, 33-37, 60 and Rusinow, op. cit., 7.

9. Ivan Laća, 'The League of Communists of Yugoslavia', *Yugoslav Survey*, Volume XVIII, No. 2 (1977), 28.

10. Statistics from Peter Jambrek, *Development and Social Change in Yugoslavia* (Lexington: Heath, 1975), 77.

11. Laća, op. cit., 29.

12. M. George Zaninovich, *The Development of Socialist Yugoslavia* (Baltimore: Johns Hopkins, 1968), 73-75.

13. Edvard Kardelj, 'Revolutionaries in Their Visions and Realists in Respect of Possibilities', *Socialist Thought and Practice*, Volume XVII, No. 5 (1977), 77-78.

14. Najdan Pašić, 'Osnove karakteristike i pravci razvoja društvenopolitickog sistema SFRJ', in Najdan Pašić and Balša Špadijer (eds), *Društveno Politički Sistem SFRJ* (Belgrade: Radnička štampa, 1976), 64 and *Programme of the League of Communists of Yugoslavia* (Belgrade: Komunist, 1977), 117 and 121.

15. Fred Warner Neal, *Titoism in Action: The Reforms in Yugoslavia after 1948* (Berkeley and Los Angeles: University of California Press, 1958), especially 47, 49, 64-69.

244   *Ralph Pervan*

16. Budislav Šoškić, 'Razvoj i suština društvene uloge Saveza komunista Jugoslavije', in Drago Roksandić (ed.), *Savez Komunista Jugoslavije u Razvoju Socialistickog Samoupravljanja* (Belgrade: Komunist, 1978), I, 105 and Rusinow, op. cit., especially 184-91.

17. Bilandžić, op. cit., 328.

18. Ibid., 328-331.

19. Ralph Pervan, *Tito and the Students* (Nedlands: University of Western Australia Press, 1978), especially 101 and 173.

20. Šoškić, op. cit., 105-106.

21. Pervan, op. cit., especially 137-138, 169.

22. Rusinow, op. cit., 296-297.

23. Bilandžić, op. cit., 418-423 and 426-430.

24. Ibid., 423-426, 431-441 and Rusinow, op. cit., 325.

25. Bilandžić, op. cit., 444; see also 442 and 443.

26. Stipe Šuvar, 'Nacije i medjunacionalni odnosi', in Pašić and Špadijer, op. cit., 464 and Bilandžić, op. cit., 404.

27. Rusinow, op. cit., 58-59.

28. Ibid., 97-98, 128.

29. Bilandžić, op. cit., especially 281-282 and Rusinow, op. cit., 63-64 and 103ff.

30. See Rusinow, op. cit., Ch. 4; Pervan, op. cit., Ch. 7; and Deborah Milenkovitch, *Plan and Market in Yugoslav Economic Thought* (New Haven: Yale University Press, 1971).

31. Rusinow, op. cit., Chs. 4 and 5, especially 135-137 and 166.

32. Bilandžić, op. cit., 310-313.

33. Ibid., 313-319.

34. Rusinow, op. cit., 284-286.

35. Bilandžić, op. cit., 396-412, and Leon Geršković, 'Istorijski razvoj društveno-političkog sistema jugoslavije', in Pašić and Špadijer, op. cit., 104.

36. Kardelj, *Democracy and Socialism*, especially 141-165.

37. Ibid., 18 and 155.

38. *Constitution*, article 130.

39. Bilandžić, op. cit., 452-453, Mirko Popović, 'Sistem socijalističke samoupravne demokratije i uloga saveza komunista jugoslavije', in Roksandić, op. cit., 166 and Pašić, op. cit., 67.

40. Kardelj, *Democracy and Socialism*, 17.

41. Ibid., 212-213 and Popović, op. cit., 163.

42. *Samoupravni Društveno Ekonomski Razvoj Jugoslavije 1947-1977* (Belgrade: Savezni Zavod za Statistiku, 1978), 100.

43. Šuvar, op. cit., 464 and Bilandžić, op. cit., 404.

44. Kardelj, *Democracy and Socialism*, 117.

45. *Statistički Podaci o SKJ Izmedju Desetog i Jedanaestog Kongresa SKJ* (Belgrade: Komunist, 1978), 12 and 36.

11 Conclusions: Whither the Party and State?

Leslie Holmes
University of Kent at Canterbury, UK

Having considered developments in both the theory and practice of the communist party and state in a number of very different countries, we can now attempt a comparative analysis of such change. Before suggesting reasons for these developments, however, it will be useful to summarize briefly the main findings of this study.

THE PARTY

The Theory of its Role

As McLellan has argued, Marx's views on the role of a communist party are neither fully consistent nor elaborated in much detail. In his early years, Marx was not particularly concerned with political parties; later, he did see some justification and need for an organized party, though this was not to be separate from and/or above the masses of the workers. He opposed the Blanquist notion of a centralized, elite party — and believed that this would not be necessary anyway by the time of a socialist revolution, since by then the working class would have a highly-developed political consciousness itself. Two very important, related points about Marx's views are of particular relevance to the present study. First, the circumstances for a socialist revolution pertained in none of the countries examined; even Germany and Czechoslovakia only partially fitted the bill.[1] Second, Marx did not produce an analysis of the role of the party *following* a socialist revolution. This applies equally to Engels, whose views on the party prior to a revolution are similarly ambiguous. Lenin, on the contrary, was far more explicit on the pre-revolutionary role of the party — at least vis-à-vis Tsarist Russia. But even Lenin's views on the party *following* the proletarian revolution are contradictory. On the one hand, he argued that *What is to be Done?* — and, by inference, the concept of an elite party of professional revolutionaries — was only relevant to the situation in Russia before the fall of the Romanov dynasty; it is also true that he favoured the enormous growth in party membership following the fall of the Tsar which accelerated still further after October. On the other hand, he later changed his policy of open admission to the party, whilst his statements at the 10th Congress in 1921 reveal that, faced with the choice of allowing more or less freedom of discussion within the party to deal with an extremely difficult situation, he chose the latter. Whether or not he was reluctant to do so is not of particular importance; the salient points are that he was prepared to claim that the 'bourgeois' revolution of February 1917 had led to a proletarian socialist revolution in October (in a situation simply not envisaged by Marx),[2] and that he was prepared to justify a highly centralized party power-structure to secure the success of such a theoretically ill-founded revolution.

Thus, although all communist parties base much of the justification for their existence and actions on the works of Marx, Engels and Lenin, the latters' views on the role of the party and Lenin's views on revolution are either almost non-existent or open to widely differing interpretations. This, in turn, means that modern communists can perpetrate all sorts of actions in the name of Marxist-Leninist ideology;[3] in all but a few instances, it cannot be shown conclusively that they have contradicted the theories upon which they base much of the legitimization of their actions.

Turning now to theoretical changes within the countries analyzed, it is clear that in most of them, the leading or vanguard role of the party has been strongly reasserted in the 1970s. In Albania, Hoxha has argued that the position of the party is to be considerably strengthened in the future, whilst in the USSR and other

European states closely allied to the USSR, new or revised constitutions of the last ten to fifteen years have for the first time included references to the leading role of the party within the state and society.[4] Even in the communist state which, over time, has gone furthest in modifying the leading role of the party — Yugoslavia — problems with both nationalism and the emergence of a 'liberal technocracy' have been used for justifying the reassertion of party control from the centre during the 1970s. And the attempt by the Czechoslovak party leadership in the first half of 1968 to democratize the party and make it more subject to popular control has been rejected and reversed by the Husák leadership-group since 1969.

Looking beyond Europe, we find that the role of the party is more fluid. In Cuba, it was not until six years after Castro took power that a communist party proper emerged, and not until the 1970s was a formalized role and structure enunciated in detail; in the past five years or so, however, the Cuban Communist Party has become increasingly like a Soviet-type party. In China, Mao never really distinguished the party and its role clearly from other organizations such as the military and the state administration; only since Mao has the Chinese leadership sought to define the party's role clearly and to distinguish this from other organizations in society, although such definition is still in progress. In Laos, the Communists have been in power for only five years, so that it is somewhat premature to discuss changes in the theory of its role; the situation is even more complex in Cambodia/Kampuchea, where we have witnessed the unusual phenomenon of one communist state (Vietnam) invading another to install a different form of communist rule (i.e. the replacement of Pol Pot by Heng Samrin). However, as Duncanson has shown, it does seem that at present, in all three states of what is still often called Indochina, the latest trend is towards the Soviet conception of the party being separate from and leading the state and society, rather than the less clear-cut Maoist (and Stalinist) picture of the party as an organization amongst many for implementing the *leader's* ideas on reaching communism. In sum, there has been a *general* trend in communist states in the 1970s for a theoretical reassertion of the party's leading role in society.

One other interesting development in the theoretical position of the party deserves special note. This is that in some of these states the party is being increasingly seen as a peculiarly *national* institution.[5] This is particularly true of Romania, but can also be observed in the GDR and elsewhere; the reasons for this will be considered later in this chapter.

Structure and Functions

Although there does seem to be a pattern of reassertion of the party's role in most communist states, this does not mean that the detailed functions currently performed are essentially identical in each country. Thus the 'interest-integrating' function now officially performed by the Hungarian party in a highly urbanized and relatively stable society, for instance, is of little relevance to the Vietnamese communists, who are primarily concerned with consolidating communist rule at home (especially in the southern part of the country) and abroad (Laos and Kampuchea). In sum, the *general* functions of party and state (the former guiding the latter) can be subsumed under the headings of 'defence of the revolution', 'allocation and adjudication' and 'socialist construction' — all of which, to avoid repetition, are considered later in this chapter — but the emphasis on particular functions will vary considerably according to a large number of factors. These include the level of economic and social development (e.g. the party's role in the transformation of the economy, nationalization of industry and the collectivization of agriculture fades into insignificance once the major part of these policies has been implemented); the political culture (e.g. the re-socialization phase will have to be more intense, prolonged and overt in a society in which pre-communist traditions and ideology were very different from communist aims, such as Czechoslovakia, than in a society where pre-communist ideologies are in closer proximity on several key issues, such as Bulgaria);[6] and the range of macro-policies dealt with by a party (i.e. the Communist Party of the Soviet Union plays a major role in the making of foreign policy because of its involvement in the affairs of so many other countries and its role in international relations as a super-power, whereas the Party of Labour of Albania is far less involved with issues outside Albania). However, whilst it is clearly the case that the concentration on specific functions varies between communist states synchronically and within individual states over time, there is no methodologically acceptable way of measuring an increase or a decrease in functions rigorously. Thus a decrease in the overt socialization function of a party does not necessarily mean that this function is decreasing — it might rather be that the party is concentrating more on less immediately visible but more effective means of harmonizing the official and dominant political cultures. This said, there have been clear indications in the past of some parties *generally* attempting to play a less dominant role in society (e.g. Yugoslavia in the 1960s, Czechoslovakia 1968) which implies a decrease in functions: however, this does not appear to pertain to any of the European communist states in the 1970s. In Cuba, too, the party is assuming more functions, partially at the expense of the army, but partially also as the clarification of the different functions to be performed within society proceeds; this is also largely true of China, and will probably become increasingly true of Indochina.

Despite these variations, there is also considerable similarity between many of the functions performed by all communist parties. Thus they are all to lead or guide society, one of the most important practical manifestations of which is macro-policy formulation ('goal-setting'); this is done primarily by the Politburo (or its functional equivalent), usually in conjunction with the Central Committee Secretariat.[7] Even in those communist states which explicitly recognize the existence of different interests in society and the right of representatives of such interests to be heard, there has been no fundamental renunciation of the concept of party leadership. Rather, some communist parties (primarily those which have been in power for a relatively long period) now realize that it is more efficient to have as accurate a conception of the mood of key groups in society as possible, which is really how concepts such as 'interest-integration' are to be understood. This point is borne out by the criticisms all communist parties make of pluralism, which they see as a political system in which the best and greatest resources are allocated to the strongest rather than one where allocation is based on certain principles of equity.[8]

Apart from policy-making, the party also has to 'check on' (the Russian word is kontrolirovat') its implementation, the latter function normally being allocated to the state administrative apparatus. Whilst such a division is reasonably closely adhered to in many of the European communist states, the Asian communist states and Cuba are either at the stage of only having very recently introduced such a division (so that it has not fully crystallized) or else they are still elaborating the detailed functions of party and state. The ways in which this supervisory function is performed are several, but include the establishment of party cells in state organs, factories etc. to see that policies are implemented; establishing various inspectorates; and ensuring that persons occupying key positions within society meet party-determined criteria, via the nomenclature system. The nomenclature system is not merely part of the essentially negative 'checking' function, however; it also serves a positive role, in promoting and encouraging those people in society whom the party feels can make an especially useful contribution (recruitment function). The party is also responsible for the political education of the population (socialization function), and for deciding on methods for dealing with those elements in society which the party feels are either not convertible to the new culture or else are useful scapegoats for unpopular policies ('class enemies'). Finally, lower levels of the party perform an important linkage function between the mass of the population and the policy-makers; in increasingly complex societies in which terror has effectively been renounced (i.e. most of the states here, with the exception of Pol Pot's Kampuchea and perhaps Vietnam, Laos and present-day Kampuchea), the flow of information *upwards* is important for efficient and popular policy-making and, as a corollary, regime legitimacy.

The basic organizational structures and principles of communist parties are all very similar, and are sufficiently well-known not to need reiteration here.[9] However, some changes have occurred and should be noted. For example, Cuba's party structure started to become considerably more complex in the early 1970s, although some organs (e.g. the National Revisory Commission) were established as late as 1979. Indeed much of the Cuban party structure was not operational until the 1970s, the first Congress being held in 1975. These changes represent a move away from the more traditional 'caudillo' element in Cuban politics towards the Soviet model, although it remains to be seen whether it will become as bureaucratized as some maintain the CPSU has done.[10] The concentration of industry — the establishment of industrial associations — in many East European states and the USSR has led to (sometimes severe) problems with the primary party organizations (ppo's). Either existing ppo's are disbanded and not replaced for some time, or else the new ppo's are felt to be remote by many shop-floor workers.[11] Although attempts have been and are being made to eradicate such problems (e.g. the strengthening of the workshop organizations), these structural changes have not yet clearly succeeded in improving on the former arrangement. A third change is the establishment of the rotation principle in Albania since 1966, and Romania since 1969.[12] According to this, high-ranking officials must periodically work at lower levels — a move which Szajkowski explains in terms of an attempt by the leader to avoid institutionalized opposition, rather than for 'democratic' reasons. The numerous structural changes at the top of the Romanian party in the 1960s and 1970s also appear to have been introduced primarily to strengthen Ceausescu's position rather than for ideological reasons.[13] Finally, there does appear to have been a more conscious policy of promoting representatives of key functional and area/national groups to the senior party organs (especially the Politburo) in some states — and generally more emphasis on collective leadership (e.g. the USSR).[14] As with so many aspects of communist politics, however, this and other changes noted could easily be reversed if a new supreme leader were to emerge in any of these countries. In sum, there is no clear pattern to structural and functional changes; those in Cuba and perhaps in the USSR represent a moderate decentralization from the leader to the central party organs, whilst some in Romania and Albania seem to strengthen the position of the individual leader;[15] in Yugoslavia, the centre has again taken on a more significant role after having decentralized in the 1960s. Developments in much of East European industry have made the primary party organization more remote for many workers, which in one sense represents centralization both within the party and society; Yugoslavia provides an exception to this particular change.

Composition

Membership of the communist party as a proportion of the total population varies considerably in the states examined from less than three per cent in Cuba, Albania and Vietnam to around twelve or thirteen per cent in Romania and the GDR.[16] Thus, there is no unified conception of what the 'correct' percentage of party membership might be, although nowhere does the party membership account for anywhere near a majority of the population. It is also clear that it is not the case, as might be expected, that states which still permit other parties therefore have smaller communist

parties (cf. the GDR with Albania). Nor is there any obvious correlation between the percentage of party membership and either the
social structure and/or the level of economic development of a
given state; for instance, a relatively underdeveloped state not considered in detail in this volume, North Korea, has a membership
comprising approximately ten per cent of the population, whilst
membership in Hungary is just under 7.5 per cent. The one relatively clear pattern is that membership generally rises the longer the
communists are in power, though purges can temporarily reverse
the general trend.[17]

In many of the states examined (including the USSR, Hungary,
Czechoslovakia, Bulgaria, the GDR and Cuba), the party has called for a 're-proletarianization' of membership in the 1970s — i.e.
an increase in the numbers and influence of the industrial working
class. Some, such as Czechoslovakia,, have been more successful in
implementing this policy than others (e.g. Bulgaria). Nevertheless
the industrial working class still does not constitute a majority in
most of the parties, exceptions including the Romanian and the
East German. However, it might be objected that white-collar
workers/employees and farm workers on state farms are wage-
earners and have the same basic relationship to the means of production as industrial workers, so that these parties are all overwhelmingly proletarian. On this point, we find a difference
between most of the European states on the one hand and China,
Vietnam and other non-European states on the other, since the latter do use this much broader concept of proletariat. However, even
the Chinese, Vietnamese, etc. subscribe to the distinction adhered
to by other parties between the 'classes' of factory workers, farm
workers and the 'stratum' of the intelligentsia.[18] Since, therefore,
communist parties themselves distinguish between the industrial
proletariat and other classes or strata in society, and since empirical
analyses reveal significant differences in life-style between groups,
we can conclude that by some definitions, there is a class distinction
between, for instance, blue-collar workers and state administrators; this point about class is explored further below. Bearing this in mind, 're-proletarianization' has not been very successful on the whole. Even where there has been an increase in industrial proletarian membership, one should distinguish between
the ordinary, mass membership of the party and its full-time, professional guiding core, the *apparat*. It is the latter which wields
most of the power in the party, and empirical research shows that

this group increasingly comprises members of the intelligentsia.[19] Moreover, we need to ask *why* there have been calls for such re-proletarianization in the 1970s. To a large extent, the explanation is to be found in the concept of elite-legitimacy. On the one hand, the party leadership can use such a policy to weaken the position of technical specialists/experts (the emergent 'technocracy') within the party, thus strengthening the position of the political vanguard (the 'reds'). On the other, such a policy can be useful in countering discontent caused by mass perception of 'bureaucratism' and 'elitism' within society. In sum, to the extent that the party guides society, communist states are still typically characterized by dictatorships 'over' or 'on behalf of' rather than 'of' (i.e. directly involving) the proletariat, and recent developments do not reveal any really significant moves towards the latter.

Other Parties

Several communist states formally have bi- or multi-party systems — among them the GDR, Bulgaria, Vietnam and China. However, in all of these countries, the non-communist parties have agreed to follow the leadership of the communist party, and none is permitted to propagate anti-socialist or anti-Marxist-Leninist ideas. In addition, there are three major limitations to the autonomy of such parties. First, the 'bloc' or 'front' system in elections means that the actual distribution of seats in national parliaments is not determined by the electorate, but by the communist party. Second, the nomenclature system — which seems to have come under official attack only once in the communist world[20] — ensures that any non-communist occupying a key position, be it within the state administration or even as editor of a non-communist party newspaper, does so only with the approval of the communist party. Finally, in all the cases examined in this study, major policy initiatives derive from the communist party, usually from the Politburo or its equivalent; obviously, only members of the communist party may be members of such bodies.[21]

There have not been significant changes in the positions of these minor parties in any of the states considered, with the possible exception of China. In the GDR, for instance, there has been a marginal downgrading of the parties, in that even the symbolically, if not politically, important post of President of Parliament (formerly occupied by the head of a minor party) has been occupied by a member of the SED (i.e. Communist party) since November 1976; but the renewed industrial drive of 1972, which all but ended private enterprise in industry has not been accompanied by theoretical justifications for the abolition of any of the 'bourgeois' parties. In China, the multi-party system meant little for two decades; there are signs that the role of the other parties has been increased since Mao's death, but there is nothing to suggest that the communist party will relinquish its dominant role or compete on a more or less equal footing with other parties in liberal-democratic style elections.[22]

Hence, the communist parties are not renouncing their vanguard role vis-à-vis other political parties.

THE STATE

The Theory of its Role

As with the party, so the role and meaning of the state *following* a socialist revolution was not examined in much detail by either Marx or Engels. Moreover, neither the distinctions between the concepts of 'government' and 'administration' (and thus between 'the state' and a classless but not disorganized society) nor the concept of the 'dictatorship of the proletariat' is spelt out by either theorist. Even the distinction between the concepts of 'abolition' (Abschaffung) and 'withering away' (Absterben) of the state is vague, since the latter could be interpreted as leading to the former, and there is no clear indication that the former (Marx's preferred term) is to be achieved suddenly rather than over a period of time.[23] However, both writers agreed that the state should take possession of the means of production as a pre-requisite to full political liberty and communism. Marx also considered the administrative apparatus or bureaucracy to be the most important part of a modern state, so that in looking for the 'withering away' of the state, concentration should be particularly focused on that part of it; this would include consideration of the revocability of officials, the relationship of their wages/salary to those of 'ordinary workmen' and the level of centralization of executive tasks within the state and society. The role of the military should also be examined, as one of the specific dimensions of post-revolutionary organization overtly considered by Marx and Engels.

Before the October Revolution, Lenin, too, emphasized the need for a post-revolutionary state (in the form of the dictatorship of the proletariat) to take over the means of production, agreed that state officials should be revocable and modestly-paid, and that the state bureaucracy should wither away. However, he too produced little further detail on the post-revolutionary, transitional state, since he was soon to be more concerned with the everyday management of it than with long-term theoretical analyses of its development. However, in the autumn of 1919, Lenin did draft a brief outline on the tasks to be accomplished under the dictatorship of the pro-letariat, in which the main role of this dictatorship was argued to be the suppression of hostile class elements within society.[24] Add to this the various specific roles of defending the new Soviet regime from external intervention and turning a basically agrarian country into the highly industrialized society both Marx and Lenin thought necessary as a pre-requisite for communism, and it becomes ob-vious why the notion of a withering state was irrelevant to Russia's needs immediately after October 1917.

Again, as with the party, the 'classical' theorists were sufficiently vague in their analyses of the state following a proletarian, socialist revolution to permit ideologists of a wide spectrum of very dif-ferent kinds of political system to attempt to legitimate these systems in terms of 'Marxism-Leninism'. However, some aspects of the post-revolutionary state were clearly specified, and can be in-corporated into the empirical analysis of contemporary communist states.

One of the most interesting points to emerge from the country-studies in this volume is that the predominantly European concep-tion of the state and its subdivisions has in the past not always been accepted in other parts of the world. Thus in China, Indochina and to some extent Cuba, the army has in the past been used as an agen-cy for implementing party and/or leadership (in the case of Cuba before 1965) domestic policy or even for making policy, at least as much as an organization for defending the country from external attack.[25] At present, however, the trend in both China and Cuba is towards the typical European division of labour between a state ad-ministrative apparatus and the military, whilst the military in In-dochina is still officially fulfilling much of the role normally assign-

ed to a state administrative apparatus. Thus, although it is possible
to argue that in Indochina the state is 'withering', it must be clearly
understood that in fact only one part of the full state machinery is
in decline, and there does not appear to have been a formal
theoretical claim that the state generally is withering. Conversely,
the formal strengthening of 'the state' in China since 1978 is in fact
only of one branch at the expense of another, so that the recent formalization of the division of labour within the Chinese state does
not in itself represent a strengthening of the state as a whole. It has
also emerged that the conception of the state held by Mao for some
of his period as Chairman — viz. an infrastructure for the non-
military command and control of the party — is in marked contrast
to Soviet theory, according to which the state is to be controlled by
the party. Finally, although this was rescinded by the 1978 Constitution, the 1975 Chinese constitution abolished the concept that
the state representative organs should be the channels through
which the people exercise power; this seems to be a unique development in recent communist theory.

In Europe, in many ways the most interesting developments of
the theory of the state have emanated from Yugoslavia, where the
self-management concept has been developed since the 1940s to its
present all-important position in the 1974 Yugoslav constitution.
Even though this concept seems to have emerged primarily as a
reaction to the Stalinist system in the USSR, it has long since
become a theoretical concept in its own right, and represents a
serious attempt to dilute the centralized, bureaucratic state.
Moreover, even where it has been argued that the state should be
strengthened, it has become more subject to the control of the
population through the delegate system. This system seems to us to
be the most interesting and significant attempt in the communist
world to combine the 'necessity' of the state whilst subjecting it to
popular control.[26]

The position of the state elsewhere in Europe varies. Thus, whilst
the Soviet-oriented communist countries conceive of the state as
subordinate to but separate from the party, the Albanians have rejected the concept of separating party and state. The Romanians,
too, have in recent years both in theory and practice begun to
merge the two institutions; although some Romanian practice is not
unlike that in Soviet-oriented systems, the theory of merging to
avoid parallelism is quite different from the formal separation of
roles typical of the latter. In one sense, the state in both Albania

and Romania is withering through incorporation into the party; but since the latter is fulfilling many functions formerly performed by the state, there can be no meaningful talk of 'withering away'. In other European states, the notion of the states 'withering' has been dismissed as irrelevant in present conditions (e.g. Hungary) or else it has been argued that the process will take far longer than had originally been envisaged (e.g. the USSR); indeed, even some left-wing dissidents within the communist world have argued that the concept of 'withering' is mere anarchistic utopianism (Harich, GDR). This said, it should also be pointed out that there have been both proposals (e.g. Czechoslovakia throughout the 1960s) and ac-tual attempts (e.g. the USSR under Khrushchev) to weaken the state and involve more of the population in state-functions; thus it cannot be argued that there have been *no* serious attempts to wither away the state, and there could well be renewed attempts in the future.[27]

But if the state is not to wither away at present, it is also the case that its role is being conceived of in different terms over time in many of these states. For instance, from being an organ primarily for the suppression of 'class enemies' and establishing the bases of socialism in the 1920s and 1930s, the modern Soviet state is seen more in terms of a resolver of 'collisions of interest' (to use their own term) within society and the machine for administering the transition from developed socialism to communism. Indeed this periodization of socialism into various stages, typical of all com-munist states, is something that has developed as the state con-tinues to exist. In the works of Marx and Engels, the distinction between communism and socialism is often hazy; Lenin clarified the distinction, but did not make the neat distinction between diff-erent *stages* of socialism that is typical of modern communist states.[28] Thus the emergence of theories of different stages of socialism has meant that official ideologists have justified the con-tinued existence and even the strengthening of the state whilst simultaneously arguing that major changes have occurred within society which mean that the state's role has altered. However some of these states disagree amongst themselves on this periodization; this emerges most clearly in the different views of the Soviets and the Chinese. Thus although even the Chinese communists now acknowledge that the class structure in China is changing, and that the role of party and state is more constructive than suppressive (i.e. in line with Soviet theory), they have consistently, vehemently rejected the Soviet concept of the 'state of the whole people'. This was introduced by Khrushchev in 1961 (when the CPSU programme was adopted), and came under attack from the Chinese.[29] Although the present leadership has modified the meaning and practical implications of the 'state of the whole people', it is still officially the description of the Soviet state and was embodied in the 1977 Constitution. The Chinese argue — correctly — that this constitutes a major theoretical revision of what Marx, Engels and Lenin had to say. Engels, for instance wrote:

> When at last it (the state) becomes the real representative of the whole of society it renders itself unnecessary.[30]

whilst Lenin argued quite unambiguously that the state is invariably a class concept.[31] In line with this, Lenin maintained that the *whole* transitional period between capitalism and the higher stage of communism must be the dictatorship of the proletariat; the Chinese accept this, and hence argue that their state is a socialist state of the dictatorship of the proletariat. Whatever the merits or demerits of this, the current Chinese position on this question is undoubtedly nearer to Lenin's views than the Soviet line.

There is one other point made by communists concerning the theory of the state's role in these societies which is obvious but often overlooked in the West — viz. they argue that the socialist state is qualitatively different from the bourgeois state, both in that it represents the interests of the workers rather than the exploiters, and that it represents the interests of the majority rather than the minority.[32] And there are a couple of points rarely made by them — viz. that state officials should be directly revocable and paid workmen's wages.

Changes in Structure and Functions

As in all countries, one of the functions of the state in socialist societies is to represent the people in international affairs and defend them; in most of them, it is also formally the sole repository of legitimate force (though this is much truer of the European than the Asian states). Hence two important branches of the state are the police and the military, who for much of the time perform similar — if more overtly class-oriented — functions to their counterparts in other kinds of political system.[33] But, as we have seen, the classical Marxists were more concerned with the state administrative apparatus (the bureaucracy) and the representative organs, so that it is on their functions that we concentrate; some aspects of representation, however, are more appropriately dealt with in the next section. Hence the major role of the state apparatus is, in the majority of cases, to implement the policies of the party. This is done through the related functions of, firstly, elaborating the details of policy and issuing instructions on the basis of these (legislation, assigning plan-tasks, etc.) and, secondly, checking that these instructions are being implemented both by its own agencies and within society generally (the control function). In the context of both of these functions, there have in recent years been interesting structural developments within the communist world. Generally, there has been an upgrading of the role of smaller, professional state bodies to the further detriment of the parliaments; this is observable, for instance, in the establishment and position of the State Council in Bulgaria, whilst even in China, the downgrading of the role of the State Council in the late 1960s was much shorter-lived and less effective than the decline of the role of the National People's Congress (which did not meet between January 1965 and January 1975). However, whilst the role of the full parliaments may still be, despite official upgrading, largely ceremonial,[34] there has been a marked increase in the role of the parliamentary committees (e.g. the USSR, Cuba); the growing complexity of social 'needs' would suggest that this increasing role for specialized state agencies is likely to continue. At the same time, the role of President is in most cases either being abolished (e.g. the position of Chairman of the Republic in China) or else converted into what is in effect a Presidential Council (e.g. the State Council in the GDR since 1960, the Yugoslav State Presidency since 1971). Of course, in many cases these bodies are probably dominated by one man; but their very existence suggests that, whilst developments outlined above suggest a centralization, it is not the case that this is invariably being pursued to the logical conclusion of one-man rule.[35] This said, there are cases within the communist world where such a pattern is currently being followed (e.g. Romania, especially since 1974).

But the very complexification of society and social provisions has led to some functions being transferred to local collectives (e.g.

welfare services in Vietnam since the 1960s) or to bodies linked with but not synonymous with the state apparatus (e.g. the welfare functions of the trade unions in the USSR since Khrushchev's time); the importance of this form of decentralization should not be overemphasized, however.

One structural aspect of the state on which there is no general agreement within the communist world is that of unitarism versus federalism. Certainly, size (either in terms of area or population) is not a useful indication of which path will be followed, since there are both large and small federal states (USSR, Czechoslovakia, Yugoslavia) and large and small unitary states (China, Bulgaria). A more useful explanation is the level of real or potential national antagonism within a communist state. Thus the federalization of Czechoslovakia in 1969 and the changes in the federal structure in Yugoslavia at about the same time represented responses by the central governments to tension between national groups; it seems improbable that federalism will be introduced in other countries unless such tensions arise.

There have also been some instances of structural changes relating to the state apparatus' control function. This has been increased again in post-Mao China, whilst in Romania, there are an increasing number of joint party-state bodies fulfilling this function; but these changes are merely in line with more general trends in the two states already discussed.

A relatively recent development in several communist states is the use of surveys for assessing public opinion. This linkage function is usually performed in conjunction with the party, and represents one of the many ways in which the older communist states in particular now attach far greater importance to public attitudes than was the case in the early years of communist rule; the majority of states may not yet be withering, but in some, consultation is increasing noticeably.

Mass Participation

Two ways in which the state might 'wither away' is through increasing involvement of the population in functions formerly performed by the state (or party) apparatus — i.e. the dilution of state power — and through increasing popular control of the state apparatus.

Considering the latter first, one channel through which the

population (or even just the proletariat) might appear to be able to control the state apparatus is elections — which potentially relate to Marx's conception of revocability. General elections in most communist states are now conducted on a reasonably regular basis and some limit the terms of office of deputies and make *formal* reference to revocability.[36] Although participation in elections is not, strictly speaking, compulsory in most communist states (an exception being the elections establishing the People's Democratic Republic of Laos), turnout is usually very high; reasons for this vary, and range from a tradition of high turnout (very relevant to the GDR) to party encouragement of voters and even, perhaps, falsification of electoral turnout figures.[37] But even if the figures are genuine, we should not attach too much significance to elections. In any state, be it liberal-democratic or communist, the fact that people show some form of approval for this or that party every four or five years can only be a minor part of the participatory process; this is even more true when there is no real choice at elections. Moreover, although elections in several states are direct,[38] they are so only for the parliamentary representatives, not for members of the government or the state apparatus; the same point applies to revocability. Thus to the extent that the party dominates and guides the state — both constitutionally, and through arrangements such as the nomenclature system — there is no formalized public control over the senior decision-making bodies within the society. Whilst both proposals for and implementation of changes in the electoral procedure in countries such as Hungary, Cuba and the USSR should be noted and are of some interest, their significance should not be overestimated.[39]

Referenda are also used occasionally in the communist world, especially before the adoption of a new constitution. Of greater importance, however, are the discussions in the mass media of both constitutional changes and, sometimes, new laws; whilst this aspect of communist politics requires considerably more research, it is already clear that sometimes significant changes are made between the publication of a draft constitution or law and the adoption of the final version, largely in response to popular reaction.[40] It does seem that this form of involving the population in the discussion of important laws is increasing, and this represents some decentralization of power. Again, however, it must be noted that the public is not being encouraged to take the *initiative* for policy-proposals, nor is the public generally involved in the final decision.[41]

Developments such as these and the increased tolerance of a limited form of criticism should not go unremarked; but, as we have seen in the case of the rise and fall of Democracy Wall in Beijing (formerly Peking), it is still the party and state apparatus which decides the parameters of such discussion in most states.[42]

So far in this section, the emphasis has been on participation relating to national issues at national level. Yet there have been developments in participation at the local and workplace level. In Hungary and to some extent the USSR, for example, the local representative organs have been upgraded in functional terms, made more autonomous of central bodies and more responsible to the local electorate during the 1970s; in Cuba, such bodies have been established for the first time following the 1974 Matanzas experiment. However, such changes have as yet not seriously affected the powers of central authorities.[43] In Hungary and the USSR, attempts have also been made to involve more workers in decision-making at the workplace. But such attempts have been less than successful, to some extent because the concept is in contradiction to the emphasis on efficiency and international integration which has been seen in most European states throughout the 1960s and 1970s. Thus the development of various forms of association (i.e. fewer, larger industrial production units) in the last ten to fifteen years has in practice made participation even more difficult for many workers than before, whilst integration plans such as the Council for Mutual Economic Aid's 1971 'Complex Programme' leave less scope for real autonomy at the level of the individual production unit.[44] Indeed, some European states (Czechoslovakia, the GDR) have in the 1970s been limiting still further the possibilities for worker-participation in the workplace. Even in those states which have been encouraging more participation, it seems that this is often of a guided nature, i.e. it is a method by which the regime encourages involvement in the *application* rather than the making of policies and decisions. The most striking exception to this general pattern has once again been Yugoslavia, which since 1971 has consciously pursued a policy of splitting production units into smaller ones with the aim of giving workforces a real possibility to be largely self-managing.

Another channel for participation is the mass organizations in these states. Formally, bodies such as the various Youth Leagues or the Trade Unions are to represent the ('non-antagonistic') interests of their members. In practice, they are usually subject to the control of the party, and are primarily organs for mobilizing members for the construction of socialism (and eventually communism) rather than promoting particular interests against other groups or the government. Moreover, such bodies have at times been relatively inactive; in China, for instance, the mass organizations have only been reactivated since Mao's death.

One final point should be made about mass participation. The moves towards greater use of cybernetics and modern technology in social administration and planning, plus the increasing codification of the legal system that is typical of most contemporary communist states, mean that ordinary citizens must have an ever-increasing knowledge of specialized subjects if they are to deal on a relatively equal basis with specialist party and state officials; the simplification of administration envisaged by Lenin is not being realized. Theoretically, the masses and/or their representatives do not have to understand the details of the official's work to be able to control (in the Soviet sense) him; in practice it will often happen that the representative becomes more technically competent and thus distant from those he represents, or else the administrator refers to the 'facts' on which his actions or recommendations are based and with which the dubious non-specialist will find it difficult to argue. Thus the 'technicalization' of society has a generally negative effect on mass participation.

CHANGES IN THE PARTY-STATE RELATIONSHIP

It has been shown that, although the main trend at present in the communist world is for a formal separation between party and state, this has not always or everywhere been so, and does not apply to all states at present. Whatever the theory, there is an abundance of empirical evidence to show that in all these states, senior party personnel also occupy most if not all of the key state offices; indeed one of the most visible recent trends has been for the General Secretary of the party to be appointed head of state and/or premier. Although such overlap is generally less obvious at lower levels, various studies of career-patterns in communist states reveal a high level of interchange between state and party, whilst the nomenclature system ensures that state positions are filled by people at least acceptable to the party.[45] Yet such de facto interpenetration has led to some important theoretical problems.

The first point relates to the question of control. Lenin's concern about who was controlling whom in terms of the party and the state bureaucracy has developed in such a way that the question has become almost academic. Clearly, in organizations of the size we have been considering, it would be absurd to assume that there is always homogeneity of interest and approach between party and state officials — and there is ample evidence to show there is not.[46] Yet when differences arise, there is no in-built effective separation of powers and neatly-defined (and adhered to) method for resolution or control. Formally, the party controls the state; in practice, interdependence makes this a highly subjective matter. One of the few situations in which a clear distinction is drawn is when the party leadership wishes to use state officials as scapegoats for a failed policy; Duncanson cites a Vietnamese example of this, whilst anyone familiar with Soviet politics will know how frequently Soviet agriculture ministers have been dismissed following a poor harvest. Beyond this, the lack of tolerance of opposition to the party and its state leaves considerable scope for corruption, and far too few channels for revealing and dealing with such corruption. Of even greater concern is the fact that communist leaderships sometimes refer to the 'errors' — occasionally 'crimes' — of their predecessors. They usually argue that these were on marginal rather than fundamental issues; but if such erroneous judgements lead to purges and deaths (often on a massive scale) and public hostility to communists and their ideology, it becomes difficult to accept that such mistakes are merely unfortunate minor deviations on the road to communism.[47] Moreover, the fact that conflicts between leaders do arise because of *fundamentally* different approaches to the building of communism puts the correctness of the Leninist concept of a vanguard party of the most politically enlightened seriously in doubt. Expressed differently, it cannot be argued that there is no *need* for public control of leadership because the latter is more conscious of the 'correct' policies; there is ample evidence that the 'correct' path is often merely the set of policies preferred by the victor in a power-struggle.[48] Of course, there is evidence of *some* control of leadership — from peers (the ousting of Khrushchev, Chervenkov or Ranković), from external forces (the USSR's involvement in Czechoslovakia in 1968-69 or in Ulbricht's 'resignation' in 1971) and occasionally through mass action (Gomulka's overthrow in 1970). But such attempts can fail, and in all events constitute a very haphazard form of control. Notwithstanding communist theories of leadership, such leadership is in fact to a large extent subjective, not the objective result of historical circumstances; personality cults and nepotism still exist in some states and could arise elsewhere in future.[49] For this reason, the de facto merging of party and state whilst mass control is still at a nascent stage has serious implications for the 'socialist' democratization of these states.

A related problem is that the raison d'être of the party — as Hill, Dunmore and Dawisha point out — is becoming ever less obvious in the older communist states.[50] With the revitalization of various state representative organs and the formal encouragement of their control function (even if this has not been seriously implemented in most cases), the role of the party comes into question. Such confusion can be seen, for instance, in the Hungarian party's references to *its* interest-integrating function, a function which should, logically, be perfomed by state representative organs. It can also be seen in the tension that has arisen, particularly in the economically more advanced states, between technically-trained state functionaries and more generalist party functionaries; when attempts have been made to reduce tension by raising the technical qualifications of the latter group, the distinction between their role and the state functionaries' has become blurred.[51] Finally, it is to be observed in the very muddled theoretical descriptions in so many states of the social and political structure — the vacillation between various forms of 'dictatorship of the proletariat', 'dictatorship of the workers and peasants', 'state of the whole people', etc. — which have implications for the party's role relative to the state and society. Having summarized the main findings of the preceding chapters, let us now consider the reasons for such developments.

EXPLANATIONS

The reasons for the persistence of what can be called the party-state complex are numerous and complicated, and the relative importance of individual explanatory factors will vary according to time and place. Bearing this in mind, a useful starting point is with functional explanations. As was argued earlier, such explanations can be sub-divided for analytical purposes into three — defence of the revolution; allocation and adjudication; socialist construction.

Communists usually face considerable hostility from various quarters for a considerable time after they have taken power. If the dominant political culture or sub-cultures at the time of the takeover differ(s) markedly from the communist culture and/or each other there will obviously be conflict.[52] The situation will be further exacerbated if the communists assume power primarily through the use of foreign (most frequently Soviet) assistance, what Burks calls 'baggage-train government'; hence the circumstances of the assumption of power are important for gauging the level of support or hostility[35]. Following the takeover, various groups will oppose major policies — many peasants will object to collectivization, and national minorities might object to a multi-national unitary state run on a centralized basis by communists of a different (dominant) nationality from a distant capital. Moreover, continuing heavy dependence on a foreign power and official tolerance of involvement of that power in the country's internal affairs will prolong or re-kindle the flame of hostility to the domestic leadership (Czechoslovakia since 1968 is a prime example). The communists must cope with many such problems if the revolution, as they define it, is not to be lost; a strong coercive state is usually considered to be one of the most effective methods.

The revolution also has to be protected from external aggression. In the early period following the takeover, this threat will often be a military one; although the threat has traditionally been from anti-communist forces (e.g. 'capitalist encirclement'), recent developments have revealed the possibility of threats from other communist states (e.g. the Sino-Soviet dispute, Vietnamese involvement in the ousting of the Pol Pot regime). Indeed the communist commitment to worldwide socialism/communism can be used by some states (notably the USSR and Vietnam, but also the GDR, Cuba and others) for justifying military intervention in other states, on the grounds that they are defending an indigenous revolution (e.g. Afghanistan, 1979). Such real and alleged threats, then, necessitate an army, which is an important branch of the state.

The external threat is not invariably military, though. For example, the rapprochement in recent years between the Soviet bloc and the West has been accompanied by an insistence from ideologists such as Suslov and Hager that there should be no ideological detente; this is the basic point of the East German concept of

Abgrenzung.[54] Under such circumstances of 'ideological encircle-ment' the party and state can justify the need for vigilance and thus for their own existence. The need for such vigilance can be used to legitimize both ideological warfare and the existence of a secret police force (to uncover spies, etc.).

In sum, until a given society building communism is safe from all counter-revolutionary forces (including the threat from pro-pagators of alternative 'incorrect' paths to communism), a case for the retention of the party-state for the defence of the revolution can be made.

Another function of the state, under guidance from the party, is to allocate resources and adjudicate conflicts that might arise from such allocation. We have seen how in Hungary, for example, the concept of 'withering' has been deferred while the central authorities have to deal with problems of shortages. Most com-munist states have, on occasion, referred to their competition with capitalism largely in terms of production and consumption; as a result, the populations come to expect as of right (justified by the ideology) constantly rising living-standards. This has two impor-tant ramifications. Firstly, as long as consumption in the West con-tinues to grow — both quantitatively and qualitatively — expecta-tions in the communist states will, *ceteris paribus*, also rise. Present shortages may be overcome, only to be replaced by new ones — so that the need for discretionary allocation will persist. Since com-munist states to a large extent reject the notion of allocation accor-ding to the free hand of the market, preferring to direct distribution consciously (the planned economy) the state's allocative function does not diminish. Indeed it *can* be argued that since allocation is to be based on 'just' social principles, and since an overview of the whole of society is required to decide what is 'just', this particular function should remain highly centralized. The second ramification pertains more to the coercive aspects of the state. Communist states are at present increasingly affected by prevailing world market con-ditions. In a situation of global recession, communist states suffer too. If such states have in the pre-recessionary period based their legitimacy increasingly on economic performance, such legitimacy comes under pressure at times of serious economic difficulties; strikes in the USSR and Poland in the spring of 1980 are one manifestation of this phenomenon. In such a situation, it is em-pirically the case that the party and state apparatuses will normally defend, according to one's perception, the revolution and/or their

position. This can be done in various ways. Occasionally, concessions will be made; these vary from improving the conditions of key
groups (e.g. the Romanian miners in 1977) to changing leaders
(Gierek's replacement of Gomulka in 1970).[55] In such cases, a
change is made which, it is hoped, will overcome a major conflict
and increase the legitimacy of the party-state. A second method is
more long-term, and involves basing legitimacy on factors other
than economic performance or merely Marxism-Leninism; it is in
this context that the increasing identification of some communist
leaderships (e.g. the Romanian, Albanian, East German) with the
national traditions of their states can be understood, whilst it is
also part of the explanation for the increasing emphasis on constitutional legality in the 1970s.[56] Finally, and most frequently,
there can be an intensification of the state's coercive functions.
Critics of the regime will be repressed in one way or another, whilst
the rest of society is made aware of the treatment meted out to
anyone who dares to question the correctness of the party-state's
leadership. In this case, the party-state becomes more self-assertive
and detached; the concept of 'withering' becomes irrelevant.

But the role of the party and state under communism is also
positive — to build a better society rather than retain a status quo.
This involves both policy-making and changing the consciousness
of the masses. Although the former function could in theory be
democratized (i.e. the masses could directly participate), there are
four closely interrelated factors which can be used to justify the
concentration of such powers in the hands of a party and state apparatus. The first is one familiar enough in liberal-democratic
theory — that the scale of modern societies precludes participation
of the majority, who must exercise power vicariously, through
elected representatives.[57] The second point is also commonly heard
in the West — viz. that society is becoming more complex, and
functions more specialized; this can also be argued to pertain to
decision-making, so that such a function should be fulfilled by
those most knowledgeable about and skilled in this area.[58] Third,
communist states are committed to building the base for communism as rapidly as possible; this, too, can be used for justifying
limitations on mass participation in the fulfilling of state
functions.[59] Finally, the ideological basis of the party and its state
in terms of the vanguard concept can be used for limiting control
by and participation of the masses; this point relates to the concept
of the transformation of consciousness, to which we can now turn.

To argue that the functions outlined above *can* be used to justify the continued existence of the party and state machinery is not to say that they *need* be. Indeed, justification of the continued existence of state and party in terms of 'functional necessity' is to a large extent based on subjective premises. Certainly there are *some* parts of the state the non-abolition of which can be objectively defended; the notion of an armed people rather than a professional army, for instance, has become increasingly utopian in an age when methods of warfare everywhere have become ever more sophisticated.[60] But what of the other functional reasons? Reference to shortages, for instance, is based on a particular conception of need. Yet the concept of need is to a considerable extent socially-determined. In most societies, the 'needs' of people become greater and more sophisticated over time; it would appear that the only way to counter such a development is through a change in consciousness, away from ever-greater consumption towards concepts such as 'the quality of life'. Although some communist states have recently placed more emphasis on the latter, it is not yet clear that this is not merely a transient policy designed to placate the populations until economic conditions improve and the call to overtake the West in consumption terms is renewed. Hence the justification for the continued existence of the party and state apparatus in terms of their allocative function in shortage situations is based on a subjective rather than an objective premise. The same applies to the state's adjudicatory role between 'non-antagonistic' (itself a subjective concept) interests;[61] such conflicts are most frequently based on disagreement about resource-allocation, which in turn is dependent on the particular conception of need. Unfortunately, it is far from clear that the *total* package of present socialization measures (i.e. including the references to better living-standards, not simply references in schoolbooks to the 'new socialist man') is aimed at a change in consciousness which will permit this allocative function to be phased out.[62] A second example of the subjective nature of these functional justifications relates to the question of mass participation in policy-making. The Yugoslavs have overtly rejected the representative form of democracy — which exists in most communist states as well as the liberal democracies — arguing that their delegate system, with all its teething problems, is a more satisfactory method of rendering mass participation significant. In this case, the *will* to involve people has overridden considerations of the possible dysfunctionality

of such participation — even though, given the intra-societal conflict which arose in the 1960s when decentralization was seriously
attempted, the Yugoslav party and state apparatus might be held to
have a more justifiable claim to retaining centalized powers than
some others. But even in Yugoslavia there are limits to participation. In other states, the party-state apparatus can and does argue
that the population is still insufficiently politically conscious to
play a major role in decision-making. Although the authors of the
chapters on Hungary and the USSR are probably correct in arguing
that the Hungarian and Soviet people are generally reluctant to participate and/or have primarily a welfare mentality, the reasons for
this need to be explored further. Cultural factors (traditions of
non-participation) undoubtedly play some role. Structural factors
— centralized planning, repression of dissident political views —
are also important, and would help to explain the higher level of
meaningful participation in Yugoslavia. But related ideological factors must also be included; here, we are again referring to the pro-
duction/consumption orientation of so many communist states. It
is often argued that one reason for workers in communist states being relatively apathetic politically is their tiredness following a long,
boring day's work; there is probably much truth in this.[63]
Theoretically, increasing automation could change this. Perhaps it
will, although the economic difficulties the communist world is
presently experiencing is severely hindering moves towards
automated production; moreover, as was argued above, the present
seemingly unquestioned acceptance of the concept of growing need
will probably more than keep pace with automation for a long time
to come. But the working week *could* be reduced if this concept of
need were to be changed in the direction indicated; opportunities
for political participation would then be greater.

Part of such a transformation of consciousness would be the
changing of attitudes towards the division of labour, including the
de-mystification of technical expertise and the abolition of acceptance of 'natural' or 'necessary' hierarchies derived from this division. It is true that some communist parties have been attempting
to reduce the status of technical specialists in recent years (e.g. the
Hungarians, the East Germans); unfortunately, however, such attempts appear to be primarily in order to reassert the special position of the party apparatus rather than to lead to greater equality.

In sum, a radical change of consciousness through the development of a new ethos is required. Such a transformation should be

the task of the ideological vanguard, the party. Yet nowhere does this seem to be happening at present. The explanation for this is largely in terms of the vested interests and the bureaucratic culture of the state and party apparatus; this point requires elaboration.

As was stated earlier, contrary to Marx's view of socialism and the dictatorship of the proletariat emerging from mature capitalism, communist takeovers typically occur in relatively underdeveloped societies, where the biggest class is the traditionally conservative property-oriented peasantry. The transformation of this society into the industrialized one necessary (according to Marxism-Leninism) for socialism is a long process. It often takes decades, for instance, before the industrial workforce constitutes a majority of the population. During this period, the revolutionary elite is typically replaced by a more conservative, administration-oriented group, whilst the interaction of communist ideology and traditional values can also blunt the knife of continuing major revolutionary change: this does not inevitably happen, as was seen in Maoist China — but even in China, many current developments can be interpreted as fitting this general picture.

Having extended the revolutionary vanguard concept from the pre-revolutionary to the post-revolutionary phases, this separation between the party-state complex and the rest of society can all too easily become part of the general post-revolutionary culture; temporary necessity becomes accepted norm. The ideology of rapid transformation is used for justifying developments and distributive practices quite different from those practised in the Paris Commune or envisaged in *State and Revolution*. Specialists of various kinds are paid much more than ordinary workers, since this is seen to improve economic growth rates;[64] important decisions are still taken according to a conception of democratic centralism which places more emphasis on the centralism than the democratic, since this is argued to be quicker and more efficient. Everything can be justified in terms of creating the base of communism as rapidly as possible; centralization and inequality is in the long-term interests of all. The apparatus perpetrating this enjoys its privileged position, develops its own identity and culture, and by some definitions — from Weberian to neo-Marxist (Djilas et al.) — becomes an entrenched class in terms both of economic and political power and of social status.[65] Since the pre-communist dominant cultures typically accept — even expect — leadership and an administrative elite, the position of these apparatchiki appears to the majority to be 'natural' or 'normal'. But it is not only the culture which supports them. The ideology — including the paucity of analysis of what communism actually means and when and how the transition to it occurs — is ideally suited to the perpetuation of such elite or class rule; it is both logically feasible and permissible for the party and state leaders to argue that only they know when mass consciousness is sufficiently developed for their own leadership positions to wither away/be abolished. Unfortunately, the Marxist-Leninist theory of control does not adequately tackle the problem. According to this, the masses cannot fully control the state in the period preceding communism, since their consciousness is at a lower level than that of the largely party-appointed state machinery; hence control (e.g. the revocation of officials) is exercised by the party on behalf of the masses. But, on the basis of the same argument about consciousness, the party is largely self-recruiting; if careerists and others are admitted to the party for whatever reason, there is no *in-built*, failsafe method for ensuring that the party does not eventually become dominated by such people.[66] In addition, in seeking to make the state operate in a maximally effective way from the party's point-of-view, the latter fills the state apparatus with people holding similar views to the party membership — and who in the majority of cases are themselves party members. This class becomes almost unassailable. If *it* fails to keep the revolutionary transformation of consciousness in motion, it is unclear that communism — in the simple sense of a society of political equals and liberated individuals in the social context — will emerge. Yet for it to lead such change would be to undermine its own privileged position; to expect this of a whole class would be highly ingenuous. This is not to state categorically that such a class must exist and will never relinquish power; it is merely to explain how it arises, why purely functional explanations for the persistence of the state are insufficient, and that there are major theoretical as well as practical problems to be overcome if the party-state is to wither away in communist countries.

SOME CONCLUDING REMARKS

With the possible exception of Yugoslavia, there are few indications that the party and/or the state is withering away in the communist world. Any signs there are, even in Yugoslavia, must be treated with caution: history has shown that a change of leadership and/or a domestic crisis could lead to a strengthening of the coercive organs of the party-state and full ideological justification for such change. Some transformation in the direction outlined by Marx, Engels and Lenin has occurred — private ownership of the means of production has been almost abolished, for instance. But party and state officials are still not properly subject to public control, appear still to receive far higher wages than the average worker, whilst the armies are for the most part professional elites. Classes persist, even if these are officially 'non-antagonistic'.

Yet this is only part of the story. Many communist states have achieved much in terms of economic progress and the development of a welfare state; the populations in many are probably better off in terms of both income and security than they would have been under the pre-communist regimes.[67] Nor is it the case that the role or the tasks or the ideology of the state in these countries is identical to that of the capitalist or mixed economy state; in theory, at least, it is generally more responsible to the population for the provision of certain rights (e.g. to work, to free medical services) than most Western states — whilst other rights (e.g. to travel, to propagate differing ideologies) are less readily conceded. And the task of transforming consciousness in these countries — which is still formally accepted by the party-state — is a priori far more difficult than the basically status quo-oriented socialization task of the liberal-democracies.

Future developments in these states are difficult to predict. One possibility is that the sum of incremental changes (including better education) over a long period will lead to a much higher level of meaningful public participation in social administration, thus weakening the position of the party and state apparatus; the 'withering' here would be gradual. Another is that the present regimes will be overthrown suddenly and by force — either in an international war or because the gap between societal expectations and regime performance has become intolerable. Only then will it become clear whether or not mass consciousness has changed sufficiently under decades of communist rule for the populations to permit and insist upon a genuine withering away of the state; at present, it is far from obvious that the majority in the communist world has experienced a fundamental change of attitude towards authority and has transcended the boundary between what Lenin criticized as 'economism' and real *political* awareness.

NOTES

N.B. Wherever possible, repetition of sources cited in earlier chapters has been avoided unless a different point from the same source is being made.

1. For instance, in terms of the level of development of political consciousness. Although the value of individual chapters varies considerably, the most comprehensive analysis of how and under what circumstances communists take power is T. Hammond (ed.), *The Anatomy of Communist Takeovers* (New Haven and London: Yale U.P., 1975).

2. For the views of Marx and Engels on Russia see W. Weintraub, 'Marx and the Russian Revolutionaries', *Cambridge Journal,* Vol. 3, No. 8 (May 1950), 497-503; R. Pipes, 'Russian Marxism and its Populist Background', *Russian Review,* Vol. 19, No. 4 (October 1960), 316-337.

3. In this chapter, Marxism-Leninism refers to the ideologies of communist parties in power — which in some cases may differ considerably from the theories of Marx and/or Lenin.

4. E.g. Czechoslovakia 1960; Romania 1965; GDR 1968; Bulgaria 1971; USSR 1977; Cuba also introduced this concept recently.

5. This development can be traced back to Stalin's concept of 'Socialism in One Country'.

6. On the political culture in Czechoslovakia see Ch. 5, esp. fn. 7. Literature on Bulgaria is much scarcer; there is a short article by John Georgeoff on Bulgarian socialization — see 'The Goals of Citizenship Training: A Bulgarian Perspective' in *Studies in Comparative Communism,* Vol. 10, Nos. 1-2 (Spring/Summer 1977), 309-314. Otherwise the reader can glean much about attitudes before and since the communist revolution from N. Oren, *Revolution Administered: Agrarianism and Communism in Bulgaria* (Baltimore: Johns Hopkins U.P., 1973).

7. The Chinese Secretariat was disbanded during the Great Proletarian Cultural Revolution, but was reconstituted in February 1980.

8. For a typical criticism of Western-style pluralism see A. Zharkov, 'Lozh' i Litsemerie Burzhuaznoi Demokratii', *Partiinaya Zhizn',* No. 3 (February) 1980, 72-76; see too Ronald J. Hill, *Soviet Politics, Political Science and Reform* (Oxford and New York: Martin Robertson/M. E. Sharpe, 1980), 181-184 and M. Schwartz, *Soviet Perceptions of the United States* (Berkeley: University of California Press, 1978), esp. 33-60. However, it should be noted that some communist states (in addition to Czechoslovakia, 1968) refer in a positive way to a form of pluralism within their own political systems — see e.g. P. Divjak, 'Composition of the Delegations of Basic Self-Management Organizations and Communities and of Delegates to the Assemblies of Socio-Political Communities, in 1978', *Yugoslav Survey,* Vol. 20, No. 3 (August 1979), 13.

9. An up-to-date sourcebook on communist party structures is B. Szajkowski, *Marxist Governments — A World Survey,* 3 Vols. (London: Macmillan, 1981).

10. For an analysis of the caudillo concept and an argument that Cuba was beginning to move away from this in the 1960s see E. Gonzalez, *Cuba under Castro: The Limits of Charisma* (Boston: Houghton Mifflin, 1974), passim and esp. 168-189.

11. In addition to sources referred to in earlier chapters, readers interested in this phenomenon in the Polish context should see J. Woodall, 'The Policy of Industrial Amalgamation and Concentration in Poland since 1958' (Unpublished PhD dissertation, University of Manchester, 1979).

12. Khrushchev introduced a compulsory turnover arrangement for party committees in 1961, but this was dropped by the present leadership in 1966. For details see Archie Brown, 'Political Developments: Some Conclusions and an Interpretation' in Archie Brown and Michael Kaser (eds.), *The Soviet Union since the Fall of Khrushchev* (London: Macmillan, 1978), 220-221.

13. The use of the term 'Permanent Bureau' since 1974 obviously bodes ill for the withering away of the Romanian party, at least under the present leadership.

14. However, as Hill, Dunmore and Dawisha point out, recent promotions of functional/area representatives also appear to strengthen the personal position of Brezhnev.

15. Little importance should be attached to the creation of the post of Chairman of the SED (in the GDR) in 1971. The post was designed as a sop to the deposed Ulbricht, carried no significant powers, and was abolished following Ulbricht's death.

16. Figures on Laos are difficult to come by, but in 1975, party membership represented only approximately 0.5 per cent of the population.

17. The reasons for such rises vary from genuine conversion to communism in some citizens to blatant careerism in others.

18. As Krug shows, Mao also referred to the 'bureaucratic class' during the Cultural Revolution. For much of Chinese communist history, however, a class analysis similar to that of other communist parties has been used. Thus the Chinese distinguish between two classes (the industrial working class and the peasantry) and two classes-cum-strata (the national and the urban petty bourgeoisie); the intelligentsia generally stems from the latter two. For details see F. Schurmann, *Ideology and Organization in Communist China* (Berkeley: University of California Press, 1971), 90-104, 119-120 and H. C. Hinton, *An Introduction to Chinese Politics* (New York: Holt, Rinehart and Winston/Praeger, 1978), 266-270. Debates on the concept of class continue in China — see the discussion which started with the article 'On Class and Class Struggle' in *Beijing Review*, No. 20 (19 May 1980), 24—26.

19. The intelligentsia in most communist states is defined broadly as those engaged in mental labour; this usually implies a completed higher — or at least secondary — level education. On the social composition of the party and state apparatuses see the various sources cited in D. Lane, *The Socialist Industrial State* (London: George Allen and Unwin, 1976) 92-97 and 120-142 and in Szajkowski, op. cit., passim. Even apparatchiki of worker or peasant origin usually adopt the attitudes of their functional peers (see the empirical analyses referred to in Note 45).

20. I.e. in Czechoslovakia, 1968.

21. The Central Committee and its Secretariat does sometimes consult outsiders for advice and/or information which is to be used by the Politburo; but the party here takes the initiative to consult, and the final decision on the given issue.

22. For an up-to-date analysis of the Chinese minor parties see Luo Fu, 'China's Democratic Parties', *Beijing Review*, No. 50 (14 December 1979), 19-27 and 30.

23. As McLellan has shown, both Marx and Engels also used other terms. For instance, Marx referred to the 'smashing' (Zerbrechen) and Engels to the 'shattering' or 'blowing up' (Sprengung) of the state, which implies a much more rapid process; but these applied only to the bourgeois state. Although Marx and Engels used different terms, Lenin believed that, 'Marx's and Engels's views on the state and its withering away were completely identical' — see 'The State and Revolution', in R.C. Tucker, *The Lenin Anthology* (New York: Norton, 1975), 370. Lenin's own

view was that 'The expression "the state withers away" (Russian: "otmiraet") is very well chosen, for it indicates both the gradual and the spontaneous nature of the process' — see ibid., 374.

24. Ibid., 489-491.

25. This is typical of the military's role in many less developed countries — see S.E. Finer, *The Man on Horseback* (Harmondsworth: Penguin, 1976) and M. Janowitz, *The Military in the Political Development of New Nations* (Chicago: Chicago University Press, 1964).

26. However, it should be noted that at the central (federal) level, 'popular' control does not mean that the various classes and strata are proportionally represented; of the delegates to the SFRY Assembly, 90 per cent are managers, executives, specialists and artists, whilst less than seven per cent are industrial workers. For details on this and the composition of lower level assemblies see Divjak, op. cit., 13-22.

27. On Khrushchev's attempts see R. Kanet, 'The Rise and Fall of the All-People's State', *Soviet Studies*, Vol. 20, No. 1 (July 1968), 81-93. For a recent Soviet reference to the CPSU's current policy of strengthening the Soviet state see M. Zimyanin, 'Marksizm-Leninizm i Sovremennaya Epokha', *Kommunist*, No. 8 (May) 1980, 11. Many communist states have introduced 'comrade's' courts, which are run fully or mainly by amateurs. These generally deal only with minor infringements of the law, however, and the legal systems of these states depend primarily on trained, professional judges who are either appointed or else elected by the state legislature. Thus the judicial wing of the state is not noticeably withering.

28. In 'The State and Revolution', Lenin argued that 'the scientific distinction between socialism and communism is clear' and that what Marx called the first or lower phase of communist society is what has come to be called socialism, whilst the higher phase is communism proper. See Tucker, op. cit., 381.

29. For an early attack see 'Letter of the Central Committee of the Chinese Communist Party to the Central Committee of the Communist Party of the Soviet Union', *New York Times*, 5 July 1963, 8. For a more recent criticism see (A Hsinhua Correspondent), 'Reactionary Essence of New Soviet Constitution', *Peking Review*, No. 25 (17 June 1977), 13-15 and 28.

30. F. Engels, 'Socialism: Utopian and Scientific' in Karl Marx and Frederick Engels, *Selected Works*, Vol. 3 (Moscow: Progress Publishers, 1970), 147.

31. Tucker, op. cit., 326-328. Lenin also explicitly rejected the concept of the 'people's state' — see ibid., 323. It is largely as a result of such a monistic view of the state that so many communist theoreticians are now experiencing difficulties in defining the state's role within their societies.

32. Some may disagree that the latter point in particular is not a feature of liberal-democracies; but the concern here is only with the official communist view of the state.

33. The special role of the military in China, Indochina and Cuba in the past has already been noted.

34. Not invariably, however, as Lourdes Casal's research into the Cuban National Assembly suggests. However, even her findings reveal an unusually high level of unanimous votes in parliament in comparison with the situation in liberal democracies. The East German parliament, however, clearly constitutes an example of the ceremonial full parliament, whilst the Yugoslav Federal Assembly is probably the most influential legislature of those considered in this volume.

35. Tito remained President of the Republic until his death in May 1980; during his lifetime, he was also President of the Presidency of the Socialist Federal Republic of Yugoslavia. The office of President of the Republic disappeared upon Tito's death, and the head of state is now the collective Presidency. The President of this may be viewed as the Yugoslav President, but his position — constitutionally at least — is much weaker than Tito's was (for instance, any one individual can occupy the post for only one year). Although it is too early to know whether a power struggle will emerge in Yugoslavia — leading perhaps to the re-emergence of the office of President of the Republic — the first change of President of the Presidency (from Kolisevski to Mijatović) proceeded smoothly at the appointed time, just a fortnight after Tito's death.

36. On limited terms of office, see for example Articles 134, 312 and 324 of the Yugoslav constitution. For a reference to the people's right to revoke deputies see *The Democratic Republic of Vietnam* (Hanoi: Foreign Languages Publishing, 1975), 38. Apart from there being a lack of evidence on the realization of this principle, see the argument below on revocability.

37. On falsification see V. Zaslavsky and R.J. Brym, 'The Functions of Elections in the USSR', *Soviet Studies*, Vol. 30, No. 3 (July 1978), passim and esp. 369-370.

38. Notable exceptions include China, Yugoslavia and Cuba. In July 1979, China adopted a new electoral law which extended direct elections to the county level; it remains to be seen whether this will be extended still further to the national level. For details see Tian Sansong, 'Election of Deputies to a County People's Congress', *Beijing Review*, No. 8 (February 25) 1980, 11-19.

39. Romania, too, has introduced changes in the electoral system in the 1970s — for a useful analysis see M.E. Fischer, 'Participatory Reforms and Political Development in Romania' in J.F. Triska and P.M. Cocks (eds.), *Political Development in Eastern Europe* (New York: Praeger, 1977), 217-237; despite such changes, aimed at 'legality, equity, efficiency, and "mass participation"', Fischer concludes that 'The success of this domestic strategy' is doubtful (221). The same volume contains analyses of Yugoslav elections by Lenard Cohen and of participation in local politics in Yugoslavia, Romania, Hungary and Poland by Jan Triska.

40. Examples of referenda before the adoption of a new constitution include the GDR (1968) and Bulgaria (1971). For a detailed analysis of the discussions of the 1977 draft Soviet constitution and the amendments that were made see E. Schneider, 'The Discussion of the New All-Union Constitution in the USSR', *Soviet Studies*, Vol. 31, No. 4 (October 1979), 523-541. Several communist states — including the USSR, the GDR and Hungary — have institutionalized the involvement of key functional groups in the legislative process if a policy proposal directly relates to such groups; as was seen in the case of the GDR, however, such involvement can often be nominal.

41. No communist state has yet rejected the principles of democratic centralism. Although the public is not encouraged to take the initiative or decision, there are occasionally instances of the public being able to block the taking of a final decision on a major issue because of opposition to official proposals; this is particularly true in Yugoslavia. See M. Dobbs, 'Three Mile Island fuels Rebellion in Yugoslavia', *The Guardian*, 24 April 1979, 9.

42. On 'Democracy Wall' see David S. G. Goodman, *Beijing Street Voices* (London: Marion Boyars, 1980).

43. The Chinese recently (1979) re-named their local executives, the former

Revolutionary Committees, 'People's Goverments'; as yet, however, there is little sign that this represents more than a cosmetic change. Although Triska (see fn. 39) suggests more popular involvement in local politics in several East European states, the significance of the findings should not at present be overestimated (Triska admits that the study is only 'a beginning'); for instance, not only is it mainly party members who are becoming more involved, but it is also unclear in most cases what sort of issues people participate in. Hopefully future research will cast more light on this.

44. On the Soviet and East German associations see L. T. Holmes, *The Policy Process in Communist States: Politics and Industrial Administration* (Beverly Hills: Sage, forthcoming); see, too, fn. 11. In addition to such changes in industry, similar concentration has recently been accelerated in agriculture in several states, including Bulgaria, the USSR and Vietnam. Although there is little evidence on this, it seems reasonable to infer that possibilities for grassroots participation in important decisions has declined as a result. On the 'Complex Programme' see Z. M. Fallenbuchl, 'Comecon Integration', *Problems of Communism,* Vol. 22, No. 2 (March-April 1973), 25-39.

45. In addition to the information and sources contained in earlier chapters, a useful starting-point for literature on career-patterns is William A. Welsh's review-article 'Elites and Leadership in Communist Systems: Some New Perspectives', *Studies in Comparative Communism,* Vol. 9, Nos. 1-2 (Spring/Summer 1976), 162-186 — here esp. 164-165. See too Carl Beck et al., *Comparative Communist Political Leadership* (New York: McKay, 1973). A somewhat dated but still useful comparative study of the apparatuses and the nomenclature system is G. Ionescu, *The Politics of the European Communist States* (London: Weidenfeld and Nicolson, 1967), passim and esp. 60-64.

46. See e.g. Welsh, op. cit., 169-171.

47. A recent example of official acknowledgement of a past 'error' was the rehabilitation of Liu Shaoqi in February 1980.

48. Well-known examples include Stalin's victory over both Trotsky and Bukharin; Khrushchev's over Malenkov and the 'anti-Party group'; Mao's over Liu.

49. At present, the personality cult is most developed in Romania and North Korea; nepotism is to be found in most, if not all, communist states.

50. This is not a *necessary* development — see the argument on political consciousness below.

51. Although the conclusions drawn are somewhat different from our own (partially because of consideration of a different period), an interesting comparative analysis of 'red'/'expert' relations within both the party and state bureaucracies in Bulgaria, Czechoslovakia, Poland and Romania for the period 1954-1971 is J. Bielasiak's 'Lateral and Vertical Elite Differentiation in European Communist States', *Studies in Comparative Communism,* Vol. 11, Nos. 1 and 2 (Spring/Summer 1978), 121-141.

52. The reference to opposing sub-cultures applies, for example, to nationality conflicts in Yugoslavia.

53. R.V. Burks, 'Eastern Europe', reprinted in L.J. Cohen and J.P. Shapiro (eds.), *Communist Systems in Comparative Perspective* (New York: Anchor, 1974), passim and esp. 49-52.

54. Suslov and Hager are the senior party theoreticians in, respectively, the USSR and the GDR. On the concept of Abgrenzung see M. McCauley, *Marxism-Leninism*

in the German Democratic Republic (London: Macmillan, 1979), 204-208 and G.L. Schweigler, *National Consciousness in Divided Germany* (London and Beverly Hills: Sage, 1975), passim and esp. 8, 89-140.

55. On the Romanian strike see A. Mihailescu, 'Miners' Strike Jolts Ceausescu', *Labour Focus on Eastern Europe*, Vol. 1, No. 5 (November-December 1977), 8-10. On Gomulka's fall and Gierek's different approach see N. Bethell, *Gomulka* (Harmondsworth: Penguin, 1972), 268—284 and A. Bromke, 'Poland under Gierek' in *Problems of Communism*, Vol. 21, No. 5 (September-October 1972), 1-19.

56. Another explanation, suggested by Bahro, is that the codification of the state's operations represents an attempt to strengthen its position.

57. The representative or delegate system of all communist states is based on this premise.

58. The emphasis of communist parties on the increasing educational and technical levels of party and state officials testifies to this.

59. Raúl Castro's statements, cited by Casal and Pérez-Stable, typify this.

60. This said, two minor related points should be noted. First, the *use* of the army is often based on subjective factors; the Soviet Army's involvement in Hungary, Czechoslovakia or Afghanistan was partially based on the Soviet view that it has the right and duty to protect socialism — as defined by Soviet theoreticians — in other states, as well as its own position. Second, some communist states are attempting to harmonize the classical Marxist idea of an armed people's militia with a professional standing army; this has been particularly true in Yugoslavia, for example, since 1969. See M. Canović, 'Territorial Defence of the SFRY', *Yugoslav Survey*, Vol. 21, No. 1 (February 1980), 53-60.

61. The concept of 'non-antagonistic' is based purely on the Marxist notion of class conflict — i.e. antagonism exists only where there is private ownership of the means of production. This notion of 'non-antagonistic' interests has been tacitly dropped by, amongst others, the Hungarians and Yugoslavs.

62. Reasons for this are considered below.

63. Several speakers made this point in a session on worker participation at the 1979 Conference of the British National Association for Soviet and East European Studies (NASEES). The point made by Casal and Perez-Stable about Cuban underemployment in the 1960s for securing full employment pertains to many communist states, and provides part of the explanation for boredom.

64. The classic statement on this was Stalin's anti-egalitarian speech of June 1931 — see 'New Conditions — New Tasks in Economic Construction' in J.V. Stalin, *Works*, Vol. 13 (Moscow: Foreign Languages Publishing House, 1955), esp. 57-62. Whilst our knowledge of income differentials in communist states is improving, there is still almost no reliable information on the salaries of party and state officials; since so many other wage statistics are published, this lack of data surely testifies to sensitivity about high incomes. However, there is evidence that some workers in these states perceive the differentials to be too great — see e.g. A. Pravda, 'Industrial Workers: Patterns of Dissent, Opposition and Accommodation' in R.L. Tökés (ed.), *Opposition in Eastern Europe* (London: Macmillan, 1979), 218 and 226. Mervyn Matthews has produced some figures on Soviet apparat incomes — which, if correct, mean that the salary of the General Secretary of the CPSU was almost seven times higher than the average national wage in the early 1970s; for further details see his *Privilege in the Soviet Union* (London: George Allen and Unwin, 1978), passim and esp. 21-28. In 1956, the Chinese passed a wage law according to

which the highest possible income for 'cadres' would be somewhat less than five times as great as that for unskilled workers, whilst in 1972 a 24-grade system for the state apparatus was operationalized. For details on communist China through 1972 see C. Howe, _Wage Patterns and Wage Policy in Modern China_ (Cambridge: Cambridge U.P., 1973), passim but esp. 39-41 and 74.

65. Weber's analysis of class and social status primarily relates to market economies — but many commentators argue that several communist states have a form of market economy; for Weber's views see H.H. Gerth and C. Wright Mills (eds.), _From Max Weber: Essays in Sociology_ (London: Routledge and Kegan Paul, 1970), 180-195. Djilas' views are contained in _The New Class_ (London: Unwin Books, 1966). On the difficulties of applying classical Marxist class analysis to contemporary Eastern Europe see G. Konrád and I. Szelényi, _The Intellectuals on the Road to Class Power_ (Brighton: Harvester, 1979), esp. 39-44. One interpretation of official designations of the intelligentsia as a stratum rather than a class is that there is sensitivity about what some perceive as the antagonistic class position of the intelligentsia, and the apparatchiki as part of this. For the generational transference of privilege (i.e. social entrenchment) in the oldest communist state see Matthews, op. cit., passim.

66. Cuba has explicitly attempted to avoid this problem with its unique approach to party-membership. However, the 1975 party statutes reveal loopholes in this system; only time will show whether the party is predominantly self-recruiting or not.

67. This is probably least true of Czechoslovakia; some of the East German population also feel that life would be better under the socio-economic and political system of the FRG. As for other states, it is not implied here that progress would not have been as great — or even greater — had they developed in the typical West European/North American fashion; not only is the consideration of this question of marginal relevance and value, but it must be remembered that such a path was not open to many countries.

Index

Notes on Contributors

Lourdes Casal was formerly Lecturer in Social Psychology at Rutgers University, New Jersey.

Karen Dawisha is a Lecturer in Politics at the University of Southampton. Her publications include *Soviet Foreign Policy Towards Egypt* (1979) and a forthcoming book on the Soviet decision to invade Czechoslovakia, as well as a number of articles on Soviet policy formulation.

Dennis Duncanson is a Reader in Southeast Asian Studies at the University of Kent. He was formerly employed in the Colonial/Administrative and Diplomatic Services. He is the author, among other works, of *Government and Revolution in Vietnam,* and *Peacetime Strategy of the Chinese People's Republic.*

Timothy Dunmore is a Lecturer in Comparative Politics at the University of Essex. He has contributed to *Soviet Studies* and is currently working on two further publications.

Hans-Georg Heinrich is a Lecturer in Political Science and Comparative Constitutional Law at the School of Law, University of Vienna. His Ph.D. on 'Constitutional Reality in Eastern Europe' has recently been published in Vienna.

Ronald J. Hill is Fellow and Lecturer in Political Science, Trinity College, Dublin. He is the author of *Soviet Political Elites* (1977) and *Soviet Politics, Political Science and Reform* (1980).

Leslie Templeman Holmes is a Lecturer in Politics and Government at the University of Kent. He has written articles on the USSR, the GDR and Bulgaria, and is the author of *The Policy Process in Communist States: Politics and Industrial Administration.* He is currently writing a textbook on Comparative Communism.

Maria Huber is a Lecturer in Political Sciences at the University of Tübingen. Her main interest in teaching is in political economy and in research is in social policy in the USSR, Hungary and the FRG.

Barbara Krug is Assistant at the Research Unit on Chinese and East Asian Politics, the Saar University, Saarbrücken. She has recently completed a dissertation on economic policy in China.

David McLellan is Professor of Political Theory at the University of Kent. He is the author of *Marx* (1975), *Engels* (1977) and *Marxism after Marx* (1979).

Marifeli Pérez-Stable teaches Political Sociology at the State University of New York, Old Westbury.

Ralph Pervan is a Senior Lecturer in Politics, University of Western Australia. He has made several lengthy research trips to Yugoslavia and is the author of *Tito and the Students: The University and the University Student in Self-Managing Yugoslavia* (1978).

Jacques Rupnik is a Researcher on East European Affairs for the British Broadcasting Corporation External Services. His Ph.D. on the 'History of the Communist Movement in Czechoslovakia' was recently published in Paris.

Bogdan Szajkowski is a Lecturer in Comparative Social Institutions at University College, Cardiff. He is the editor of the three volume *Marxist Governments: A World Survey,* published by Macmillan, and also the editor of the annual *Documents in Communist Affairs,* also published by Macmillan.